MFA

HIGHLIGHTS conservation and care of museum collections

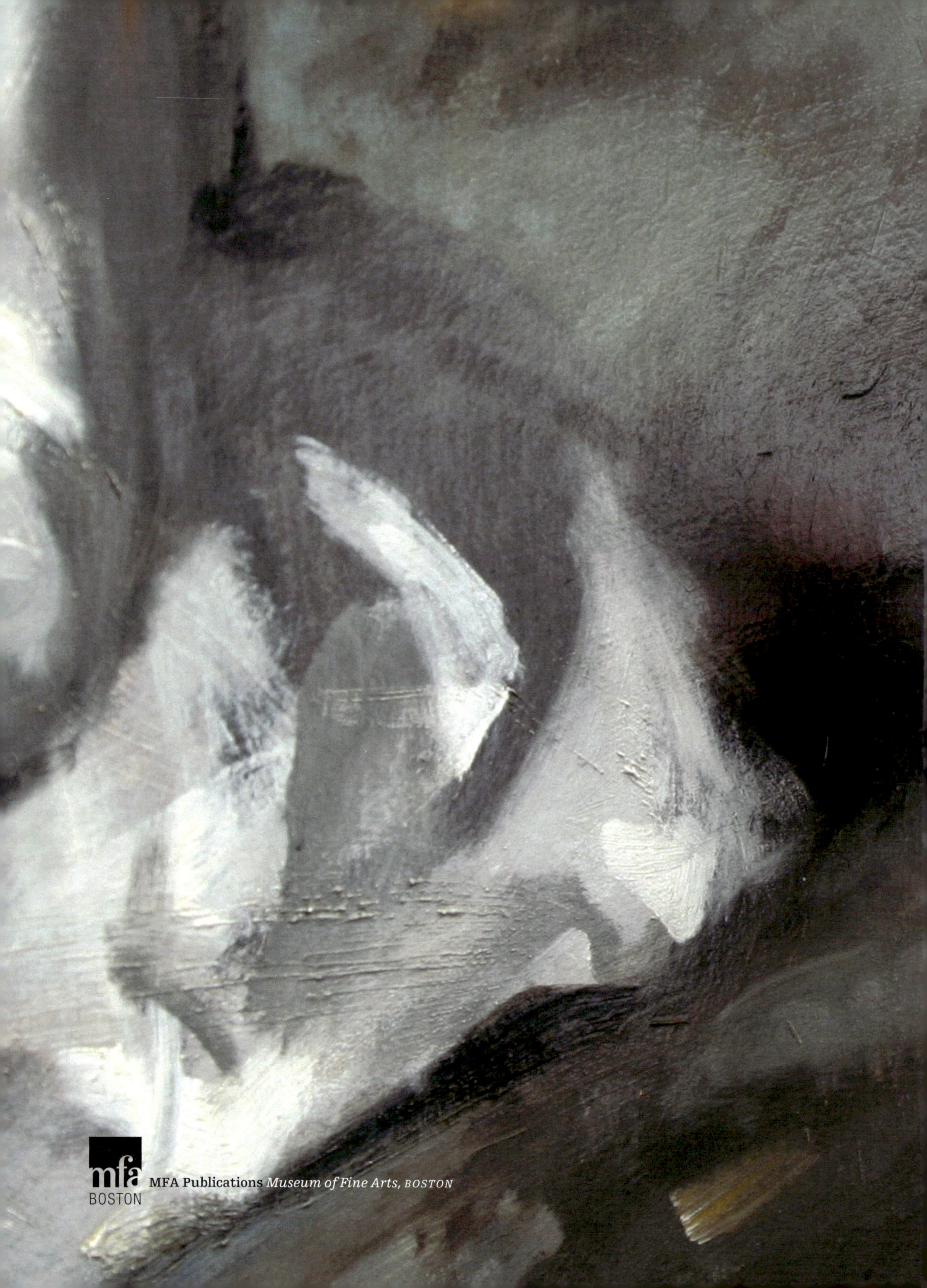
mfa
BOSTON
MFA Publications Museum of Fine Arts, BOSTON

MFA

HIGHLIGHTS conservation and care of museum collections

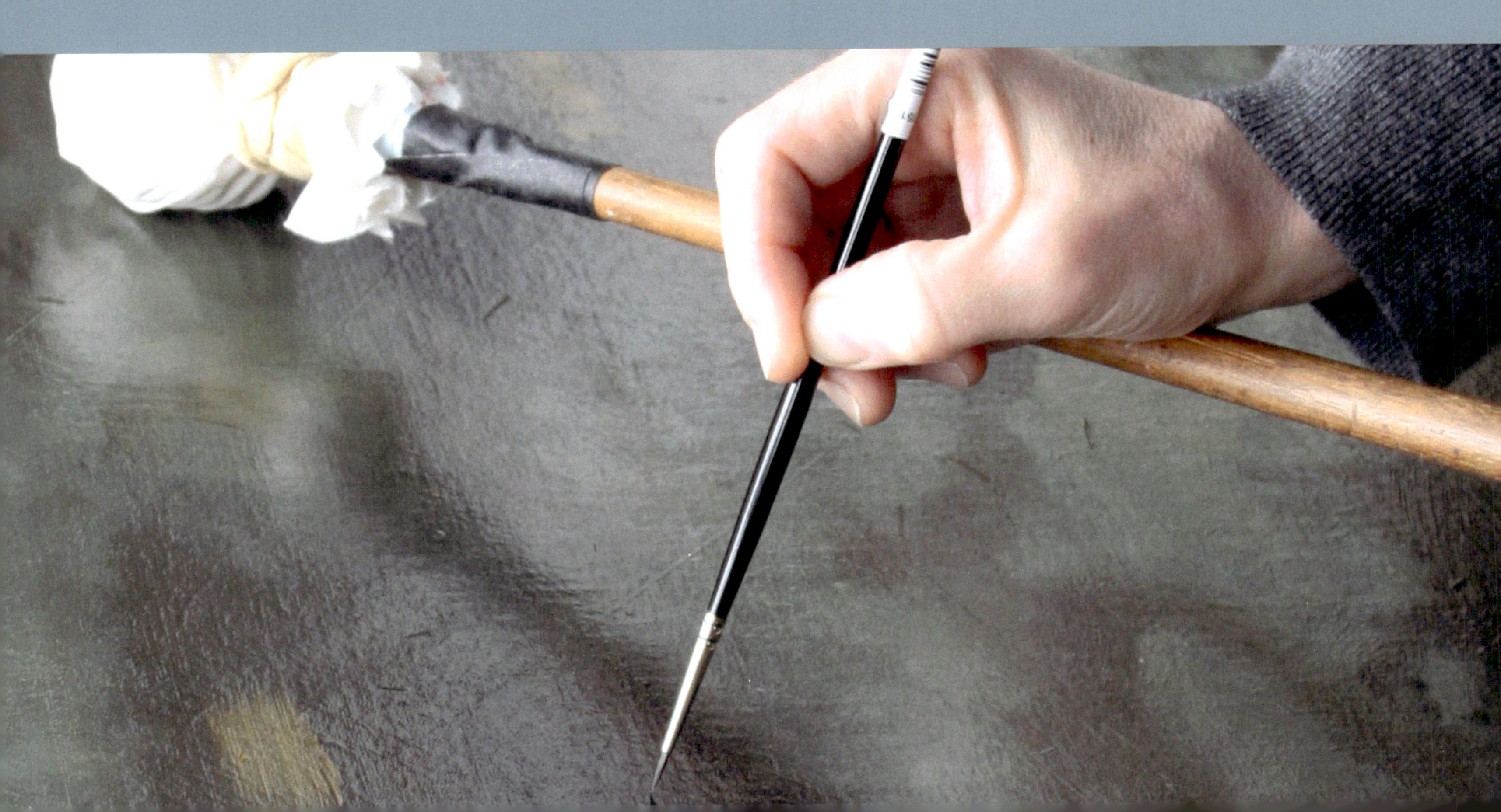

MFA PUBLICATIONS
Museum of Fine Arts, Boston
465 Huntington Avenue
Boston, Massachusetts 02115
tel. 617 369 3438 fax 617 369 3459
www.mfa.org/publications

ISBN 978-0-87846-729-7
Library of Congress Control Number:
2011922450

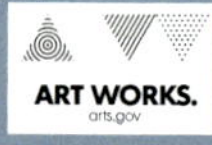

This publication is supported in part by an award from the National Endowment for the Arts.

While the objects in this publication necessarily represent only a small portion of the MFA's holdings, the Museum is proud to be a leader within the American museum community in sharing the objects in its collection via its Web site. Currently, information about more than 330,000 objects is available to the public worldwide. To learn more about the MFA's collections, including provenance, publication, and exhibition history, kindly visit www.mfa.org/collections.

For a complete listing of MFA publications, please contact the publisher at the above address, or call 617 369 3438.

All photographs are by MFA staff, unless noted otherwise.

Grateful acknowledgment is made to the copyright holders for permission to reproduce the following works:

Joseph Beuys, *Capri-Batterie,* 1985, © 2011 Artists Rights Society (ARS), New York / VG Bild-Kunst, Bonn

Cerith Wyn Evans, *"Flicker" by Ian Sommerville (1959)*, 2004, courtesy Jay Jopling / White Cube (London)

Edited by Emiko Usui and Julia Gaviria
Copyedited by Dalia Geffen
Proofread by Julia Gaviria
Design and composition by
Lucinda Hithcock and Jay Peter Salvas
Produced by Terry McAweeney
Typesetting by Matt Mayerchak
Printed and bound at
CS Graphics PTE LTD, Singapore
Series design by Lucinda Hitchcock

Trade distribution:
ARTBOOK | D.A.P.
155 Sixth Avenue, 2nd floor
New York, New York 10013
Tel. 212 627 1999 Fax 212 627 9484

First edition
Printed in the United States of America
This book was printed on acid-free paper.

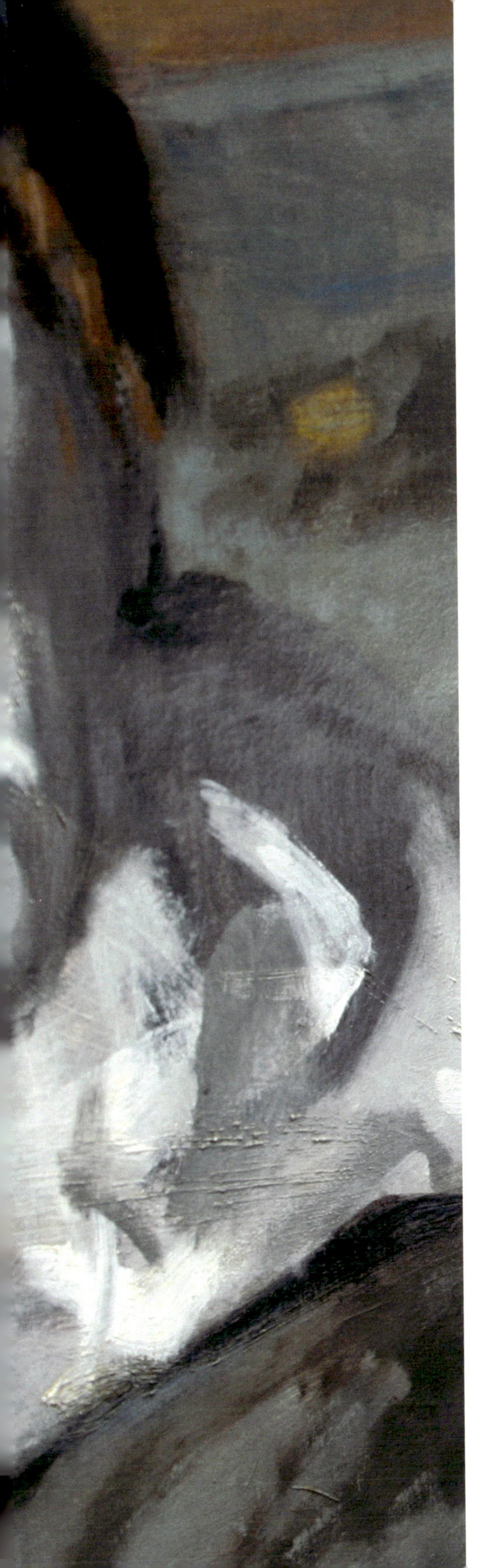

Contents

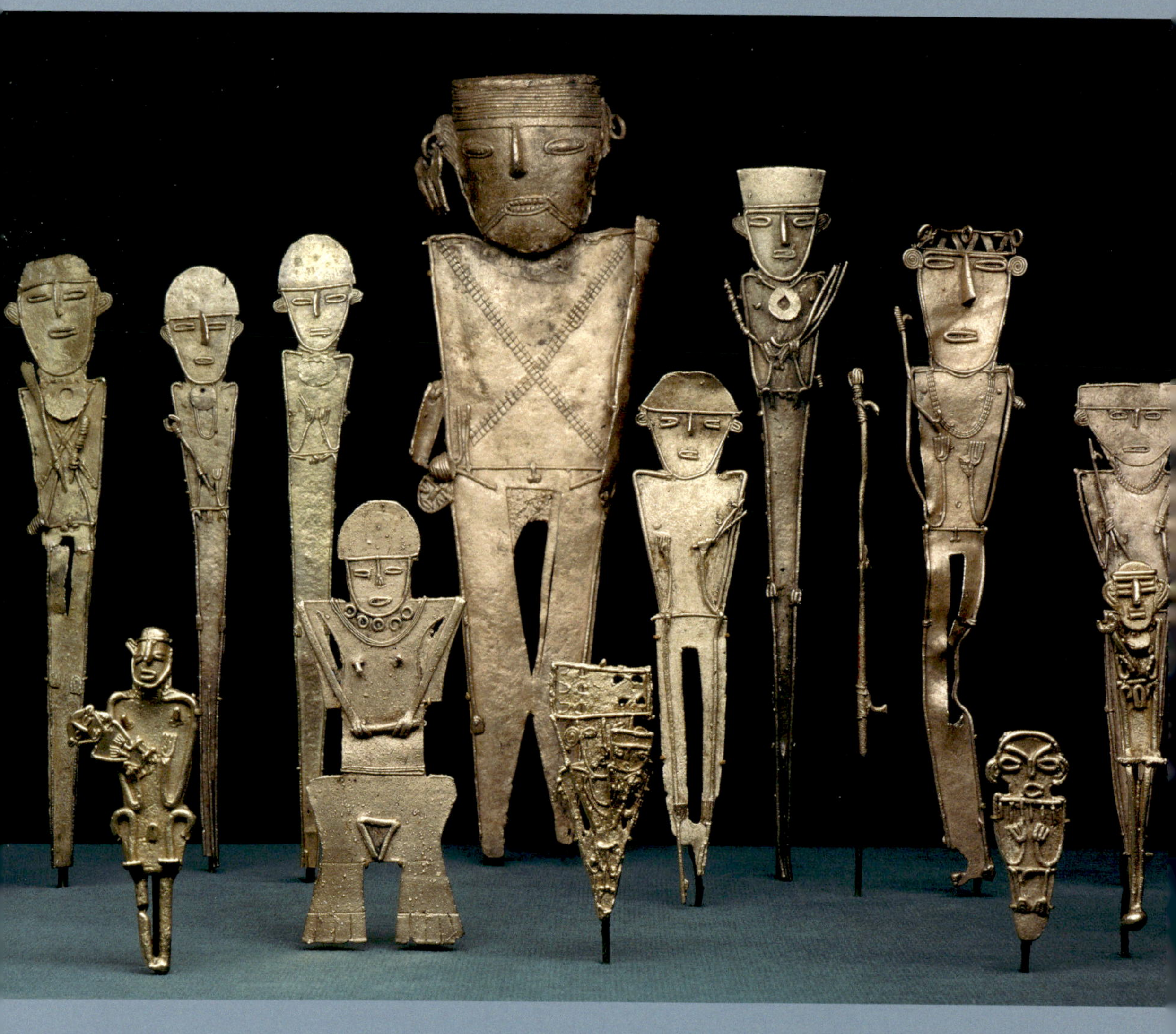

Director's Foreword

Art is for everyone, and it is in this spirit that the MFA Highlights series was conceived. The series introduces some of the greatest works of art in a manner that is both approachable and stimulating. Each volume focuses on an individual aspect of the Museum and its collections, allowing fascinating themes—both visual and textual—to emerge. We aim, over time, to represent every one of the Museum's major collections in the Highlights series, thus forming a library that will be a wonderful resource for the understanding and enjoyment of world art.

It is our goal to make the Museum's artworks accessible by every means possible. We hope that each volume of MFA Highlights will help you to know and understand our encyclopedic collections and to make your own discoveries among their riches.

Malcolm Rogers
Ann and Graham Gund Director
Museum of Fine Arts, Boston

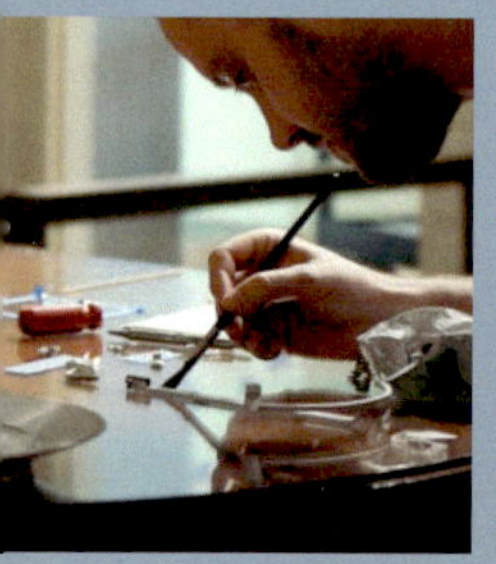
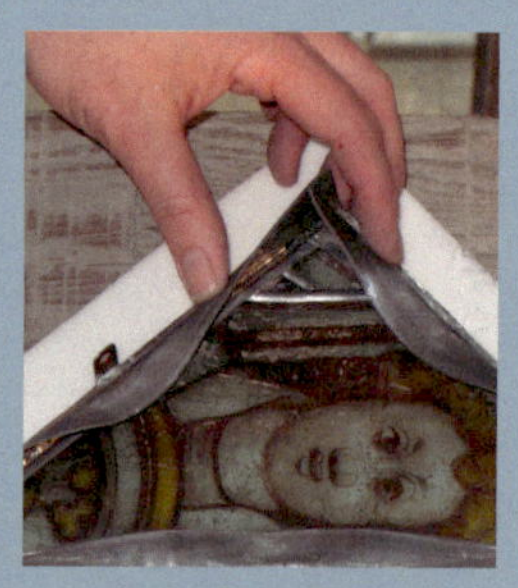
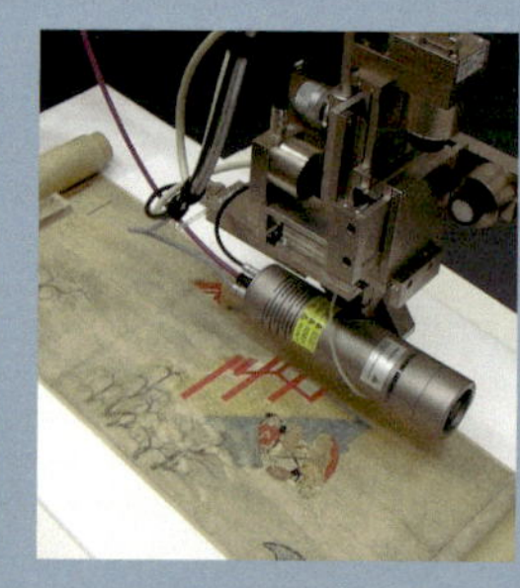
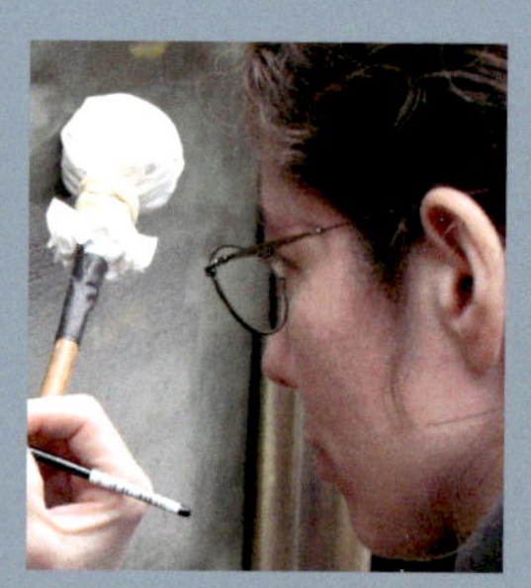
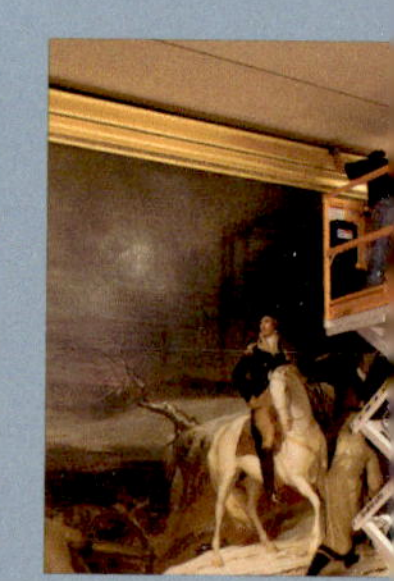

Acknowledgments

This book provides the briefest of glimpses into the activities of conservators, scientists, and collections care specialists at the Museum of Fine Arts, Boston. The fifty-one examples were distilled from projects carried out by current conservation and scientific staff, past staff, conservation fellows, and conservation interns. Included are some projects from decades past to give a sense of how the principles and aims of restoration and conservation have changed over time.

Many individual conservation stories are so complex and rich, they could fill several pages; given the numerous stories to tell, here we devote only a few hundred words to any particular case study. I have written the entries, but Emiko Usui, Director of MFA Publications, has been invaluable in reshaping and refining them to best fit the format of this book in the MFA Highlights series. Dalia Geffen copyedited the manuscript, and Julia Gaviria proofread and helped to finish the final pages of text. Terry McAweeney, Production Manager, orchestrated the book's production. Lucinda Hitchcock and Jay Salvas executed the book's beautiful design.

My role in creating this book is really that of reporter, and I hope that I have been a good one, not unduly distorting the facts that conservators have provided through conversations or written reports and publications. All entries have been checked for accuracy by curatorial staff, and I also hope that their input has been fairly represented. Current and recent conservation staff who have been instrumental in creating this book include Charlotte Ameringer; Meta Chavannes, Andrew W. Mellon Fellow for Advanced Training; Jacki Elgar; Susanne Gänsicke; Jing Gao, Cornelius Van der Starr Conservator of Chinese Paintings; Andrew Haines; Gordon Hanlon; Pamela Hatchfield, Robert P. and Carol T. Henderson Head of Objects Conservation; Abigail Hykin; Sandra Kelberlau, Cunningham Assistant Conservator of Paintings; Jean-Louis Lachevre; Rhona MacBeth, Head of Paintings Conservation and Eijk and Rose-Marie van Otterloo Conservator

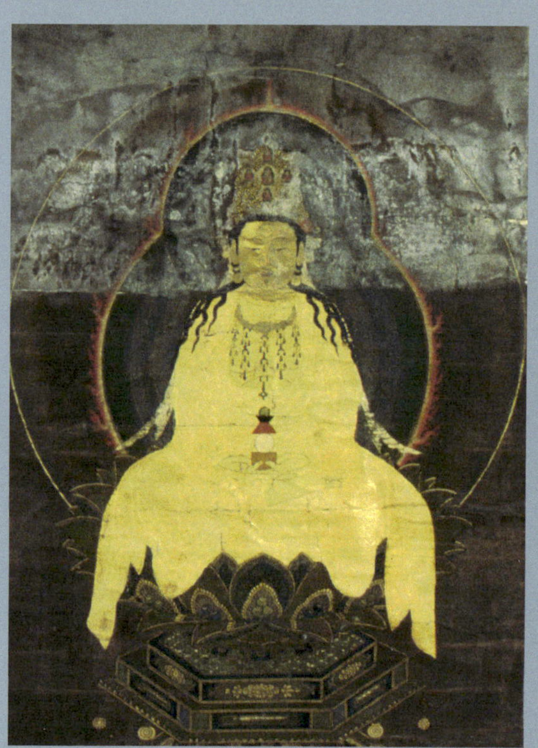

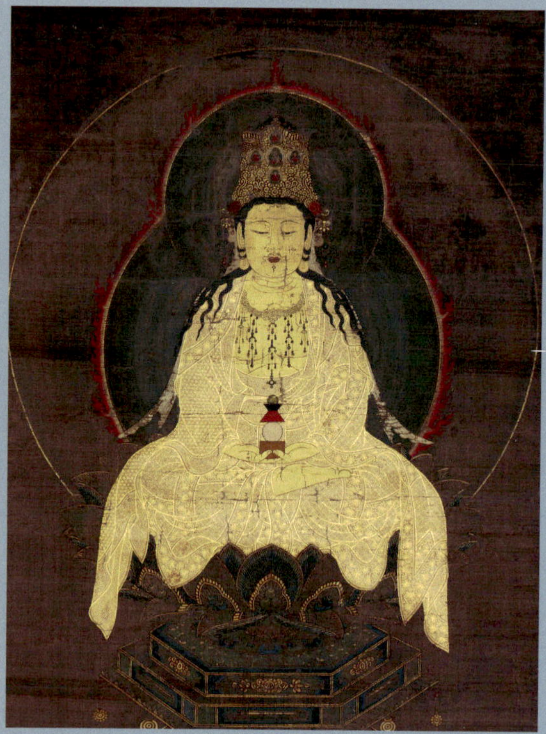

Detail, *Miroku, the Buddha of the Future*, before and after treatment (see pp. 42–43)

of Paintings; Annette Manick; Angela Meincke; Philip Meredith, Higashiyama Kaii Conservator of Japanese Paintings; Meredith Montague; Katrina Newbury, Saundra B. Lane Associate Conservator; Flavia Perugini; Heather Porter; Gerri Strickler; Joel Thompson; Hsin-Chen Tsai, Andrew W. Mellon Fellow for Advanced Training and Sherman Fairchild Fellow; Mei-An Tsu; Tanya Uyeda; Lydia Vagts; Dante Vallance; and Joan Wright, Bettina Burr Conservator, Asian Conservation. Many others, who cannot be individually mentioned, have participated in the projects included in this book. Special acknowledgment is given to Arthur Beale, Emeritus Chair of Conservation and Collections Management, who oversaw conservation, collections care, and scientific research at the MFA for many years. I wish to recognize my colleague in the Scientific Research Laboratory, Michele Derrick, Schorr Family Associate Research Scientist. I would also like to acknowledge William Young, who started out in 1929 as one of the Museum's earliest staff conservators and retired in 1976 as director of the Research Laboratory, which oversaw objects conservation and scientific research during his tenure.

The publication of this book was made possible through an award from the National Endowment for the Arts. I also thank the Sherman Fairchild Foundation and the Andrew W. Mellon Foundation for generously supporting conservation training and scientific research activities at the MFA over many years.

Richard Newman
Head of Scientific Research
Museum of Fine Arts, Boston

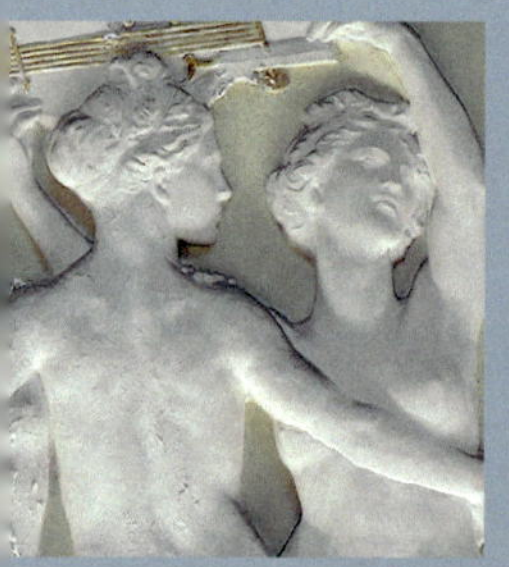

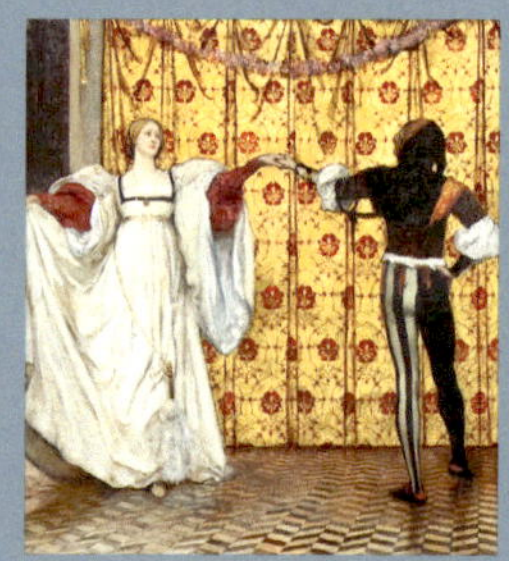

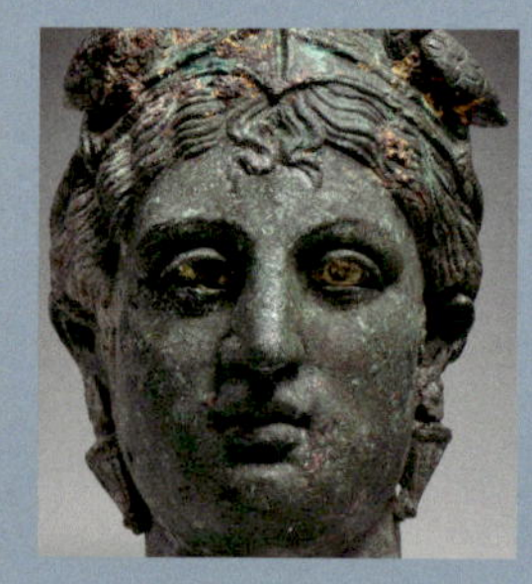

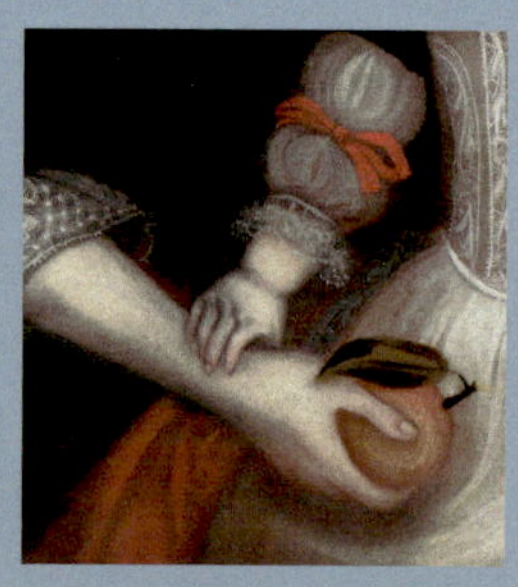

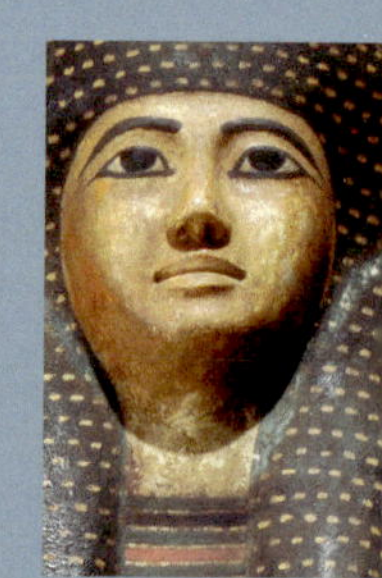

The Art and Science of Museum Conservation *Richard Newman*

Nothing lasts forever. Like everything else in our civilization, the works of art we treasure and study will eventually turn to dust. Nearly all objects change in appearance as they age. Simply putting a work of art in a gallery exposes it to variations of light, moisture, temperature, and air pollution, all of which can have damaging effects. Moving a fragile object or even storing it involves other risks. And no institution can be completely free of art-eating pests such as silverfish or moths. Most major art museums have a staff of conservators dedicated to finding solutions to these problems. Their job is to ensure that art objects in the collection are kept in the best possible condition, at the same time serving the Museum's mission to bring art before the public.

Many people think of "restoration" as a synonym for "conservation," but the word describes only one of the conservator's tasks (figs. 1a and 1b). The American Institute for Conservation of Historic and Artistic Works (AIC) defines "restoration" as "treatment procedures intended to return cultural property to a known or assumed state, often through the addition of non-original material."[1] However, there are usually many "known or assumed" states to which an object might be restored. Aside from the manner in which it was originally made (a

before treatment

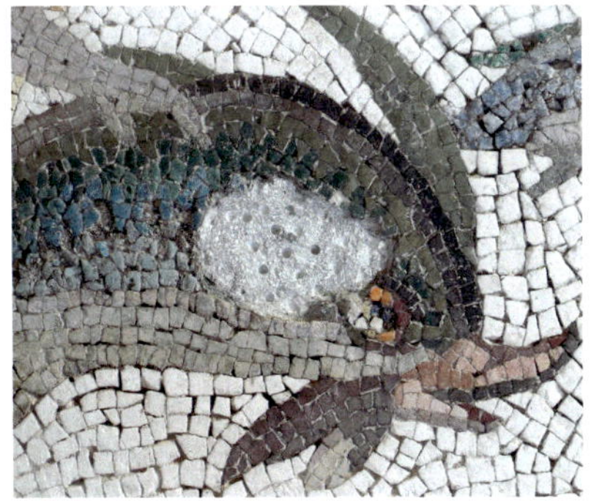

after treatment

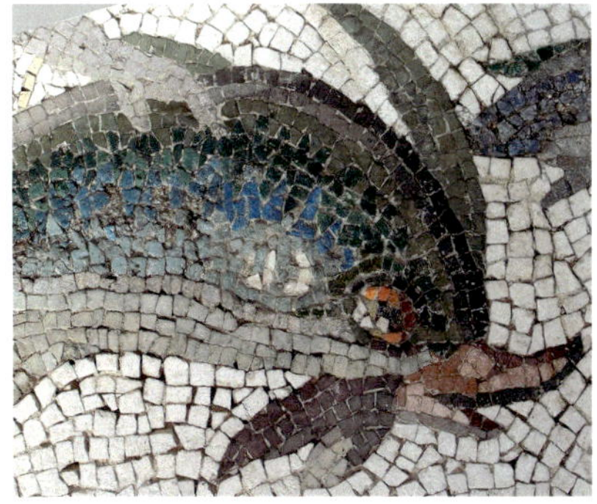

figs. 1a and 1b. **Conservators restored this section of an ancient mosaic floor from Antioch (Turkey, A.D. 200–230) by filling in missing stone and glass tesserae with pieces of pigmented plaster and tinted acrylic resin. They used an intact dolphin in another part of the floor as a model.**

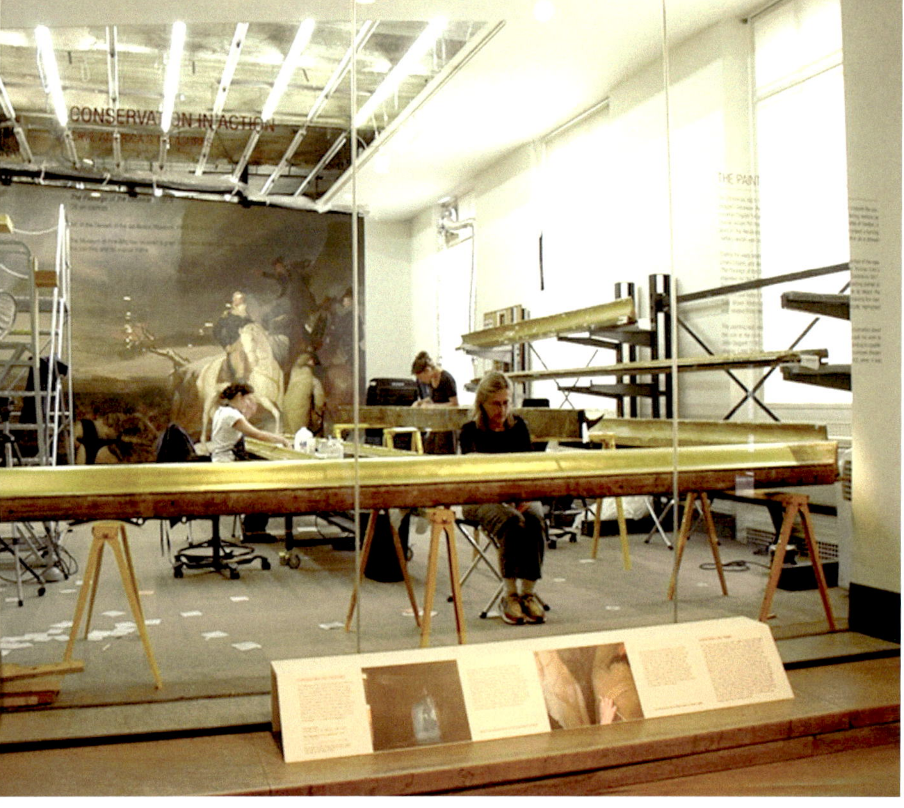

fig. 2 Thomas Sully's 1819 painting *The Passage of the Delaware* during conservation treatment in a temporary studio created to accommodate the painting's large size. Glass walls made the process visible to the public. Pieces of a frame that had been made for the painting in the early 1820s are being cleaned and restored in the foreground.

process that might be difficult to determine, if it can be determined at all), it may have been exposed to significant historical events that changed it in some ways, sometimes several times over. When a conservator is called on to restore an object, how is he or she to choose which point in time is the most important?

Two well-known nineteenth-century writers took opposite positions on this question with regard to architectural monuments. The French architect and theorist Eugène Viollet-le-Duc argued in 1854 that restoration was a legitimate "means to reestablish a [building] to a finished state, which may in fact never have actually existed at any given time."[2] One of his best-known projects was the restoration of Notre Dame Cathedral in Paris, where he added a third tower and carried out many other smaller structural changes. The English art historian and critic John Ruskin condemned restoration, arguing that old architectural monuments should be left with their marks of time or damage. In 1849 he wrote that the greatest glory of a building "is in its Age, and in that deep sense of voicefulness, of stern watching, of mysterious sympathy, nay, even of approval or condemnation, which we feel in walls that have long been washed by the passing waves of humanity."[3] Although the attitudes of the two writers were not as strict or extreme as these quotations might suggest, their statements reflect two different points of view toward restoration that have long produced tensions in the field. Most modern conservators would argue that taking an extreme position in either direction is undesirable. For each unique work of art, the conservator must decide where between the two poles its treatment should fall.

In a few very special cases, the MFA has made an effort to bring museum visitors behind the scenes as the process of conservation is undertaken. In 2010, Thomas Sully's famous military painting of George Washington, *The Passage of the Delaware,* was treated in a gallery that had been temporarily converted to a conservation studio to allow the public to watch the conservators' daily progress. The restored painting was then reunited with a period frame for the first time in one hundred years (figs. 2, 3a and 3b).

Determining the goal of a given conservation treatment may also require careful consideration of the culture that created the object and of the role the object originally served or still serves within that culture. For example, a work of art created for religious purposes may have been handled with great frequency and restored more than once. Evidence of devotion or worship, such as residues from libations once poured or offerings burned, may be an important part of that object's history. A more politically charged but familiar example is the Liberty Bell. Would it be the same symbol of the United States of America if a conservator were to mend its famous crack?

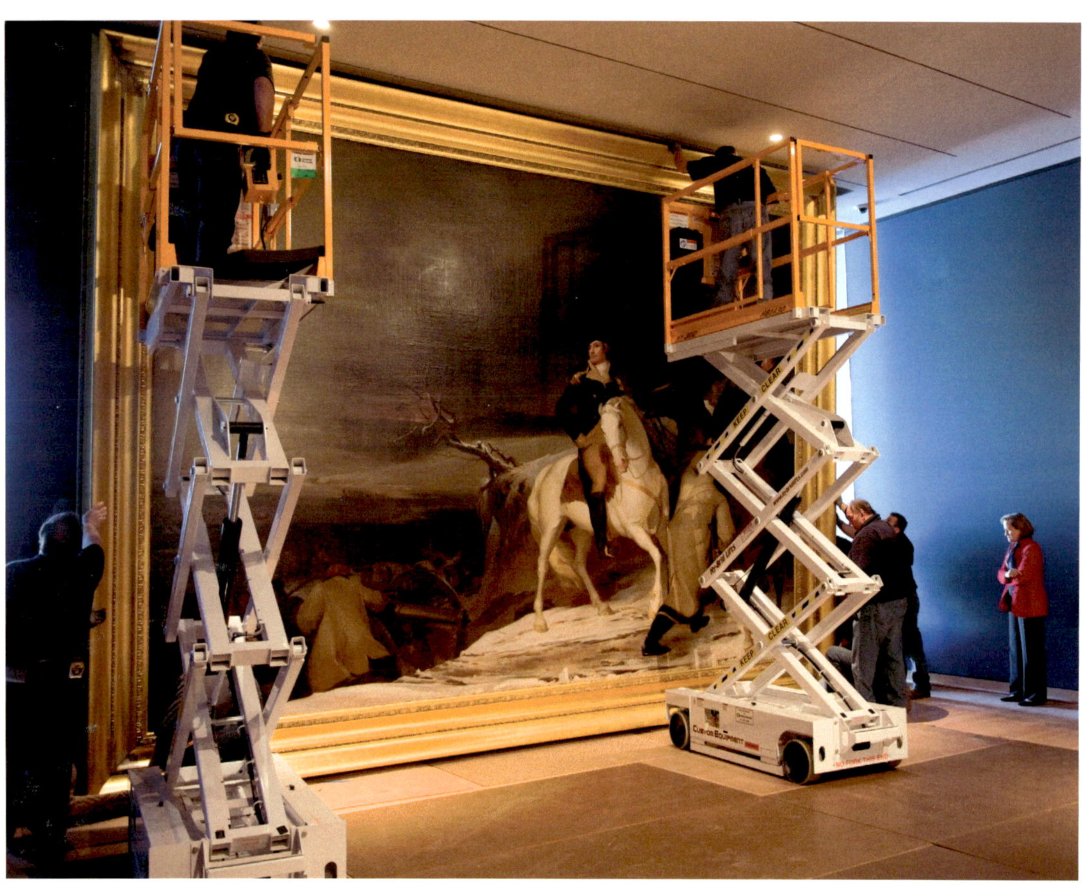
KEEP CLEAR

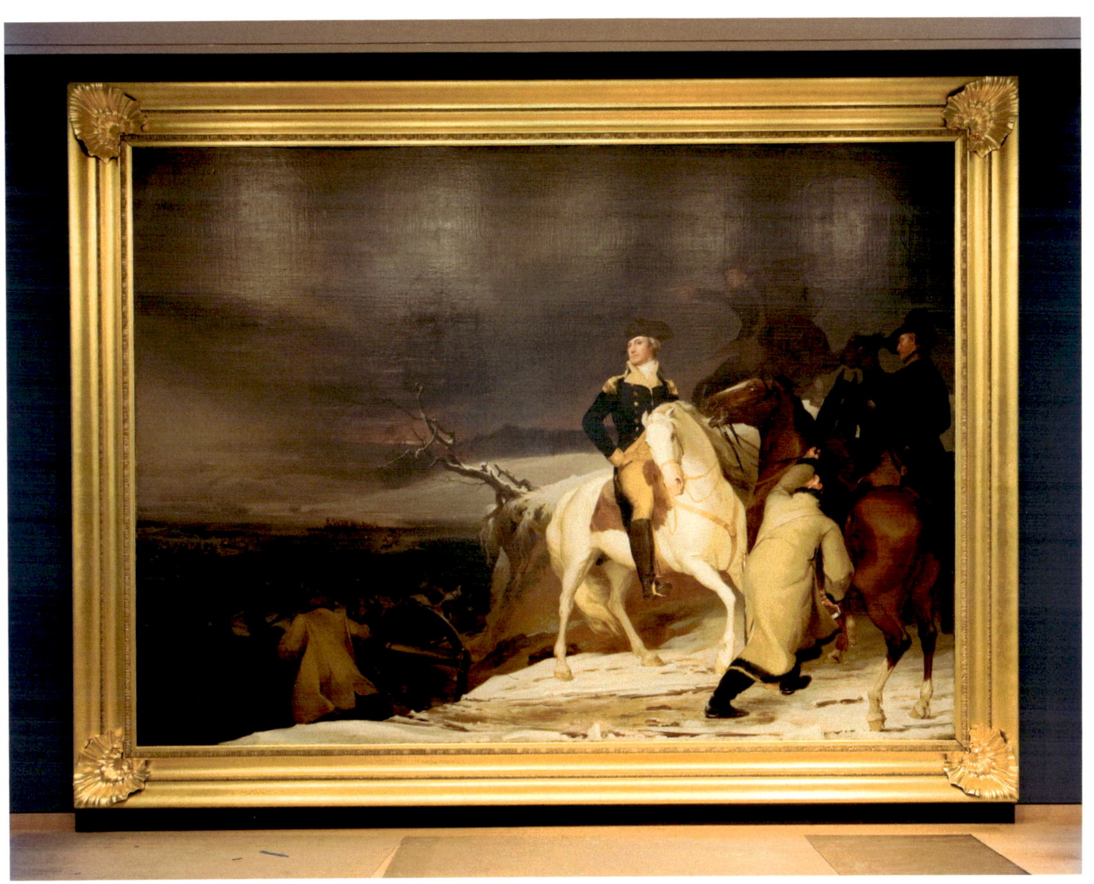

figs. 3a and 3b. **The newly restored painting during installation in the gallery. It is now displayed together with its early frame for the first time in more than a century.**

Traditional conservation has focused on the material aspects of art, and respect for original materials remains a crucial element of the field's ethics. In contemporary art, however, artists sometimes create objects with transient substances, expecting them to deteriorate as part of the meaning they are trying to convey in their work. Preserving an object such as Joseph Beuys's *Capri-Batterie*, in which a fresh lemon plays a crucial part, may be impossible and even inappropriate. For other contemporary works of art that use computers, such as Cerith Wyn Evans's *Flicker*, conservators may need entirely new skills and ways of thinking.

Restoration, as it is now defined, is largely the "hands-on" part of a conservator's work. There are many activities that are termed "hands-off" because they require no direct action to be taken on the art object. Often referred to as "preventive conservation," these include making improvements in the display or storage environments and minimizing direct handling as objects are transported around their home museum or to other institutions as loans. Conservators strive to balance the environmental needs of museum visitors with those of the collections. Light, for example, is necessary for people to see, but it causes cumulative and irreversible damage to some artworks. Most visitors and collections can coexist comfortably at a temperature of seventy degrees Fahrenheit and a relative humidity (RH) level of about 50 percent, but some objects (such as certain metal ones) may deteriorate under such conditions (figs. 4a and 4b). In those situations, conservators design cases or frames that maintain separate microenvironments to fulfill any special needs. They also must be careful with the materials used to make those cases, however, because some paints, adhesives, and woods contain chemical or biological agents that can release damaging particles into the air. Such agents can become trapped in closed cases and damage the artwork in them.

Conservators constantly reevaluate the environmental conditions in which objects should be stored and displayed, and they weigh different priorities against one another. Relaxing environmental conditions inside museums by allowing seasonal variations in temperature and relative humidity may shorten the life of certain works of art, but the positive effects on the earth's environment of saving energy and reducing the pollution caused by the expenditure of that energy (such as that from air conditioning and heating) may be worthwhile in the aggregate and over time.

As the field has evolved, conservation methods and materials have changed, along with attitudes toward how far a conservator should take a treatment. Repair and cleaning are two of the earliest known conservation activities, for broken Neolithic ceramics mended with bitumen have been found in Syria.[4]

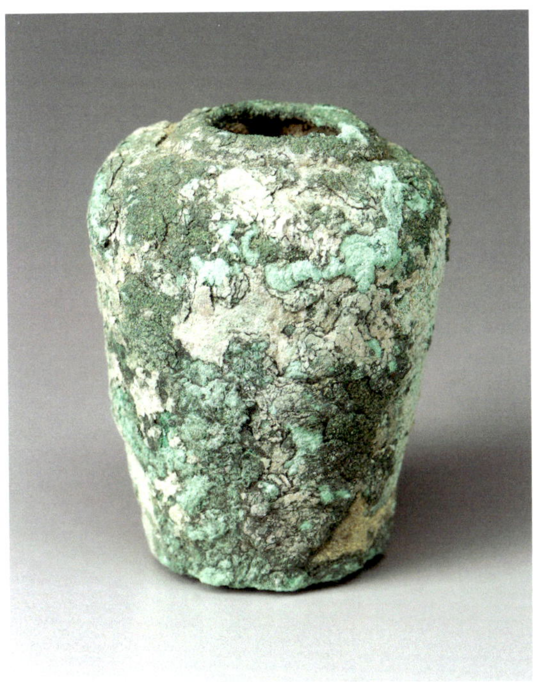

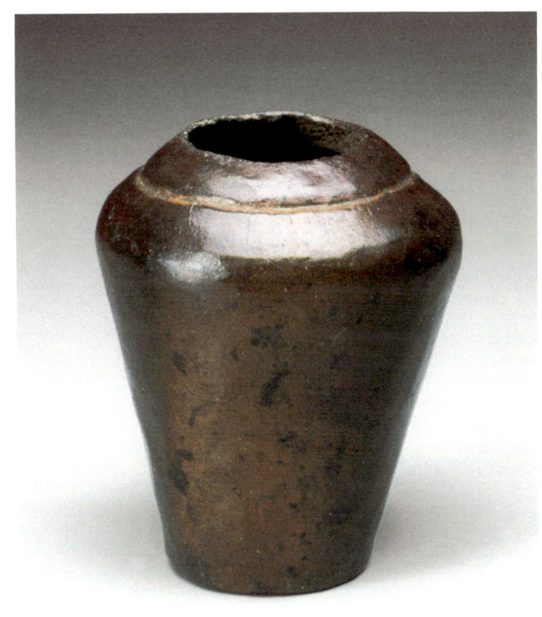

figs. 4a and 4b. **Two ancient Egyptian copper vessels made about the same time. Harsher burial conditions resulted in much greater corrosion of the one on the left. The powdery green material on this object is active corrosion that can be halted if the relative humidity of its surroundings is kept below 35 percent.**

Unfortunately, some substances used for mending in the past have more recently been found to react with the materials that make up the art object, damaging the object in the long term. Cleaning, another seemingly benign task, can be taken too far by removing some of the object's original surface, or it can be done too lightly, leaving materials that can contribute to further deterioration. Although many methods give the conservator considerable control over how much material to remove during cleaning, decisions about how extensively a technique should be carried out are still ultimately made on a case-by-case basis. Such decisions sometimes become the subject of public controversies, as in the cleaning of Michelangelo's Sistine Chapel frescoes.

Most museums have retained few, if any, records of conservation treatments before the 1960s, but now thorough documentation is considered a professional obligation. Documentation ensures the careful recording of treatment procedures and materials so there can be no misunderstanding in the future about what is part of the original work of art and what has been added or altered by the conservator. As accumulations of many individual works, period rooms prove a particular challenge in this regard (figs. 5a and 5b). Although unrecorded treatments can sometimes be untangled by examination and analysis, it may

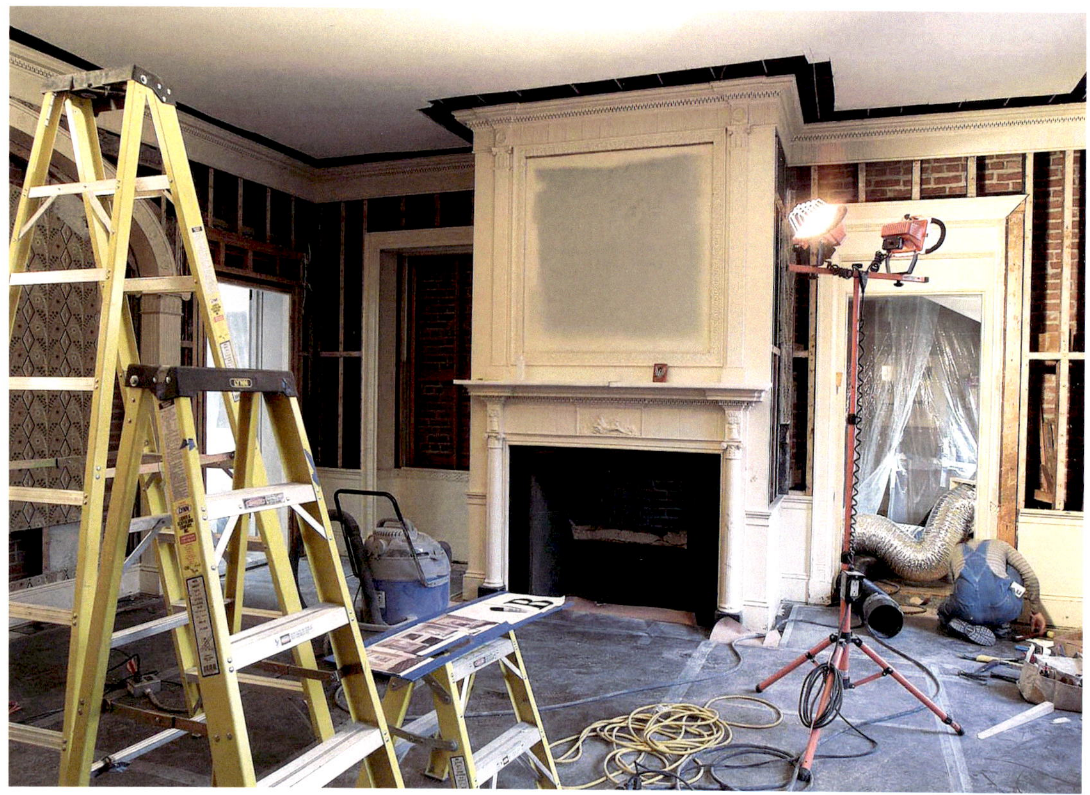

figs. 5a and 5b. **The dining room from Oak Hill, the early-nineteenth-century Danvers, Massachusetts, estate of Elizabeth and Nathaniel West. Detailed documentation was carried out during its recent deinstallation (above) so that the condition of the room could be understood and its reinstallation in the Museum's Art of the Americas Wing (opposite) could be carried out seamlessly.**

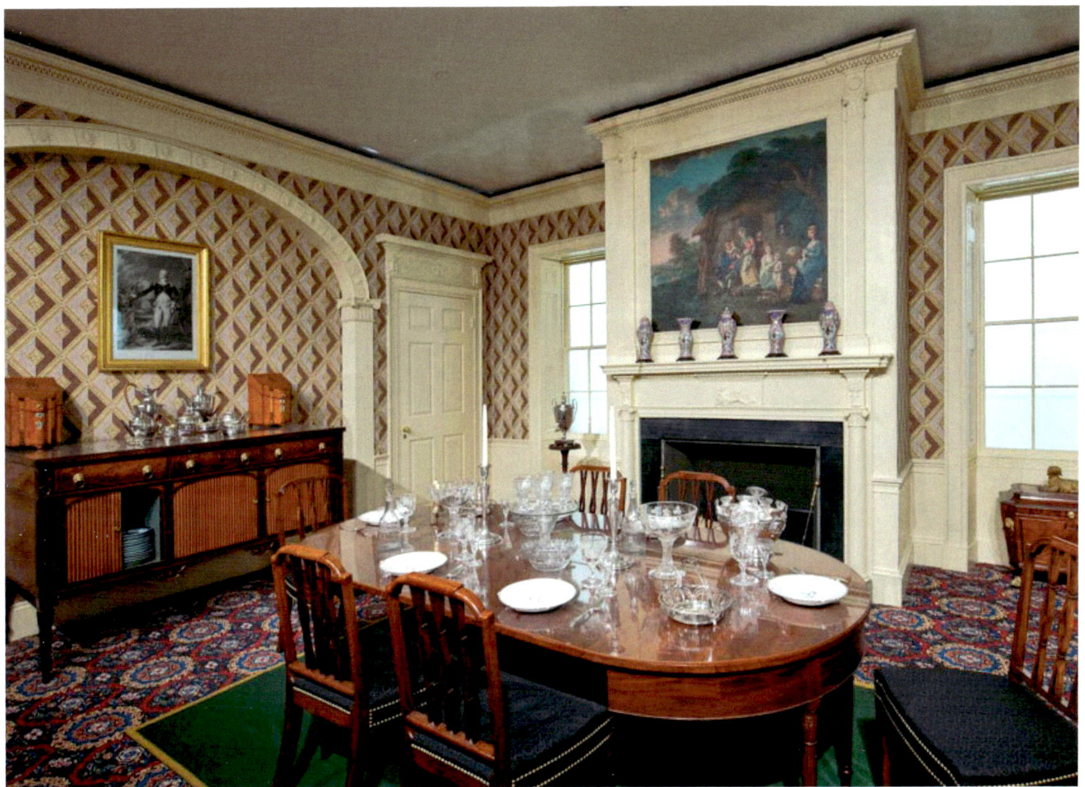

be impossible to know what the effects of earlier treatments have been on the integrity of the original. A principle in the code of ethics that modern conservators follow is that treatments should be reversible—one must be able to undo any treatment in the future. In practice, however, many treatments can never be completely reversed. Conservators can strive only to minimize interventions.

Scientific research is another revolutionizing force in conservation. Conservation science (sometimes called museum science) aids every aspect of a museum's mission to study its collections, both inside and out of the laboratory. For example, research on varnishes has helped to determine which ones deteriorate, possibly causing damage to the object to which they are applied (whether a painting, a piece of furniture, or another work of art), which ones can be counted on to last for many decades, and which are easiest to safely remove. The scientific study of materials and techniques can also help us understand how artists made objects in the first place or shed light on their geographic origins. Armed with specific material information, conservation scientists can sometimes help resolve questions of authenticity or carry out "virtual treatments" with which one can visualize the original appearance of an art object that cannot be brought back by real conservation treatment (figs. 6a and 6b).

Conservation of any work of art is a fine art of balancing competing factors. A relatively young profession—less than one hundred years old—it continues to evolve. Ultimately, just as every object is unique, every conservation decision must be considered on its own. The highlights here—selected from the vast and varied collections of the Museum of Fine Arts, Boston—illustrate diverse aspects of conservation work and the issues they raise. They are divided into three categories that reflect the different aims or goals of conservation: revealing the true nature of art objects, investigating how works of art were made to learn more about them, and preserving them now and for the future.[5] We hope that these objects show how the art and the science of conservation come together in multiple ways, and how caring for an encyclopedic collection can involve complicated decisions that balance different ideas about how a work of art should be cared for and presented to the public.

1. American Institute for Conservation of Historic and Artistic Works, "Definitions of Conservation Terminology," http://www.conservation-us.org/index.cfm?fuseaction=Page.viewPage&pageId=620 (accessed January 25, 2011).
2. Eugène-Emmanuel Viollet-le-Duc, *The Foundations of Architecture*, trans. Kenneth D. Whitehead (1896; repr., New York: George Braziller, 1990), 195.
3. John Ruskin, *The Seven Lamps of Architecture* (New York: John Wiley and Sons, 1886), 173.
4. Jacques Connan, "Use and Trade of Bitumen in Antiquity and Prehistory: Molecular Archaeology Reveals Secrets of Past Civilizations," *Philosophical Transactions of the Royal Society of London B: Biological Sciences* 353 (1999): 33–50.
5. These three broad categories were developed and discussed by Chris Caple in his *Conservation Skills: Judgment, Method, and Decision Making* (London: Routledge, 2000).

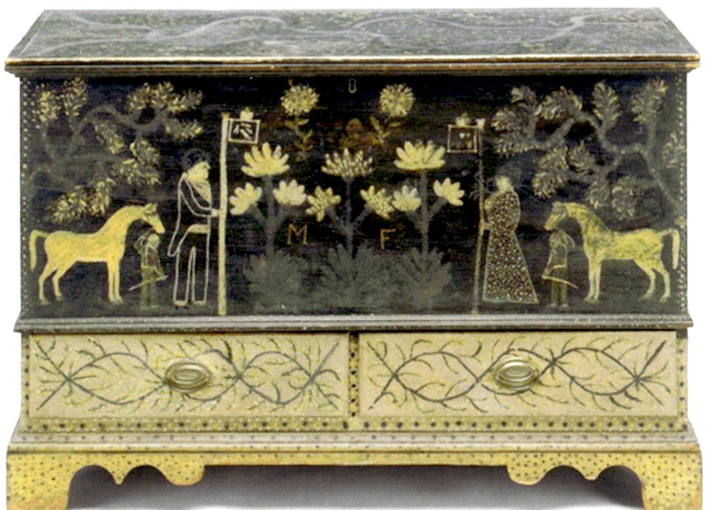

current appearance

figs. 6a and 6b. **Conservators are not able to restore the faded pigments on this American chest with drawers from about 1840–69, but they were able to digitally reconstruct the original colors by analyzing the surviving paint.**

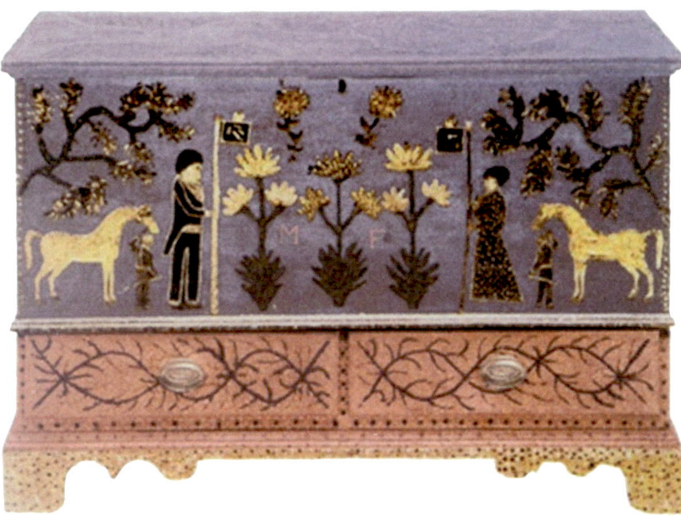

computer reconstruction

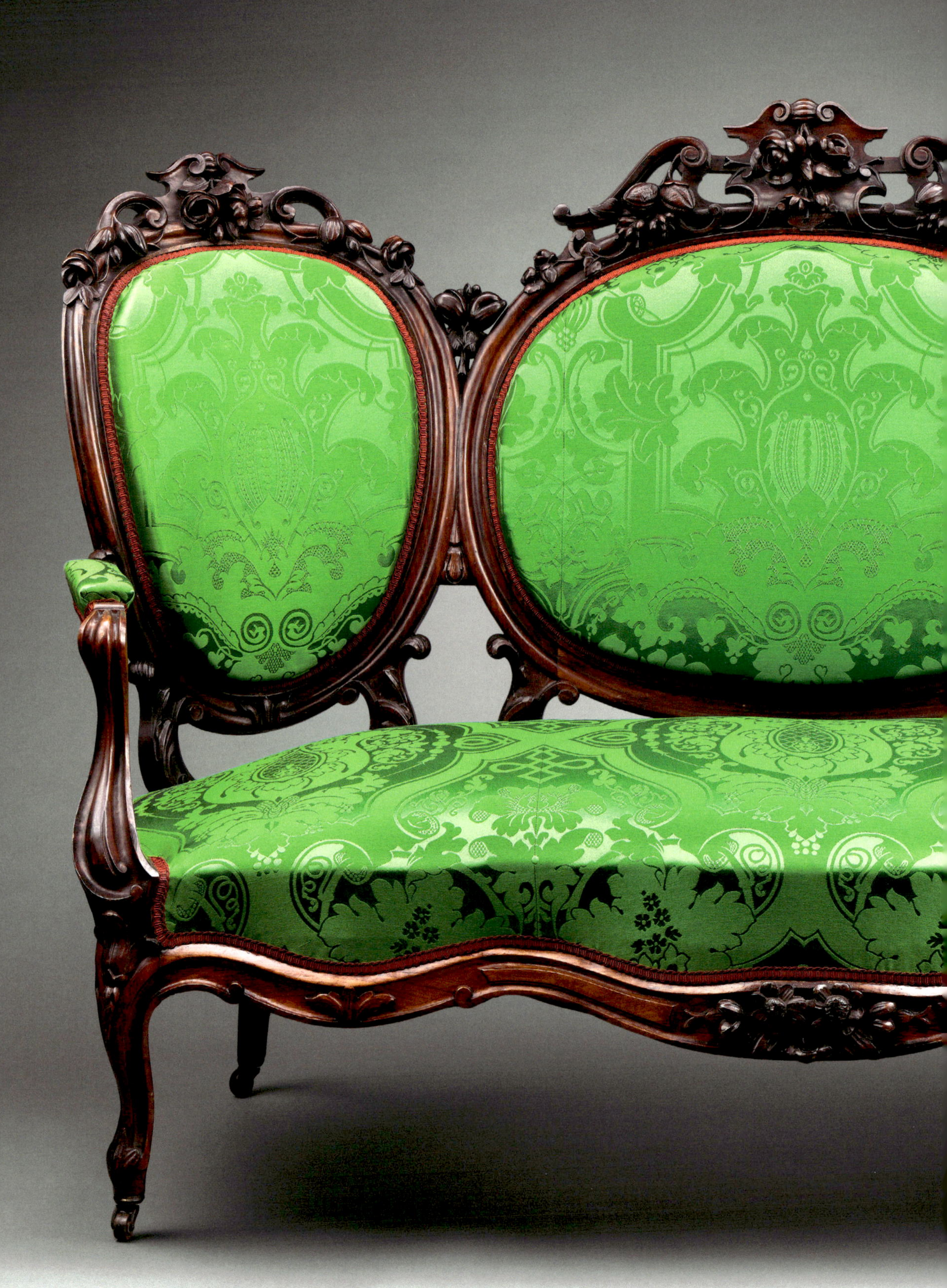

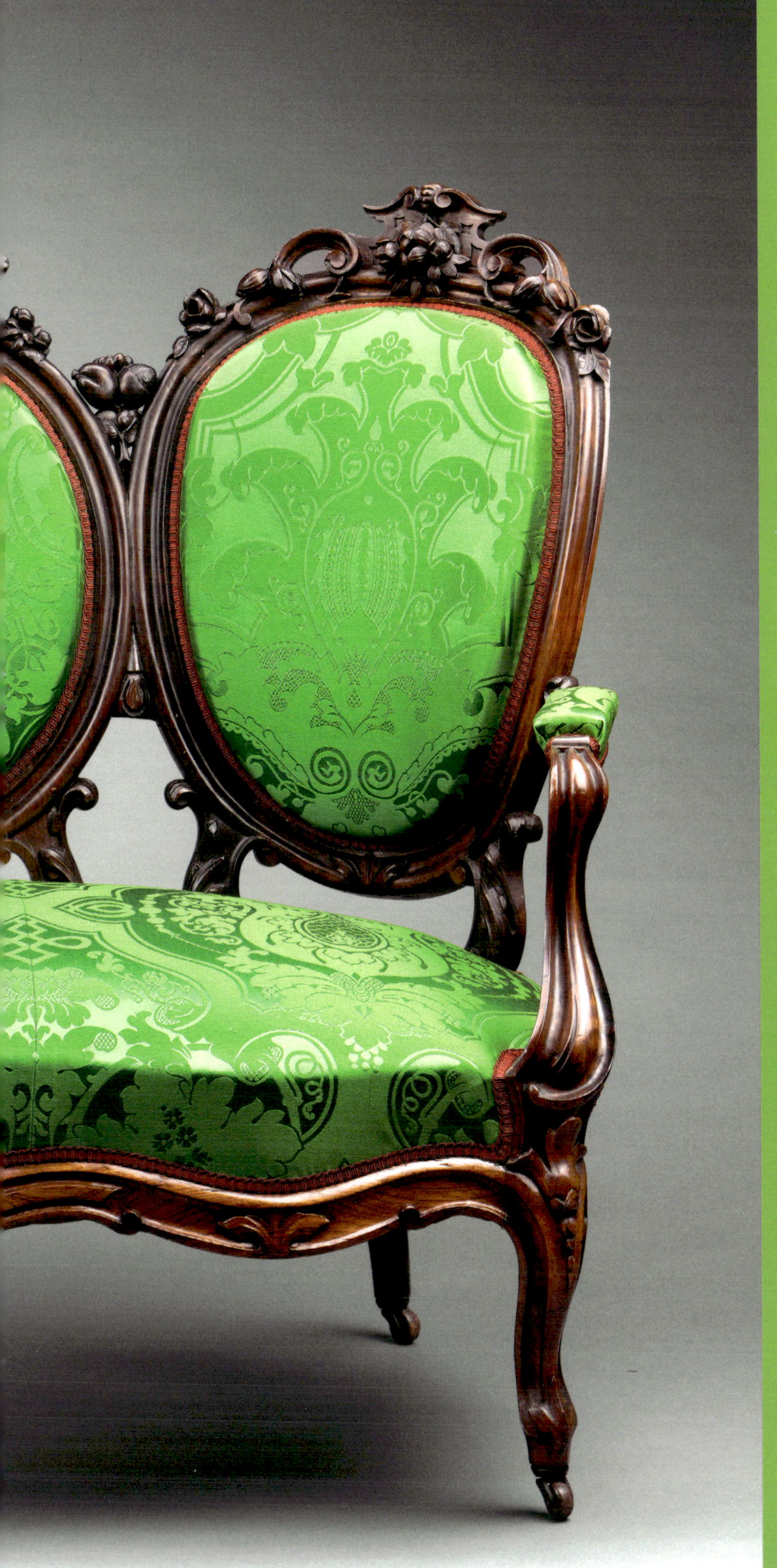

1 REVEALING works of art

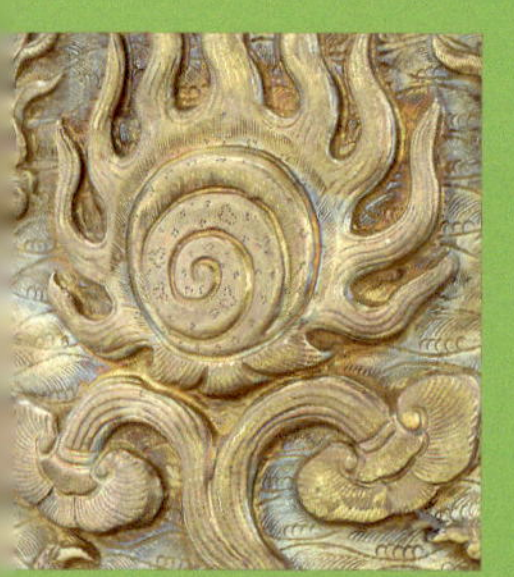
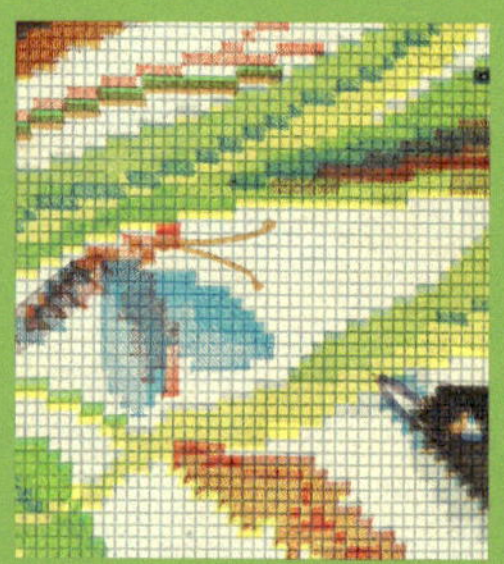
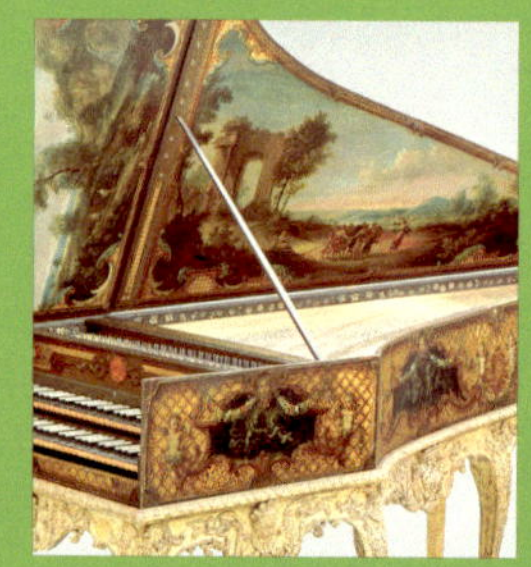
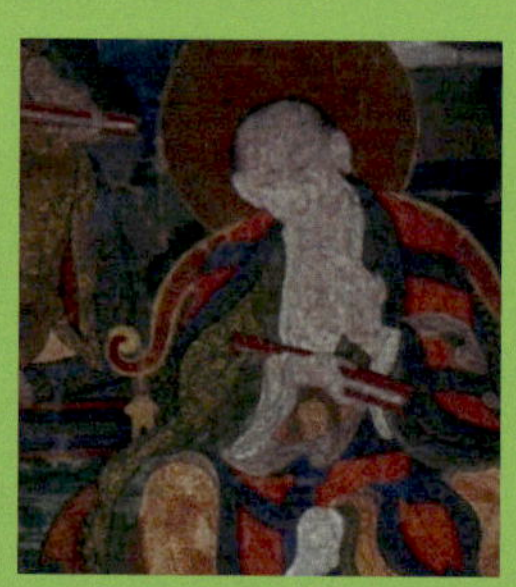
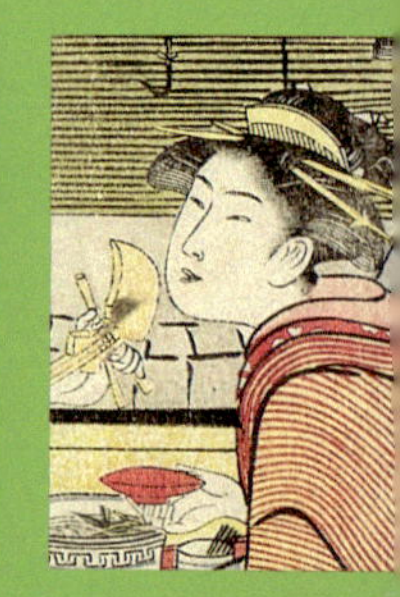

Revealing Works of Art

There are many stories behind every work of art in a museum—stories about what it means, how it was used, where it was originally displayed. Conservators contribute to revealing some of these stories and, when possible, often attempt to return works of art to their original appearance. For example, Egyptian blocks of rock that were once displayed as sculptural relief are reconfigured as part of a three-dimensional gateway, based on the latest archaeological research and conservation techniques; musical instruments, such as a medieval French harpsichord, are treated in such a way that they are not only cleaned and made beautiful but can be played again; and easel paintings are conserved so that they are brought back as close as possible to how they appeared when newly painted.

Sometimes, for various reasons, conservators leave an object in a state that says something about how it was used or how it has aged since it was made. They may intentionally let it remain worn, abraded, or covered with accretions. For example, the blackened area on a Buddhist statue reveals the use of incense in ritual worship and tells us something about the object's religious importance and history. Red and green corrosion develops on the surface of objects made from copper alloys that have been buried for long periods of time, such as ancient sculpture. Although this corrosion took place well after the object was used by the culture that created it, and although conservators are able to remove the discoloration (and often have in the past), the patina is now often left in place because collectors value it for its pleasing color and antique appearance. In many cases it also serves to protect the underlying metal from further chemical reaction.

There are no set rules by which conservators determine what state or final appearance should be a treatment's goal. Each object is unique, and decisions are made on a case-by-case basis, with conservators collaborating with curators to weigh the story or stories the object should tell as it is displayed in a particular museum setting. There are also instances where a work of art can never be returned to its original appearance. Furniture that is now considered within the

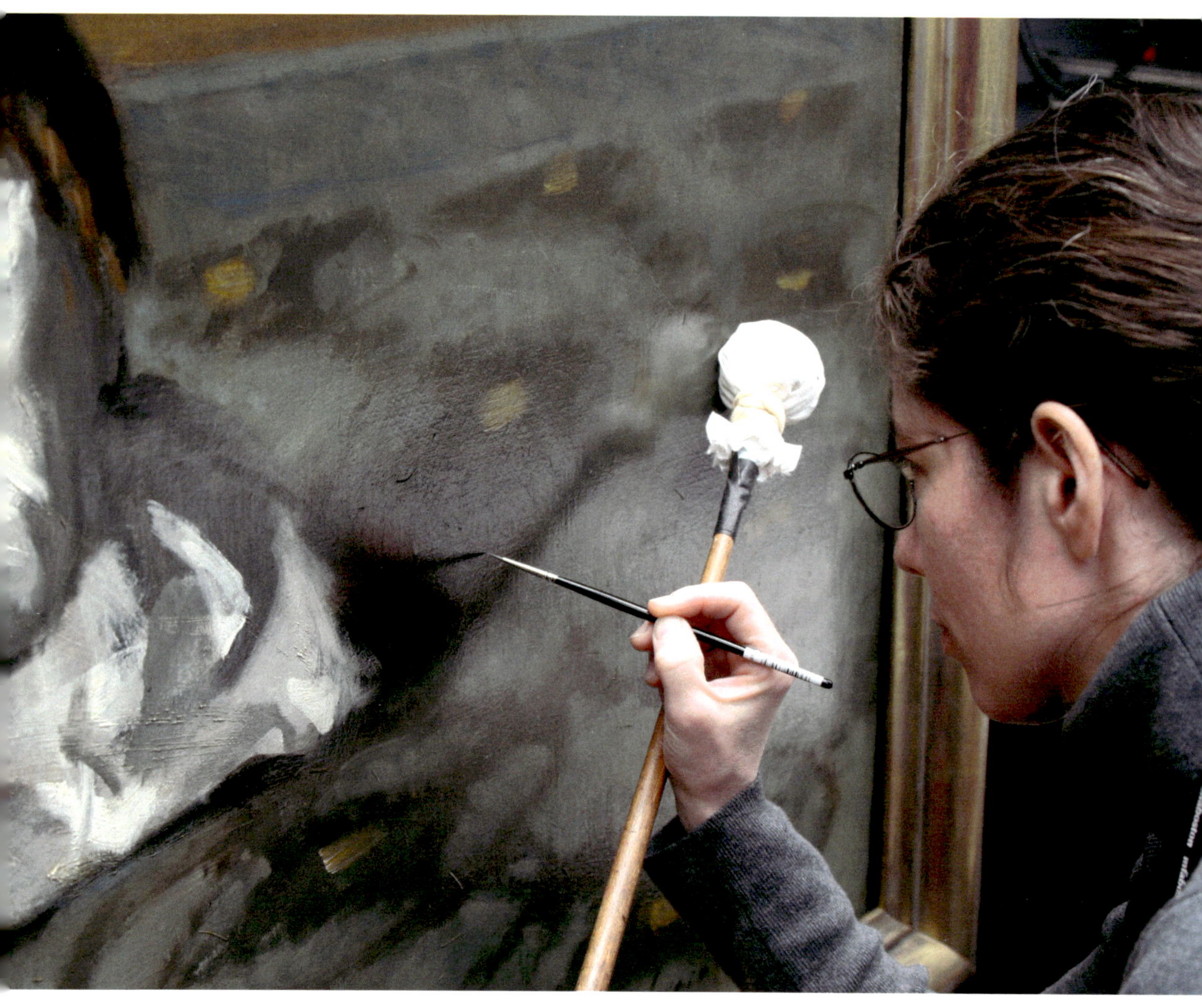

fig. 7. A conservator inpainting a loss during treatment of a painting

scope of the decorative arts may have been frequently reupholstered when in use. Conservators who wish to re-create how it first looked must turn to what traces of the original materials they can find. Alongside curators, they must then consult secondary sources and similar pieces to provide examples and context.

There are a number of common conservation procedures that reveal new information about a work of art or return it to an earlier state of appearance. Conservators remove coatings, varnishes, and corrosion products, and perform other treatments that involve cleaning, slowly and meticulously so as to avoid damage to the underlying work of art. Losses in an artwork may be left untouched, but in a fine arts museum they are often filled to present the object in a more complete state. Such restored losses may then be tinted or painted to better blend with surviving original materials. These treatments may be carried out in different ways and to greater or lesser degrees. In making decisions, the museum staff must carefully balance the story a work of art is to tell with how to best convey such revelations to visitors.

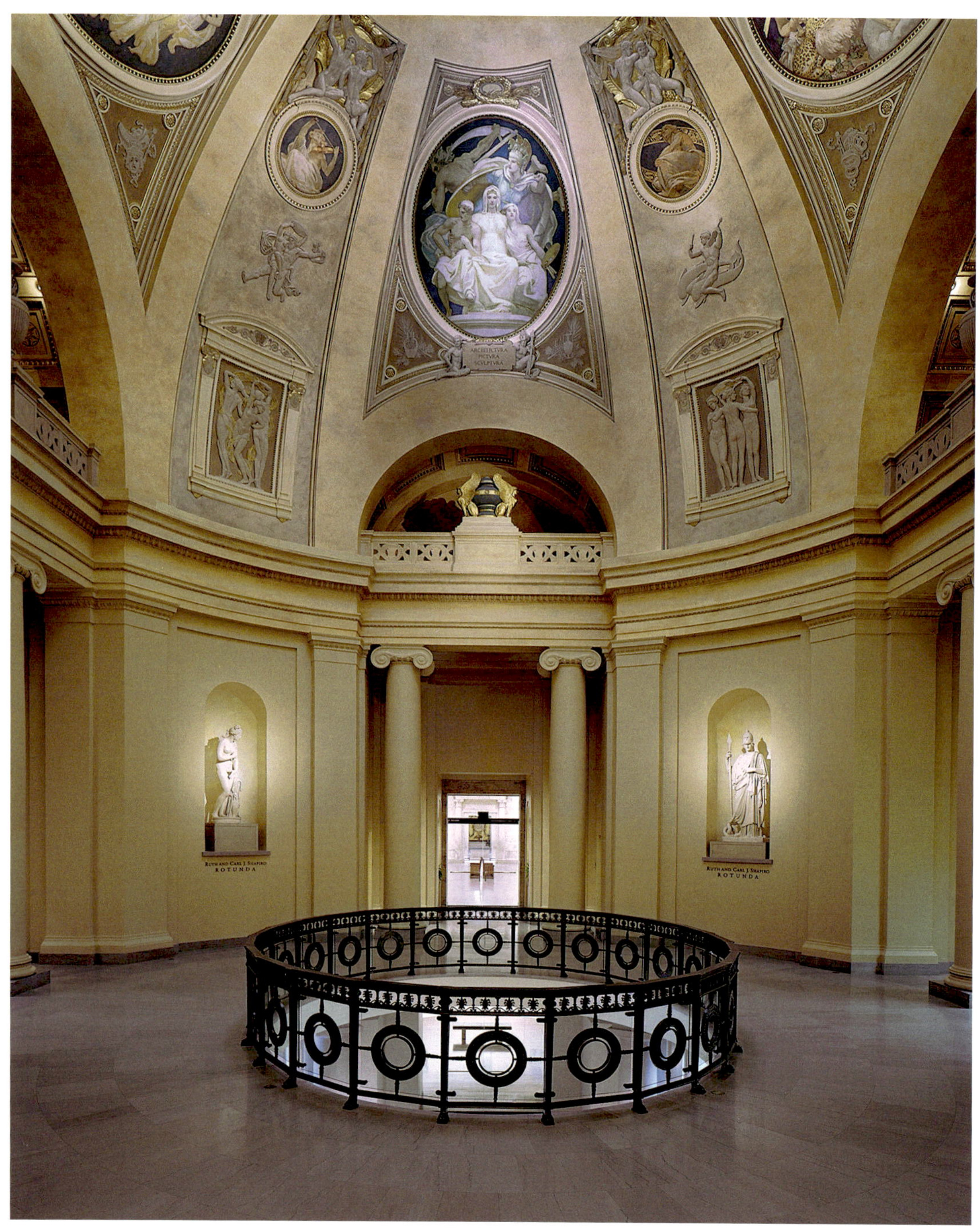

The rotunda after restoration. The *Three Graces* bas-relief is at the right. *Apollo and the Muses* is on the opposite side of the rotunda, not included in this view.

Ruth and Carl J. Shapiro Rotunda and Colonnade

John Singer Sargent (American, 1856–1925)

Three Graces

1919–20
Painted plaster
201.9 x 114.3 x 19.1 cm
(79 ½ x 45 x 7 ½ in.)
Francis Bartlett Donation of 1912
21.10502

Apollo and the Muses

1921
Oil on canvas
283.2 x 428.6 cm (111 ½ x 168 ¾ in.)
Francis Bartlett Donation of 1912
and Picture Fund
21.10512

In 1916 the MFA's trustees approached John Singer Sargent, a world-renowned portrait painter with personal connections to Boston and the Museum, about painting murals for the rotunda in its seven-year-old building. Sargent proposed a far more ambitious program than what the trustees originally had in mind, one requiring modifications to the architecture and the creation of murals and decorations to transform the space into a unified whole. Sargent completed this work, which included eight paintings, twelve bas-reliefs, and numerous urns, sphinxes, and other decorations, in 1921. It proved to be so successful that the Museum asked him to design additional murals for two other areas nearby, a job he completed to great acclaim just before his death.

In 1998 a team of conservators began a yearlong project to clean and restore the rotunda and colonnade. Careful examinations revealed that most of the architectural elements had been repainted in the 1940s and again in the 1970s, but the paintings themselves, such as *Apollo and the Muses* (pp. 34–35), had probably not been touched since Sargent first installed them. Conservators consolidated flaking paint and painstakingly removed years of accumulated dirt, grime, metal residues (perhaps from car exhaust), and nicotine (from earlier days when smoking had been permitted in the Museum), using gentle detergents, soft sponges, brushes, cotton swabs, and a great deal of purified water. Everything had to be hauled up and down the scaffolding every day.

Treating the bas-reliefs, such as the *Three Graces* (pp. 32–33) and surrounding architectural elements proved to be the greater challenge. Early black-and-white photographs and a terse written description were the only documentary evidence of their original appearance. Since the 1940s, the reliefs had been an even white against a pale yellow background, with walls a flat, rosy taupe. By examining exposed underlying paint and studying paint cross sections under a microscope, conservators determined that the background of the reliefs had originally been a pale, warm gray. The surrounding walls had also been more highly colored, with glazes that created livelier surfaces.

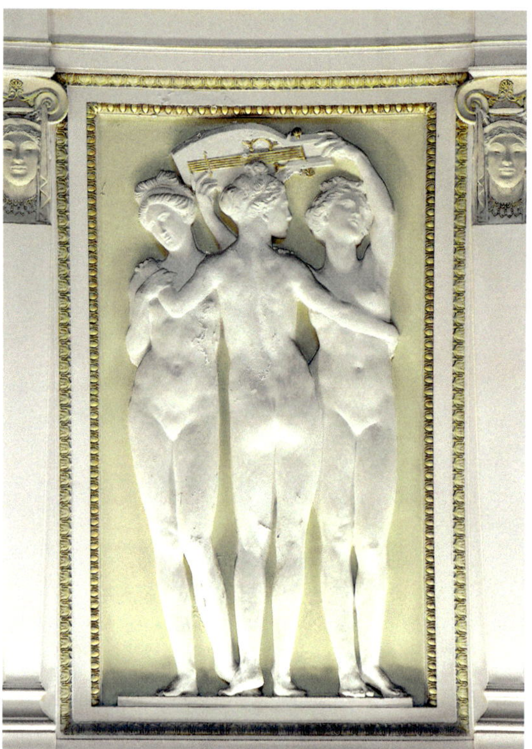

John Singer Sargent's original conception of the *Three Graces* was marred by a campaign in the 1940s to brighten the rotunda in which the artist placed them. The reliefs were painted over, changing the artist's colors and shading.

While planning the restoration, the conservators discovered full-size plaster models for some of the large relief sculptures stacked outside the dome, still wrapped in their original paper. Sargent had shaded and toned these models, enhancing the surfaces and providing clues about his intentions for the actual sculptures and the architecture around them.

Because of the large area that had to be treated, as well as the surviving paint's sensitivity to solvents and overall fragile condition, the conservators decided to repaint the reliefs and walls. (Repainting to re-create an original appearance is common in architectural conservation, where, for many practical reasons, overpaint cannot be removed to reveal original paint.) The conservation team also redesigned the lighting—which had been replaced with fluorescents in 1955—to duplicate Sargent's original plan. Although it is impossible to know exactly what the colors and lighting of Sargent's original installation once looked like, the conservation team used all available evidence to restore, in spirit and detail, the rotunda and colonnade according to the artist's original intent.

The *Three Graces* after conservation. The treatment re-created Sargent's original intentions as faithfully as possible.

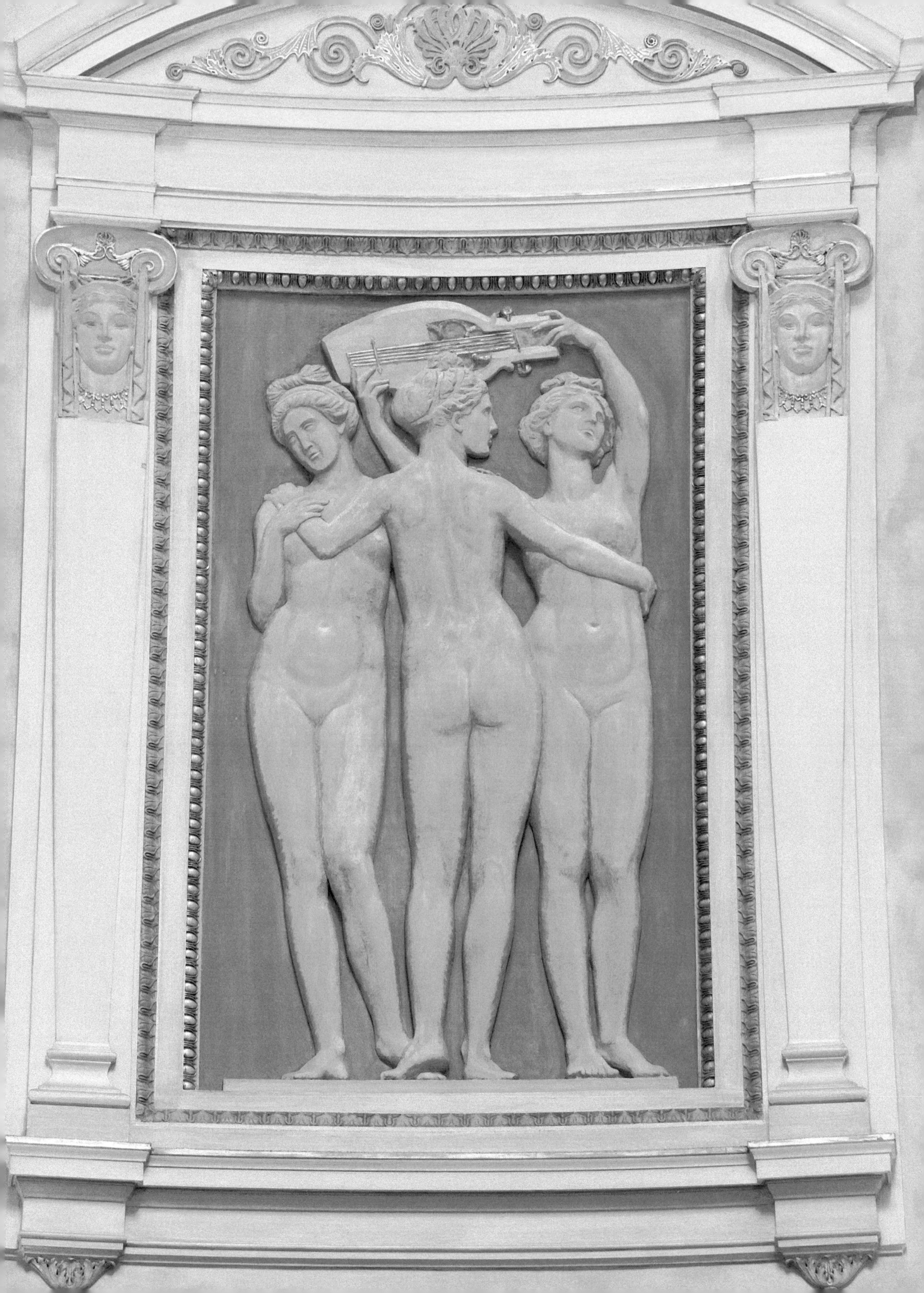

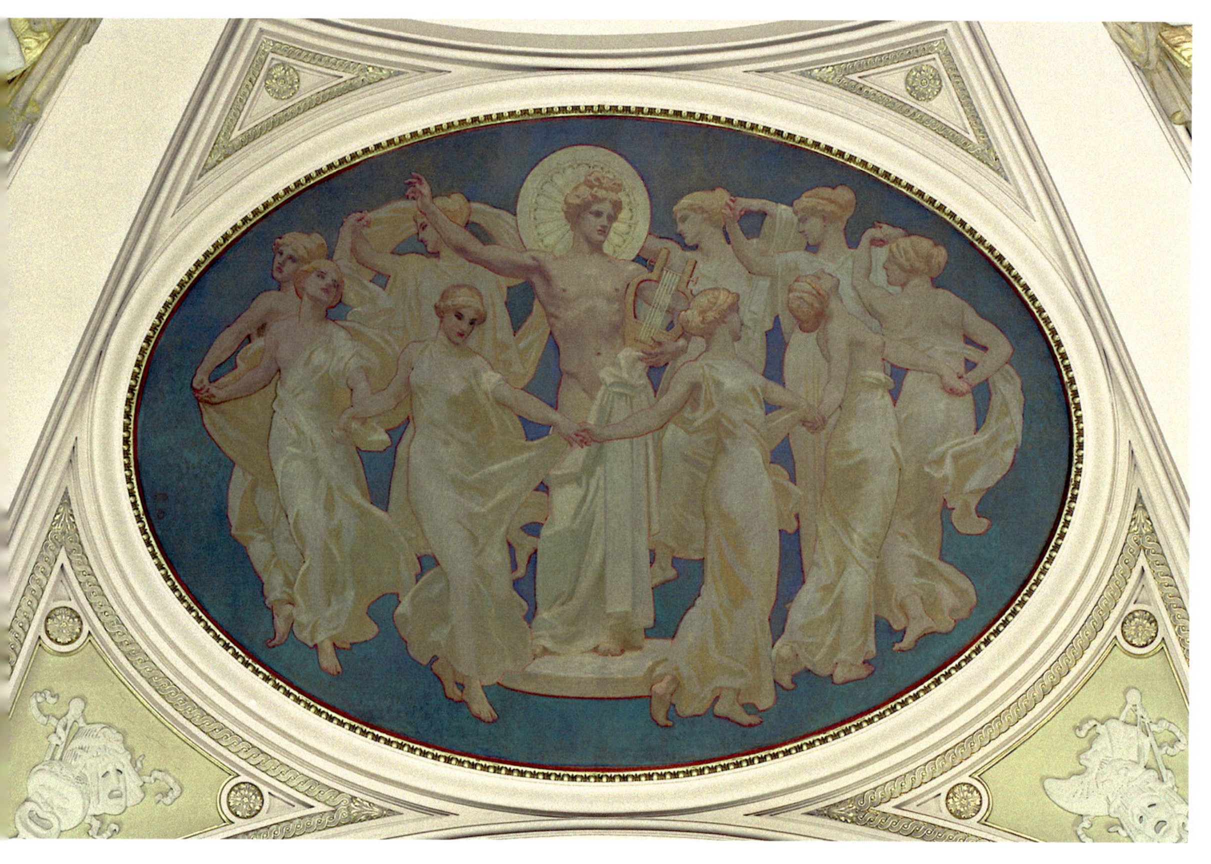

Apollo and the Muses, before treatment (above) and after (opposite). Treatment removed surface grime but did not radically change the painting's appearance. The difference between these images is mostly attributable to changed lighting conditions.

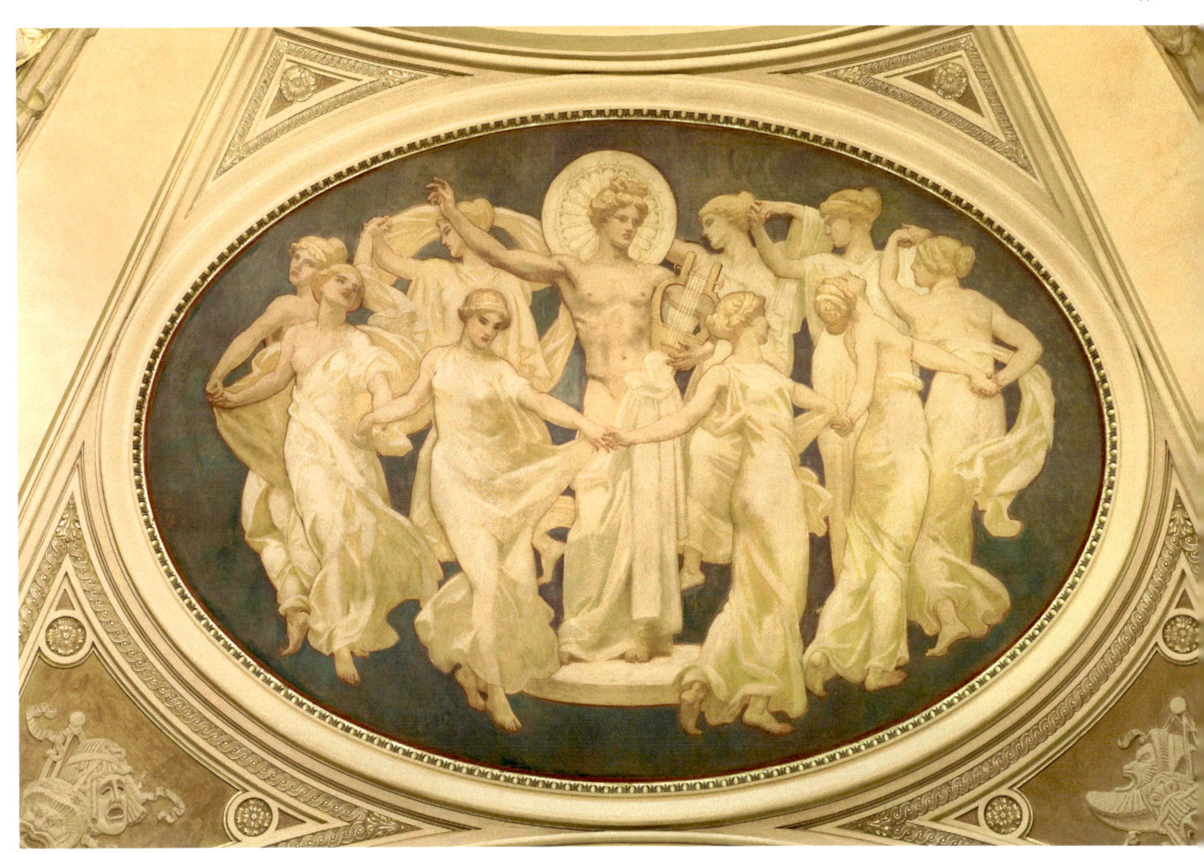

Appeal to the Great Spirit

Cyrus E. Dallin (American, 1861–1944)

1909

The surface of this monumental bronze sculpture appears to have a rich patina, as if the elements reacted with the metal and turned it from dark brown to green. In this case, however, the color is mainly from paint, not corrosion. Primarily because the artist expressed a preference for this look years after he first created the work, MFA conservators regularly restore the sculpture, so that its surface appears to have weathered.

Cyrus Dallin had *Appeal to the Great Spirit* cast in Paris in 1909, and then brought it to Boston in 1911. A movement to raise funds for its purchase had already begun. Originally, it was to have been turned over to the city of Boston for installation in a public park, but in 1912 the subscribers to the fund decided to donate the sculpture to the Museum of Fine Arts instead. It has been a prominent feature of the Museum's grounds since 1913.

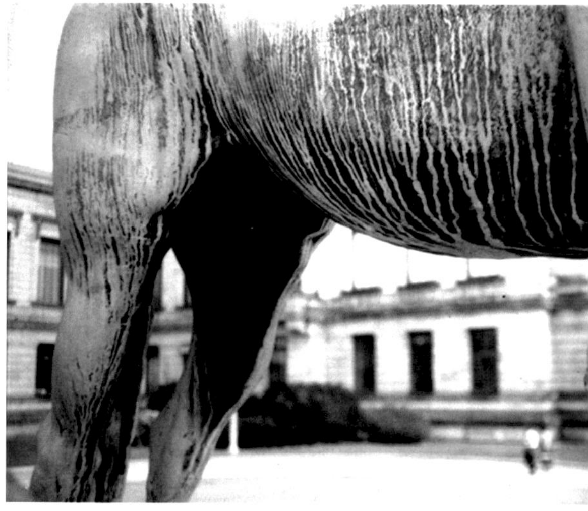

detail of the sculpture in the early 1970s

In keeping with common practice for outdoor bronze sculpture in the early years of the twentieth century, Dallin patinated the surface of his work a brown or brown-black color by treating it with chemicals. Unfortunately, the original patina was thin. Soon after it was installed outdoors, acid rain and other precipitation attacked the sculpture, leaving behind streaks of green corrosion and etched channels in the original metal surface. When Museum conservators treated the sculpture in 1933, they removed the green corrosion and repatinated the surface brown in an effort to re-create the artist's original intent. Dallin, who was teaching in Boston at the time, expressed admiration for the treatment but said that he preferred the green of the damaged surface. Because of his wishes, the conservators repatinated the sculpture green.

After that, the sculpture was left alone for many years. It again developed disfiguring streaks, this time with areas of black corrosion. Museum conservators therefore carried out another extensive treatment in the late 1970s. After cleaning the work, they applied dry pigments in a synthetic resin containing a copper-based corrosion inhibitor to turn the black areas to green. Then they applied green paint over the entire surface and added a coating of wax. The paint and wax provide good protection for the sculpture, but MFA curators were dissatisfied with the even look of the surface, so a year later the conservators added more paint in brown tones to variegate it. Conservators now regularly remove and reapply the wax coating and replace any underlying paint that becomes damaged from exposure.

Bronze, green patina, lost-wax cast
309.88 x 111.12 x 260.35 cm (122 x 43¾ x 102½ in.)
Gift of Peter C. Brooks and others 13.380

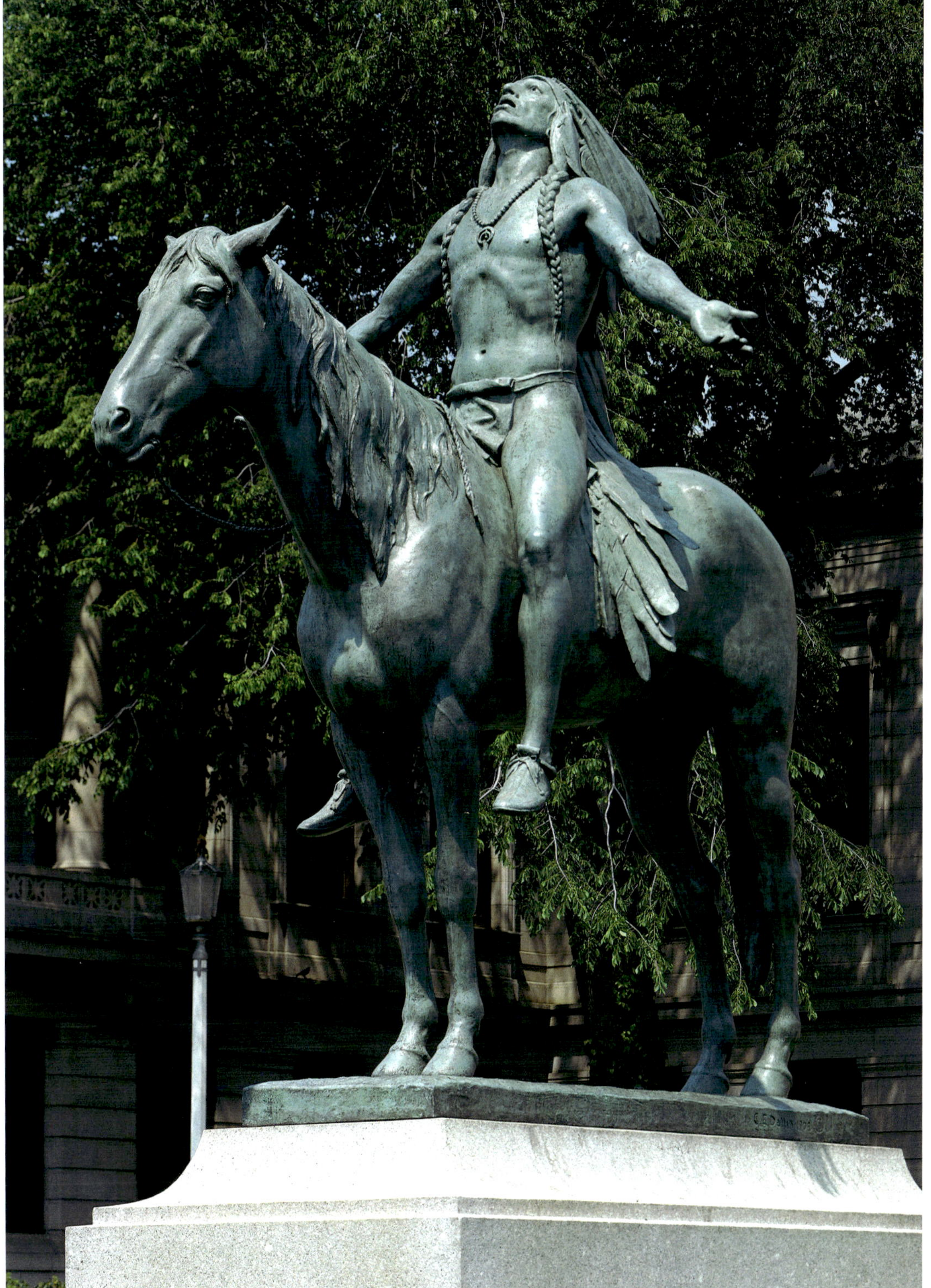

after treatment

Window with eight apostles, the pietà, and other saints

England, medieval (Gothic), about 1400–1425

The MFA first installed this medieval stained-glass window, the largest of its kind outside Europe, in a specially designed gallery in 1927. Modern stonework for the installation imitated the design of a grand country estate, Hampton Court House in Herefordshire, England, from which the window had been removed three years earlier. The window is believed to have been made originally for the nearby Hereford Cathedral. It likely depicted all twelve of Christ's apostles at that time. Eight of these came to the MFA.

In its new home in Boston, the window was exposed to the outdoors on one side, as it had been in England. In January 1942, just weeks after the bombing of Pearl Harbor, fear of attack led Museum officials to remove it (along with many other objects) to a remote storage location for safekeeping. They reinstalled the window in the same gallery toward the end of World War II in 1944. Museum staff then moved it again for the construction of a new wing in 2003. This last event provided an opportunity to clean and repair the window and redesign its installation.

The window suffered some damage from its hasty disassembly and reassembly during the war, as well as from its previous transfers. In addition, centuries of exposure to the weather had resulted in chemical changes that caused the outer surfaces of the glass to flake or break off in chips. (This type of corrosion is typical of medieval glass.) The pitting of the glass on the window's exterior made it more difficult to see the scenes painted on the interior. Some of the lead channels holding the pieces of stained glass together, called cames, had corroded over time and were no longer safe. Cames that had been added to the window as part of earlier programs of repair obscured important details, such as faces and inscriptions.

The Museum hired a team of specialists to detach the entire window from its modern stonework and to clean and repair it. After studying the window carefully to determine which parts should be preserved as evidence of its history, the specialists replaced unstable cames and removed old repairs that greatly disrupted the picture. In certain cases the conservators used new cames or made repairs with thin copper foils; in others they adhered pieces of glass together using special adhesives.

Although the conservators reused the stone tracery from the Museum's 1927 installation, they applied hardware instead of mortar to attach framed sections of stained glass to it. Now each frame can be removed without disturbing its neighbors. The conservators also replaced a clear glass barrier that the Museum had installed in 1970 to protect the window from the elements. The new isothermal glazing, which represents advances in glass technology and manufacturing, provides insulation against the elements while allowing the window to exchange air inside the gallery through vents at the top and bottom of the window. Such an installation

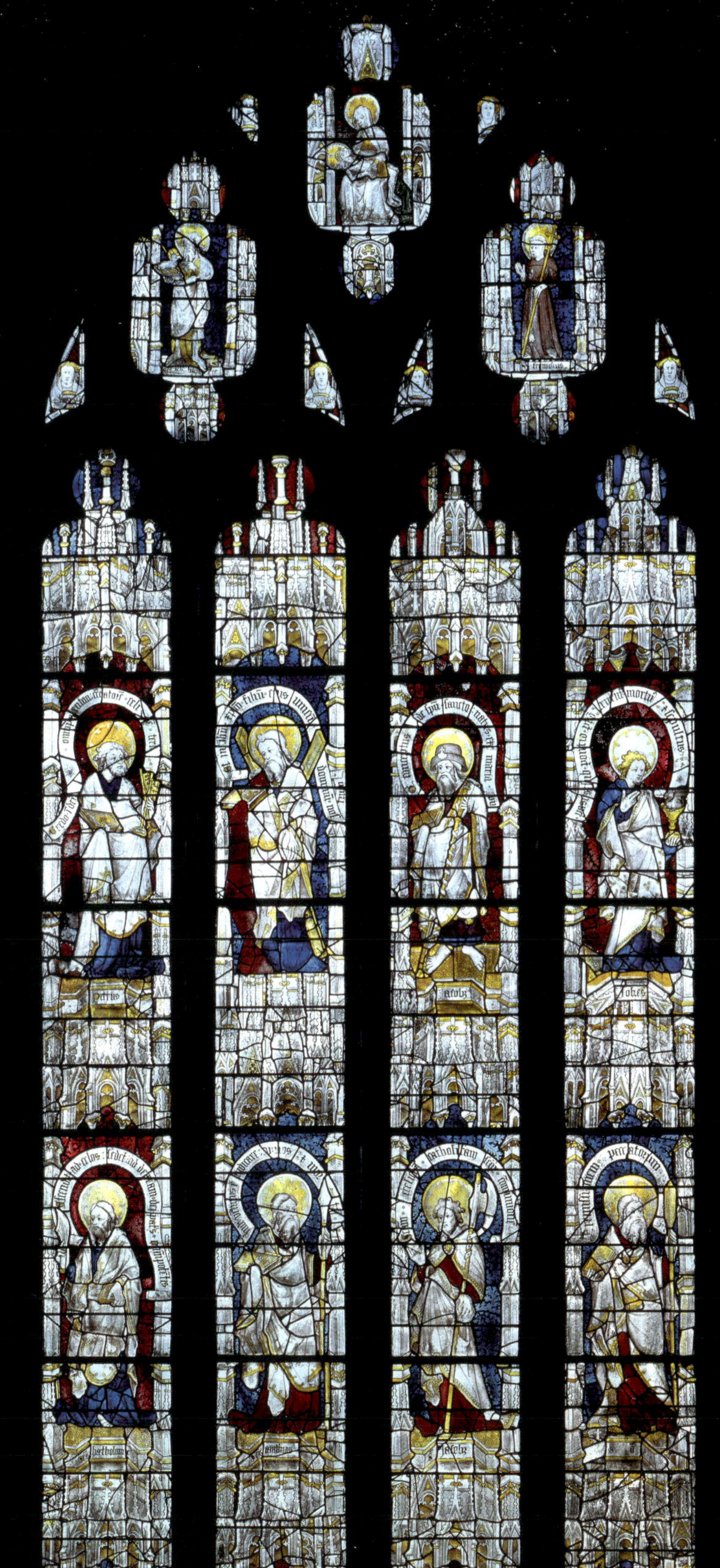

before treatment

detail, before treatment

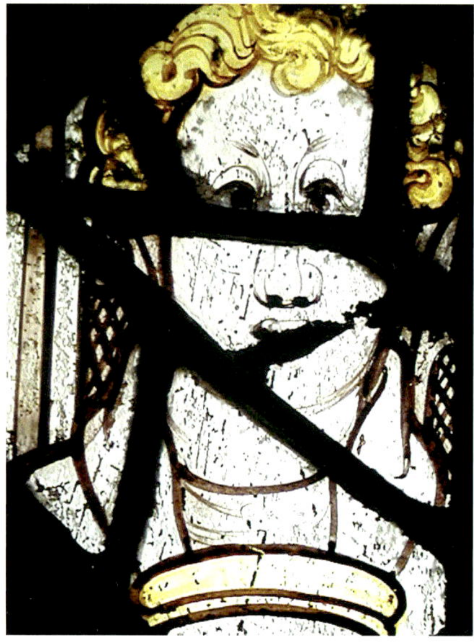

detail, during treatment

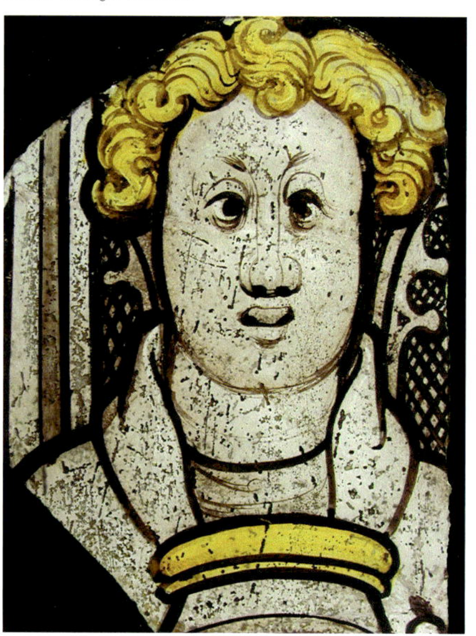

creates equal environmental conditions on both sides, which is important for preventing harmful condensation on the exterior surfaces. The glazing still allows natural light to filter through the window so that visitors can view the window as it was originally meant to be seen.

While the window was still in its disassembled state, the conservators took small samples of glass and paint from it and analyzed them for their chemical compositions. This ongoing research has the aim of exploring the relationship between this stained-glass window and the great east window at York Minster Cathedral, which dates from the same period as the MFA's and resembles it stylistically. Further scientific research may shed more light on this window's origins.

Pot-metal glass, flashed glass, and white glass with silver-oxide stain; modern limestone tracery
263 x 563 cm (103 9/16 x 221 5/8 in.)
Maria Antoinette Evans Fund 25.213.1–21

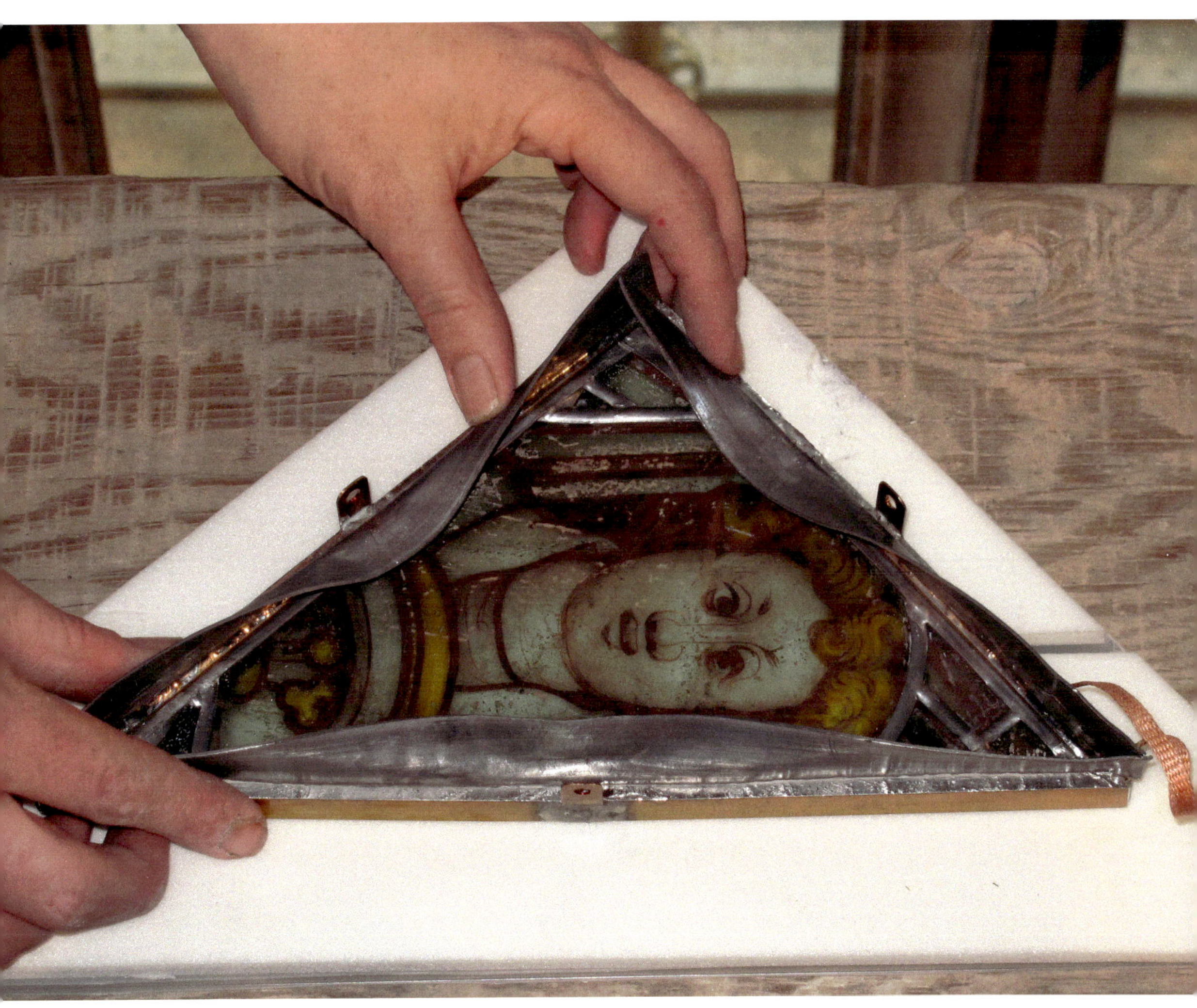

restored angel in its new mount

Miroku, the Buddha of the Future

Japan, Kamakura–Nanbokuchō period, 14th century

detail, before treatment, showing distortion of the fabric and mold damage

The hanging scroll is a flexible Asian painting format with origins going back more than two thousand years. Traditionally made of multiple borders of fabrics adhered to paper backings, it allows a painting to be rolled up for storage or transportation. Even under the best environmental conditions, however, repeated handling and display weaken a scroll's structure and materials. Most scroll paintings therefore need to be remounted at least every one to two hundred years.

This fourteenth-century Japanese painting is mounted in the Japanese Buddhist style, with double borders of gold brocade and gilt metal fittings, all incorporating religious motifs. MFA conservators specially trained in Asian mounting methods removed the scroll's old fabrics and paper linings and replaced them with new, stronger ones that can better support the painting and allow the scroll to be rolled and handled safely. Although conservators prefer to reuse the textiles from an old mounting provided that they are in good condition and are stylistically, historically, and aesthetically appropriate for the artwork, they could not do so in this case because mold had rotted the earlier brocades. Thus, they selected the replacement mounting silks in keeping with the Buddhist subject and period of the painting.

Hanging scroll; ink, color, and gold on silk
113.5 x 57.3 cm (44 11/16 x 22 9/16 in.)
Gift of Mr. and Mrs. Wilbur D. Canaday 1980.466

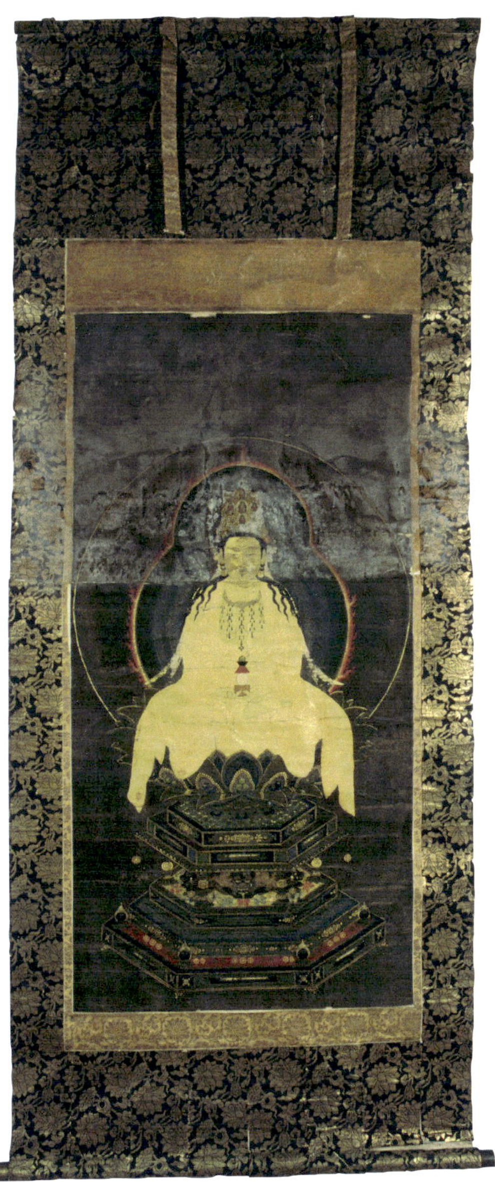

before treatment

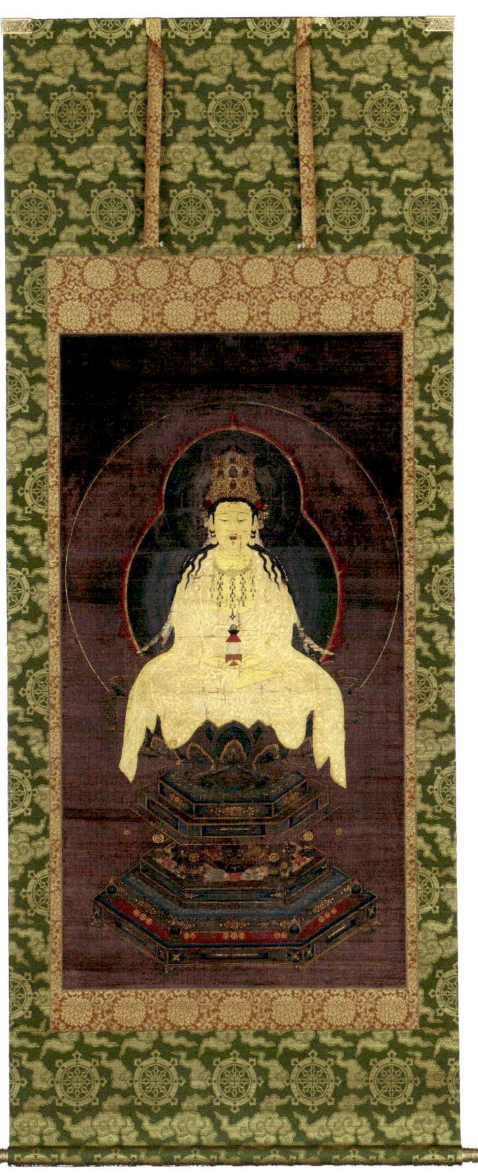

after treatment

The Arhats Hva-sang, Gopaka, and Pantaka with Two Guardian Kings, Virudhaka and Dhritarashtra

Tibet, 19th century

Someone altered the format of this Tibetan painting before it entered the MFA's collection in 1904. He or she gave it silk borders in the proportions of a Japanese hanging scroll, and then fitted the combination into a framed panel behind glass in the style of an American or European painting. The panel was probably the idea of the Japanese dealer from whom the MFA purchased the work; it is likely that the dealer needed a functional and familiar format for his Western clientele. At the turn of the twentieth century, few dealers or collectors in the United States understood the significance of the painting's original format. Even as recently as the 1980s, well-meaning museums and private collectors turned Tibetan paintings into panels in the belief that they were better preserved that way.

This image of arhats and guardian kings was originally mounted as a Tibetan *thangka*, a type of flexible hanging scroll that derives its structure and materials from Indian cloth paintings and Central Asian banner paintings. Tibetan Buddhists consider a thangka a devotional object depicting the ideal bodily forms of enlightened beings. Its design includes a veil that reveals those sacred forms to devotees or protects them from the uninitiated (as well as from light and insects), depending on whether the veil is gathered up or left to hang down over the painted image. Unlike other hanging-scroll formats from Korea, China, or Japan, stitching rather than pasting creates the thangka; therefore, it has no paper backing. The painted image on cloth is stitched into a framework of cloth borders usually made of silk and given a wooden stave at the top and a wooden dowel at the bottom. The dowel allows the painting to be rolled up for storage or transport.

When conservators from the MFA's Asian Conservation Studio returned this painting to thangka format for an exhibition in 2009, they first determined that the appropriate form for the mounting should be Eastern Tibetan, based on the style of the painting. They selected a mixture of old and new silk brocades in keeping with that style, then hand stitched every part of the new thangka according to traditional practice. In Tibet, where there is no separate occupation devoted to conservation, tailors, artists, or monks do the stitching. For the exhibition, the conservators used a monofilament thread to hang the thangka and secured two transparent thermoplastic hooks shaped to the curve of the bottom rod into the display wall to support the weight of the scroll. They tied the veil and let the streamers hang down, respecting the integrity and functionality of the thangka's original context.

Thangka; distemper on cotton with silk borders
190 x 76 cm (74 13/16 x 29 15/16 in.)
James Fund 04.61

The painting with Japanese-style fabric borders and mounted as a panel, before treatment (opposite, left), and in a Tibetan-style mount, after treatment (opposite, right)

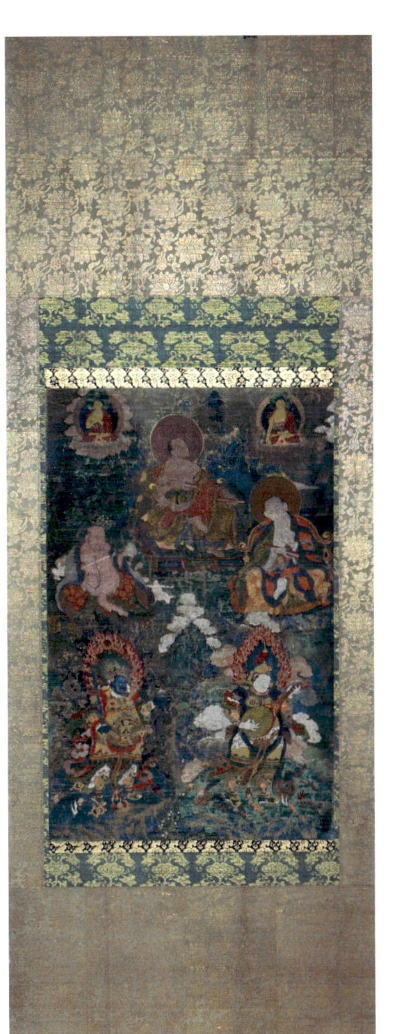

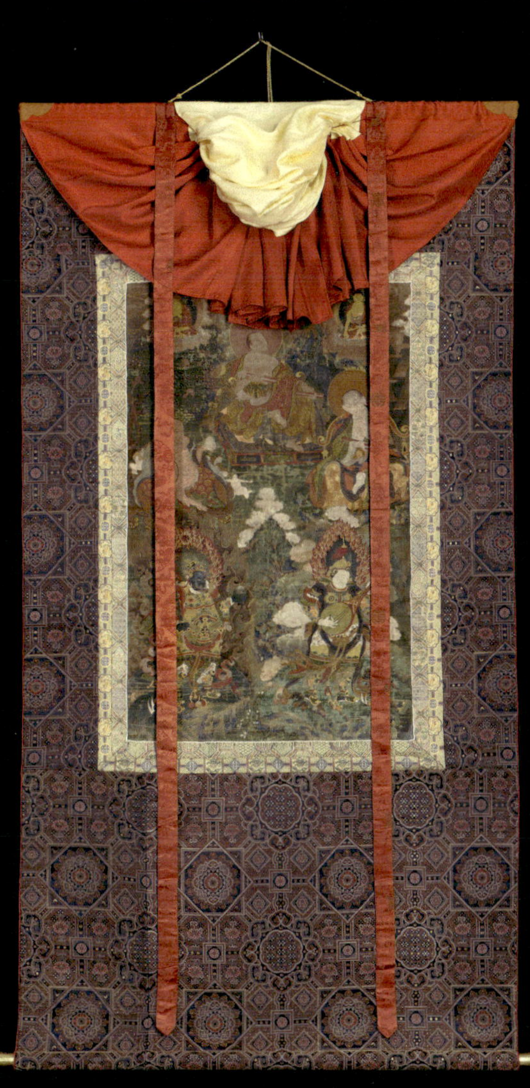

Architectural elements

Egypt, Hellenistic Period (Ptolemaic Dynasty), reign of Ptolemy VIII, 170–116 B.C.

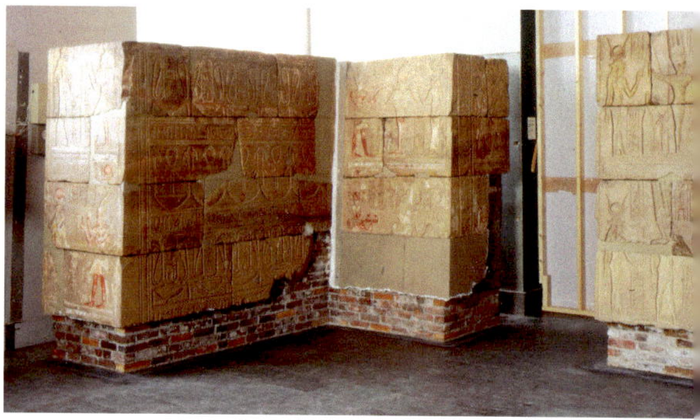

The stone blocks during deinstallation

In 1923 an archaeological expedition team jointly sponsored by the MFA and Harvard University found twenty-five large painted sandstone blocks at Koptos (also known as Qift), about twenty miles north of Luxor. Although the blocks were discovered among the ruined foundations of a Roman tower built in the late third or early fourth century A.D., they had been taken from an enclosure wall surrounding a temple dating to the reign of the great builder Ptolemy VIII. The temple was still standing in the reign of Nero when that Roman emperor added his name to it, but it had long been destroyed by the time of the MFA-Harvard expedition.

Lacking further information about the blocks' original architectural context, the MFA had them mounted in two groups, rather like wall paintings, in 1930. In 1995, funded by a generous grant, Museum staff undertook an extensive conservation and restoration project to reinstall the blocks according to the latest research on Ptolemaic gateways. Conservators carefully removed the blocks from their gallery wall and cleaned them of the cement used in the 1930 installation, which was causing areas of sandstone to deteriorate. They also consolidated the polychrome pigments on the blocks' surfaces to protect them from further damage and to allow the decoration to stand out more clearly. Finally, with the aid of engineers, they specially designed and built a mounting system that minimizes stress on the fragile sandstone blocks when they are in position. The design called for drilling vertical holes through the blocks so that they could be fitted with steel rods. The rods attach to a steel frame above, suspending each block individually without exerting any pressure on the blocks below. The missing portions of the structure were made from plywood painted to resemble the original color of the stone.

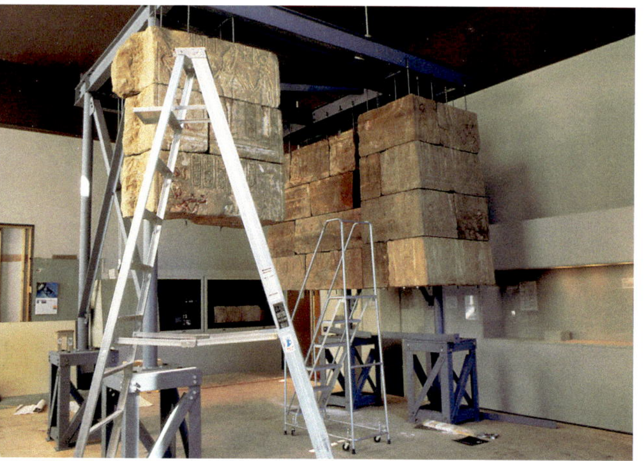

Installation of the stone blocks on a new steel mounting system that suspends each block without exerting pressure on blocks below

Painted sandstone

544 x 458 x 378 cm (214 3/16 x 180 5/16 x 148 13/16 in.)

524 x 458 x 378 cm (206 5/16 x 180 5/16 x 148 13/16 in.)

Harvard University—Boston Museum of Fine Arts Expedition 24.1632–3

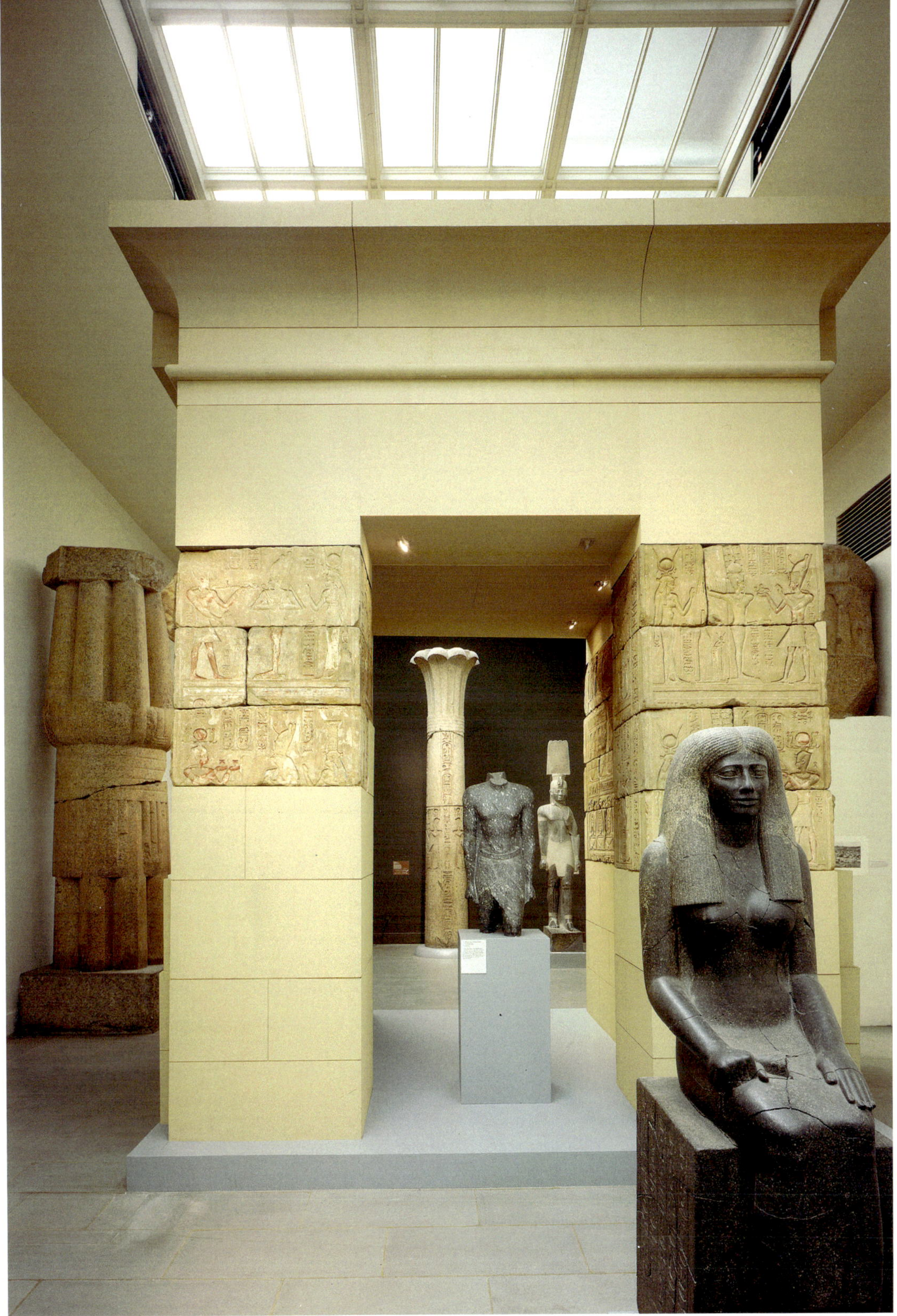

The blocks installed in the configuration of a gateway in the Museum's gallery

Headdress decorated with two dragons confronting a flaming jewel

China, Liao Dynasty, late 10th–early 11th century

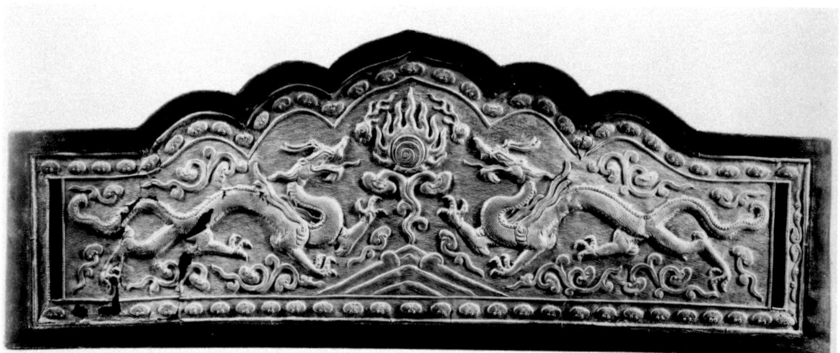

before treatment

When this object came to the Museum in 1940 in the form of a low-relief, gilt-silver plaque, Museum curators identified it as an eleventh- to early-twelfth-century Korean work of art from the Goryeo Dynasty. They noted that the plaque once ornamented the side of a rectangular receptacle, which probably had been made of wood, for the ashes of an important person. This attribution seemed reasonable based on a comparison of the object with surviving examples of Goryeo-period caskets.

Then in 1960, Chinese archaeologists published a photograph of a headdress that had been excavated in Liaoning Province, a region of northeastern China that had been a part of the Liao Dynasty from the tenth through the early twelfth centuries. The headdress, found in a tomb dated by the archaeologists to the late tenth or early eleventh century, bore a close resemblance to the MFA's plaque. On the basis of this new discovery, a Museum conservator gently manipulated the plaque into its present headdress shape.

Because even a sheet of new silver becomes brittle when it is hammered or bent due to stresses that build up in the atomic structure of the metal, and because of weaknesses in the structure caused by old corrosion, the conservator most likely used a process called annealing. Annealing, which involves heating the material to a red-hot temperature, relieves the stresses and makes the metal ductile again. Today conservators avoid this treatment because it alters the metal structure and erases most if not all clues about original manufacturing techniques. The object's new identity provides a possible explanation for its vertical slits at either end—they may have held ribbons or broad bands that the wearer used to adjust the headdress's fit.

Gilt silver with repoussé decoration
H. 20.6 cm, diam. 62 cm
(H. 8⅛ in., diam. 24 7/16 in.)
William Sturgis Bigelow Collection, by exchange 40.749

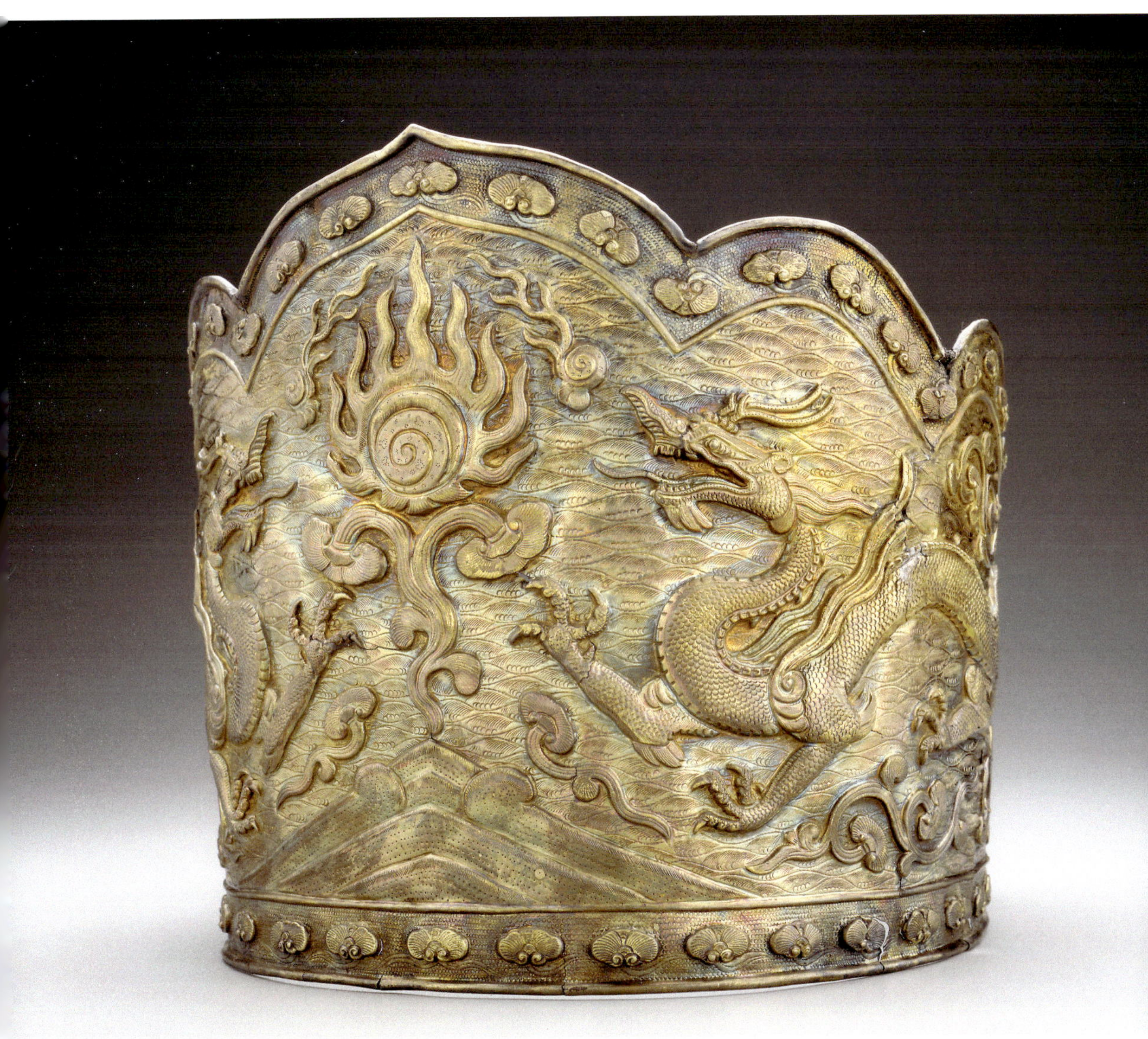

after treatment

Sofa

Probably Boston, 1850–70

Rosewood and upholstery

108 x 161.3 x 78.7 cm (42½ x 63½ x 31 in.)

Gift of John Fenn Brill 1982.479

Side chair

George Hunzinger

(American, born in Germany, 1835–1898)

New York, about 1870

Walnut and upholstery

81.9 x 44.5 x 53.3 cm (32¼ x 17½ x 21 in.)

Harriet Otis Cruft Fund 1979.625

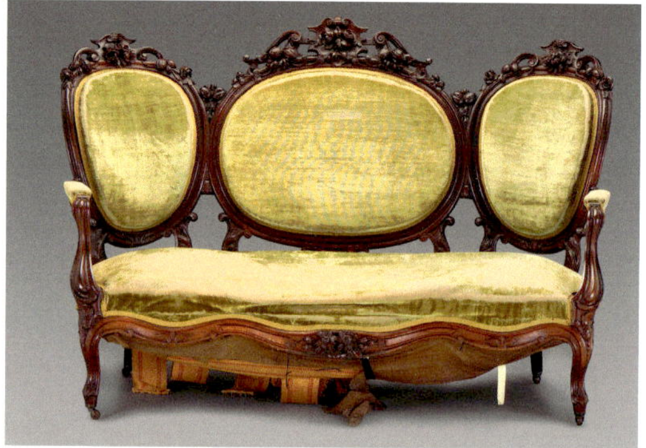

American furniture from the mid-nineteenth century probably received new upholstery about every thirty years. Sometimes new fabric was placed on top of the old, and at other times worn upholstery was entirely removed before the new covering was applied. When MFA curators and conservators decided to restore this mid-nineteenth-century sofa to the way it appeared when it was first manufactured, a few green and red threads in a tack hole on the frame were their only clues to the original upholstery's color and fiber type.

In 2009 the conservators were able to identify the type and weave structure of the green threads as silk satin by looking at them under a microscope. The curators therefore chose a green damask fabric for the restoration. Because the red threads had been on top of the green ones in the tack hole, the curators concluded that they came from the original trim. They were guided in their decisions by their knowledge of period tastes and design. The combination of green and red was a popular decorative scheme in the mid-nineteenth century, and color theorists of that time recommended creating harmonies with such contrasting complementary hues. Once the fabric and trim had been selected for the restoration, the conservators were able to reconstruct the shape of the original seat because all of the underuphol-

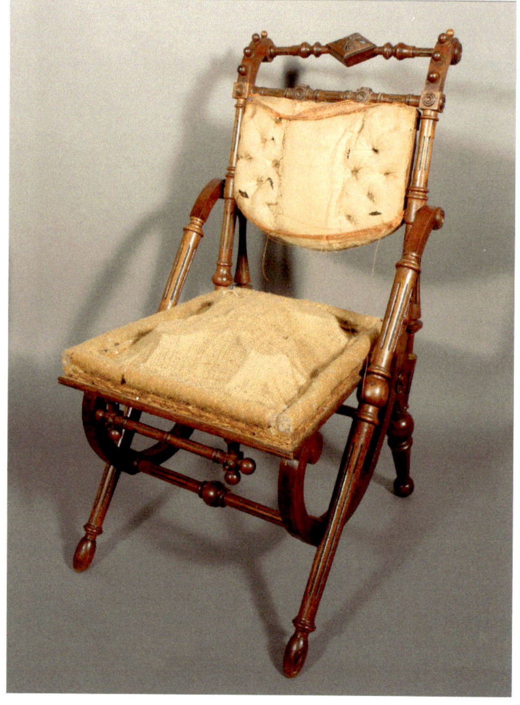

before treatment

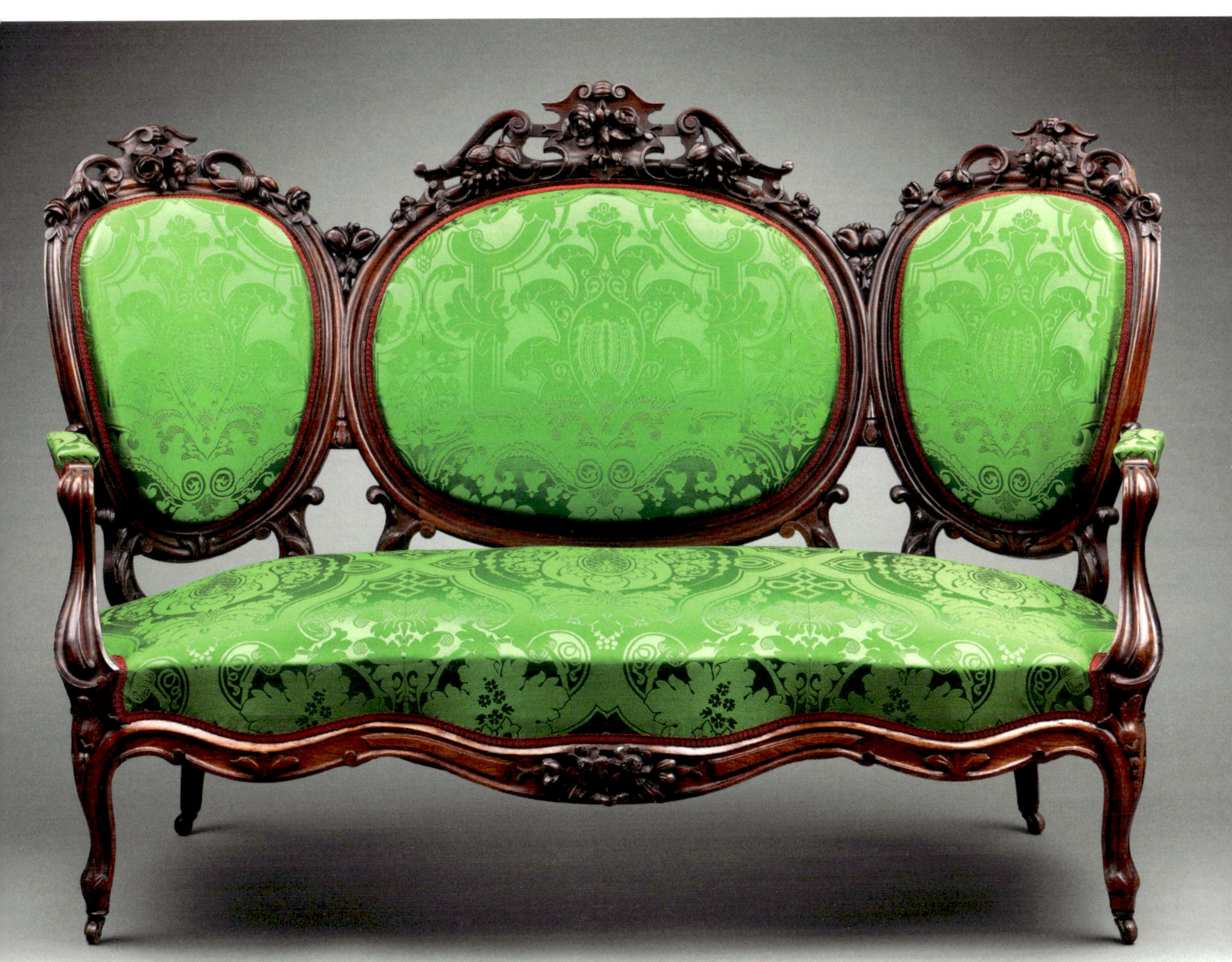

after treatment

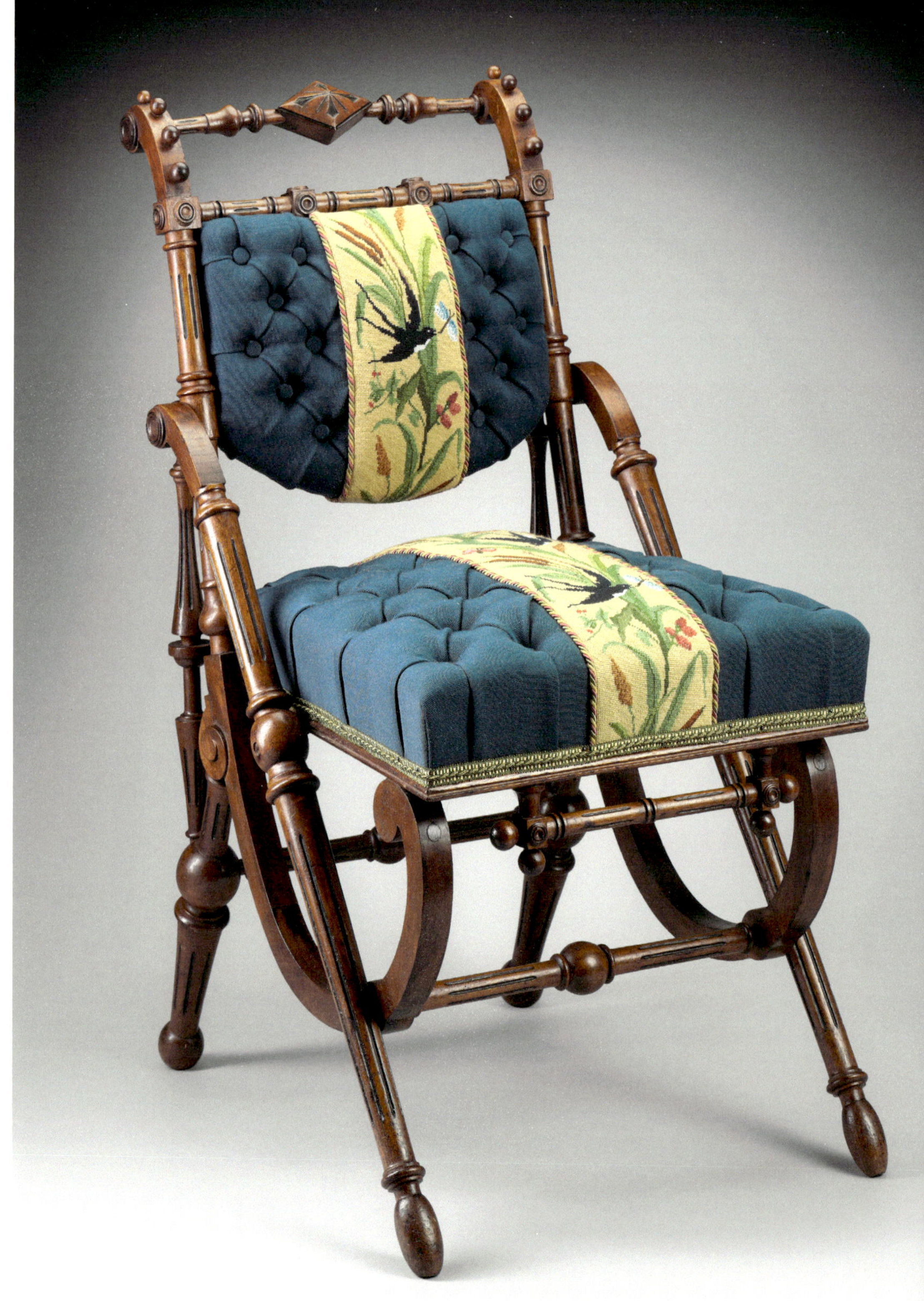

after treatment

stery, including the jute webbing, steel springs, horsehair filling, and a filling cover, survived. Significant work was needed to support those materials and return them to their original profile.

The side chair by George Hunzinger retained its original underupholstery, but only on its back. The conservator of the chair therefore adapted the proportions of its three-part design to re-create the seat, which was a later restoration (except for its springs) out of keeping with Hunzinger's work. By comparing the design with surviving original examples, curators knew that it usually included a woven or handmade decorative stripe in the center. Because no suitable commercially woven stripe could be found, curators and conservators worked with a skilled volunteer to make a needlework stripe adapted from a pattern published in the December 1877 issue of *Peterson's Magazine*. The color blue was chosen for the reproduction show cover because of fiber evidence on the chair frame and the finished upholstery.

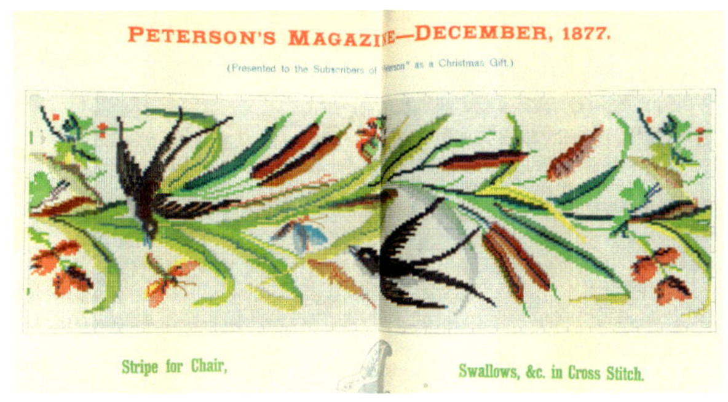

Needlework pattern used as a model for the new decorative stripe on the restored chair

Reproduction furnishings after a suite from the tomb of Queen Hetepheres I

Joseph Gerte (American, working 1920–1955)
Boston, 1929–38
Bed, canopy, and armchair
Wood, gold, copper, silver, leather, faience, ebony
Headrest
Wood, silver, gold

Ahmed Youssef (Egyptian, died 1996)
Egypt, 1939
Curtain box
Wood, gold, copper, silver, faience, ebony

Unique reproductions can be valued parts of a museum collection and require the same conservation care as original works of art. This suite of reproduction furniture faithfully represents a set from the tomb of Egypt's Queen Hetepheres I, who lived during the reign of King Sneferu (2575–2528 B.C.). Although the wood of the original furniture had mostly deteriorated by the time of the tomb's excavation in 1925, its copper and gold sheeting survived relatively intact. This casing revealed many details of the furniture's original configuration, as well as the joining methods the ancient Egyptians had used to assemble their furniture. By referring to thousands of documentary photographs taken at the archaeological site, MFA archaeologists working with British and Egyptian conservators were able to reconstruct the 4,500-year-old suite from the excavated pieces. The magnitude of this undertaking can be imagined from a photograph of the tomb when it was first opened. Parts of the bed canopy were stacked on a stone sarcophagus on one side, and crumbled parts of the other pieces of furniture were mixed with debris on the other side of the burial chamber. The reconstructed furniture was put on display in the Egyptian Museum in Cairo and may be seen there today.

When making the MFA's reproductions, the cabinetmaker Joseph Gerte and conservator Ahmed Youssef chose materials—gold leaf applied over a layer of gesso on wood—that were faithful to the originals. Unfortunately, they could not predict the conservation problems that would arise when they put the new furniture on display in galleries without climate control. Now more than seventy years old, the MFA's suite has required several treatments to address damage caused by environmental shifts in relative humidity. Conservators have had to strengthen and readhere lifted areas of gesso and gilding and remove corrosion from metal pieces, all of which reacted with moisture in the air. They performed the conservation treatments in much the same way as they would have done for authentic objects made from similar materials. The furniture suite is now in a temperature- and humidity-controlled environment, which should help to prevent future deterioration.

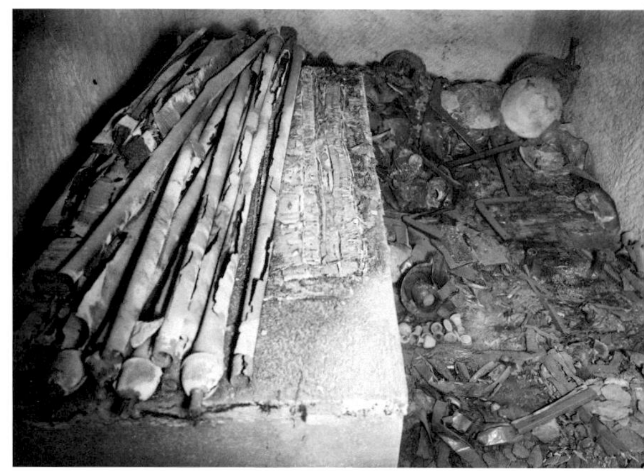

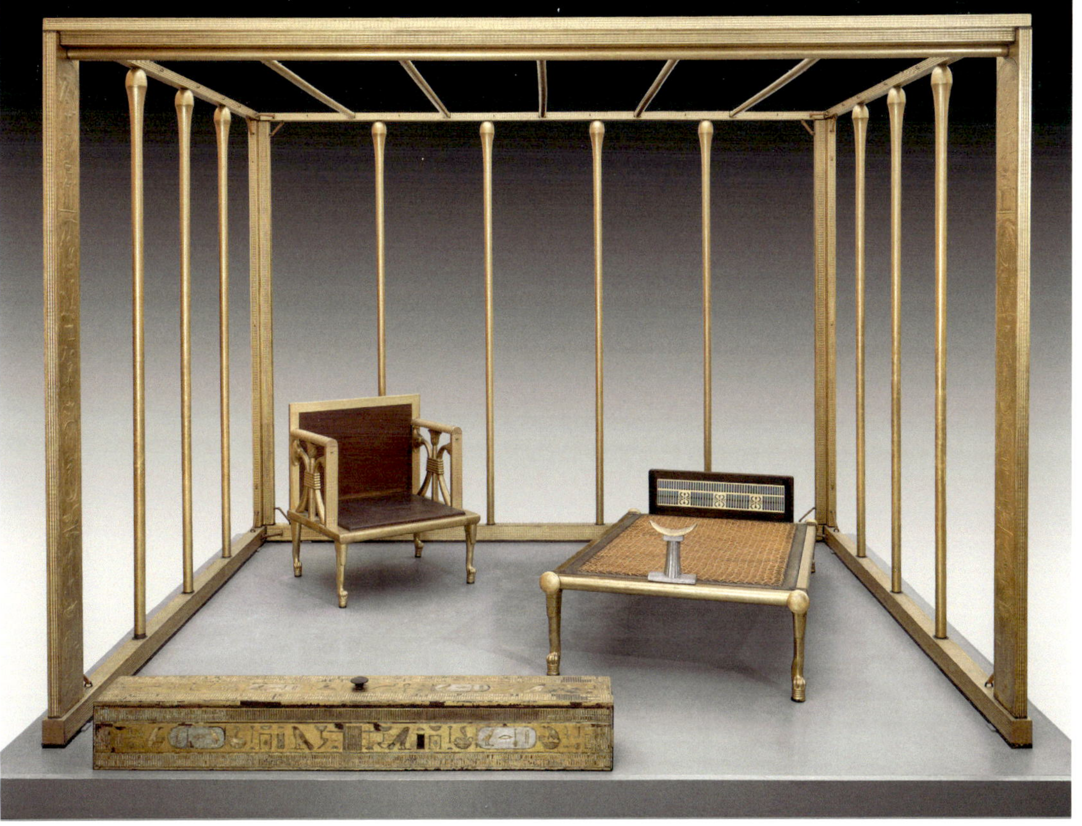

(opposite) The tomb in 1926, with parts of the original furniture mixed in with debris

Bed: H. 43.5 cm, l. 177 cm, w. 97.5 cm (H. 17⅛ in., l. 69 1/16 in., w. 38⅜ in.)
Harvard University—Boston Museum of Fine Arts Expedition, 1929 29.1858

Canopy: H. 221.5 cm, l. 313.7 cm, w. 258.8 cm (H. 87 3/16 in., l. 123½ in., w. 101⅞ in.)
Departmental Appropriation, 1938 38.873

Armchair: H. 79.5 cm, w. 70.7 cm, d. 66 cm (H. 31 5/16 in., w. 27 13/16 in., d. 26 in.)
Gift of Mrs. Charles Gaston Smith and Group of Friends, 1938 38.957

Headrest: H. 20.5 cm, w. 17.2 cm, d. 7.8 cm (H. 8 1/16 in., w. 6¾ in., d. 3 1/16 in.)
Harvard University—Boston Museum of Fine Arts Expedition, 1929 29.1859

Curtain box: H. 18.5 cm, l. 157.5 cm, w. 21.5 cm (H. 7 5/16 in., l. 62 in., w. 8 7/16 in.)
Harvard University—Boston Museum of Fine Arts Expedition, 1939 39.746

Harpsichord

Made by Henri Hemsch

(French, born in Germany, 1700–1769)

Paris, probably 1736

Poplar, fir, ebony, ivory, brass, iron

92.5 x 89 x 238 cm (36 7/16 x 35 1/16 x 93 11/16 in.)

The Edward F. Searles Musical Instrument Collection; given by Edward S. Rowland, Benjamin A. Rowland, Jr., George B. Rowland, Daniel B. Rowland, Rodney D. Rowland, and M. A. Swedlund in memory of their father, Benjamin Allen Rowland 1981.747

Arched harp

Burma, mid-19th century

Padauk wood, shà wood, glass, deerskin, cotton cord

66 x 16 x 81 cm (26 x 6 5/16 x 31 7/8 in.)

Samuel Putnam Avery Fund 1992.5

Restoring an antique musical instrument to make it whole and pleasing to the eye is usually straightforward, but returning an instrument to a state of playability often raises concerns about removing, replacing, or altering original material. Some instruments are logical candidates for this latter treatment, and others are best left in a more original state and enjoyed from a strictly visual standpoint.

Conservation in 1987 for the Museum's beautiful French harpsichord posed challenges due to its complex structure and multitude of moving parts. But as the instrument's original keyboard and jacks (the mechanism that plucks the strings) were replaced in 1885 with ones of inauthentic design, both curators and conservators felt compelled to construct new ones. In addition, the thin fir soundboard that amplifies the strings' vibrations was riddled with splits. Like a broken drumhead, the soundboard could not function properly until the cracks were carefully shimmed with pieces of new fir. Music lovers are now able to hear the wonderful sound of this harpsichord, both live and via recordings.

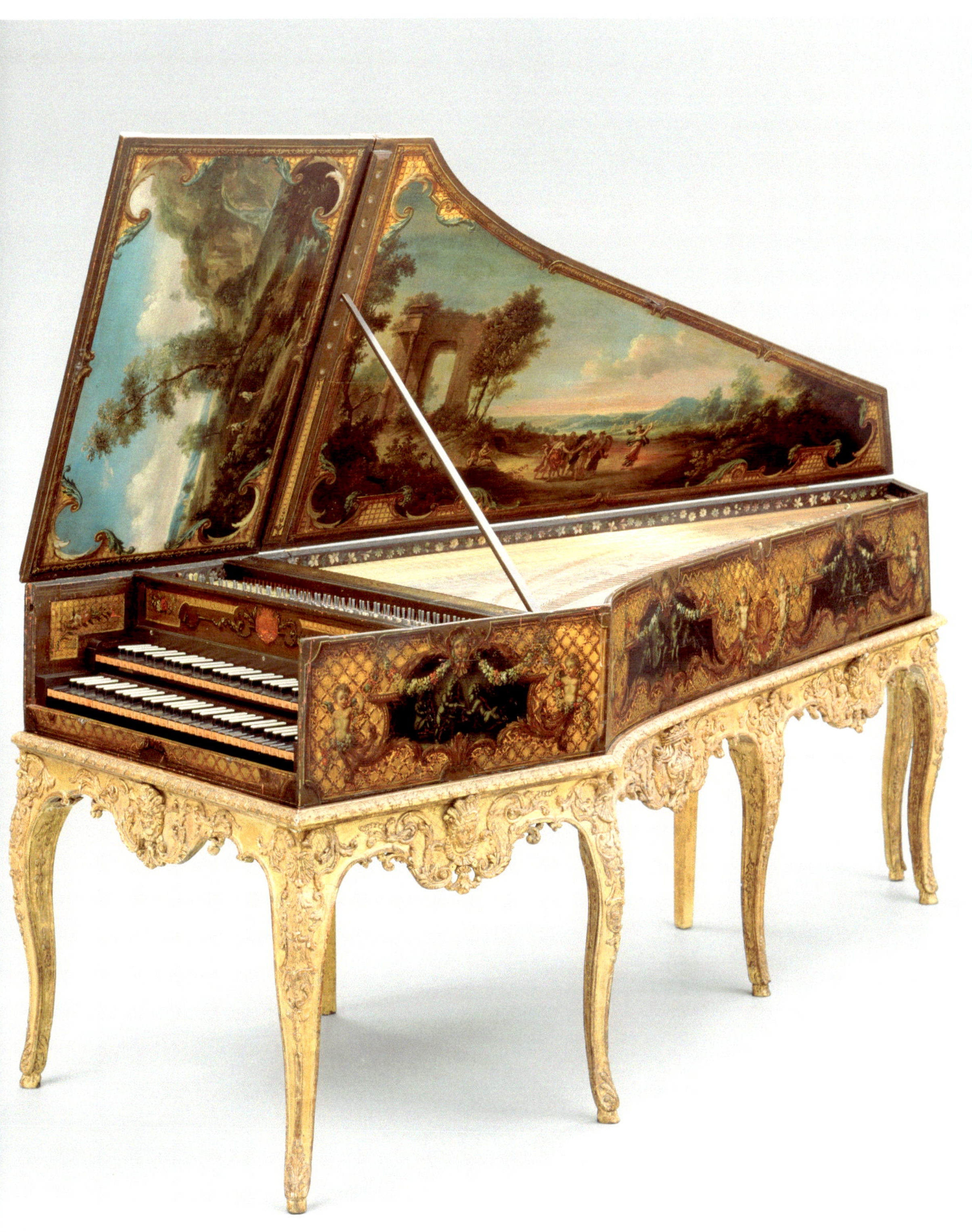

By comparison, a Burmese arched harp (*saung gauk*) received treatment only to make it appear complete, as the slender curved neck and original deerskin covering the body could not be trusted to bear full string tension. The instrument was missing all of its original silk strings and many of the tasseled cords that wrap around the neck and are used to tension the strings. The Museum procured new silk strings from a specialist instrument dealer but left the creation of replacement tuning cords and tassels of appropriate style and color to skilled textile conservators. The conservators matched cotton thread to the original cords as closely as possible and simulated an aged and faded coloring for each of the sixty-six strands required for each cord. Although the harp regrettably cannot be played, replacing its missing musical parts allows viewers to both appreciate its beauty and understand its function.

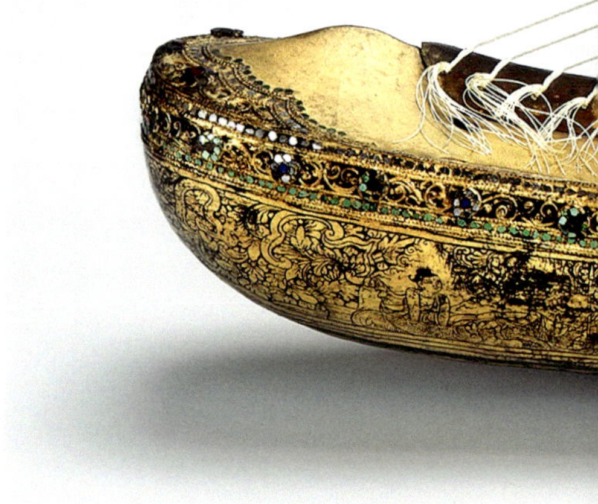

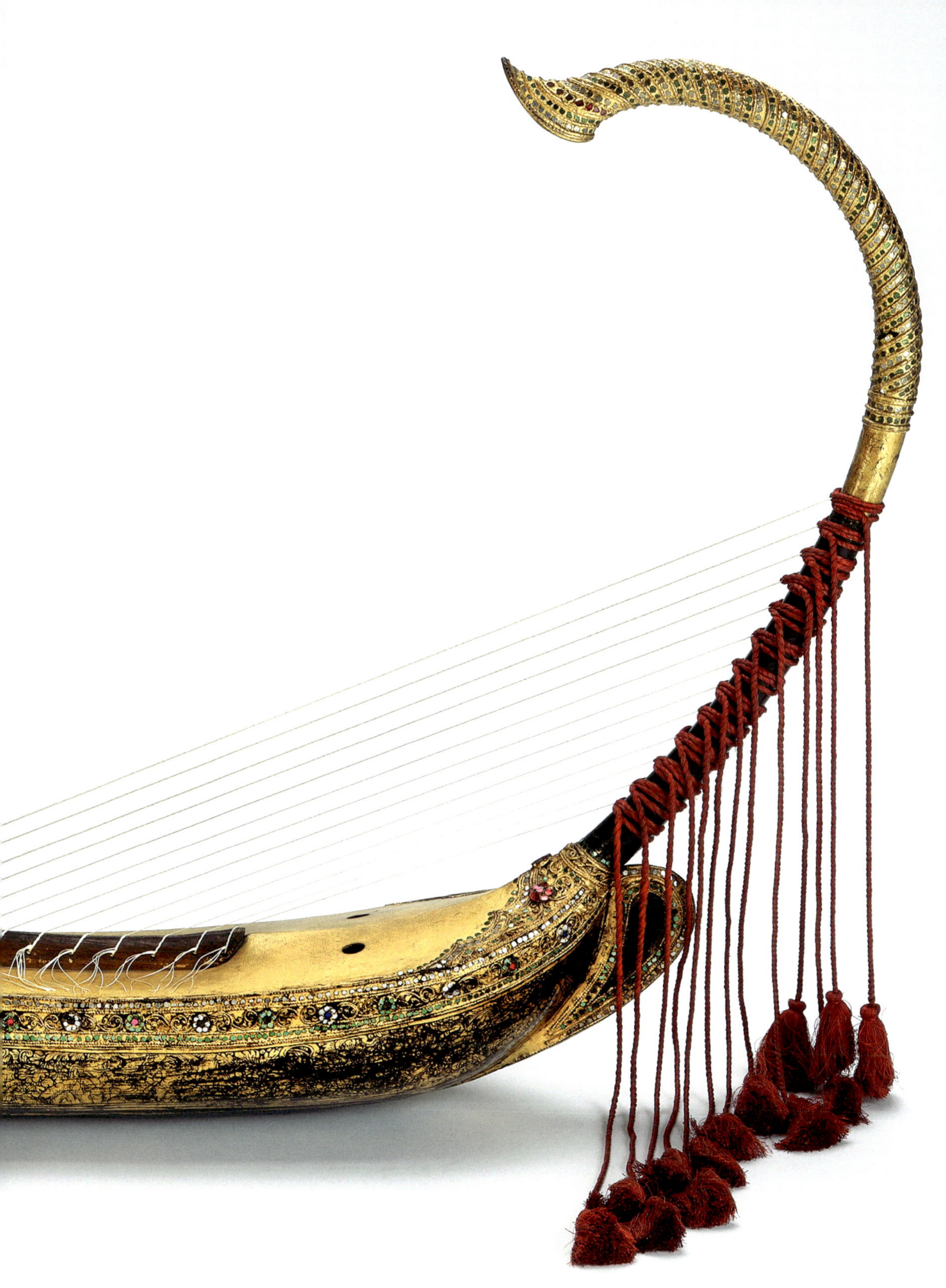

Dionysos and Maenad

Roman Empire, Imperial Period, about 1st–2nd century A.D.

When the MFA acquired this small sculpture in 1968, it did so with the full knowledge that it is a pastiche. Only the body and right leg of the male figure, and the body and left knee of the female figure, were made in ancient times. (The female's right hand and wrist remain on the male's draped back.) These fragments come from a first- or second-century Roman copy of a Hellenistic Greek sculpture carved several centuries earlier.

Documentary evidence shows that about 1770, an Englishman purchased the fragments in Rome, shipped them to his home in Cheshire, and hired an artist to make the fragments whole again. With so little of the original sculpture to go by, the owner or the restorer had to decide which ancient personages would be represented. The restorer then carved the missing parts of the composition in marble. He cut the broken surfaces of the original fragments straight to more easily fit the old and new pieces together. Even now, one can readily see the difference between the two because the new marble lacks the original's weathered surface.

The eighteenth-century restorer fashioned them as Dionysos and Ariadne, but unknown to him, two other fragmentary replicas of the same Hellenistic original (now in museums in Athens and Berlin) show that the male should be the god Priapus, a rustic fertility god characterized by a large, permanent erection. The female should be a maenad, a follower of Dionysos. Priapos-maenad figural groups were popular in the Late Hellenistic period.

Modern conservators no longer consider such extreme re-creations as this sculpture ethical. This type of restoration involves too much guesswork on the part of the restorer and damages the original fragments. The MFA preserves this sculpture in its collection as an example of an early chapter in conservation and collecting history.

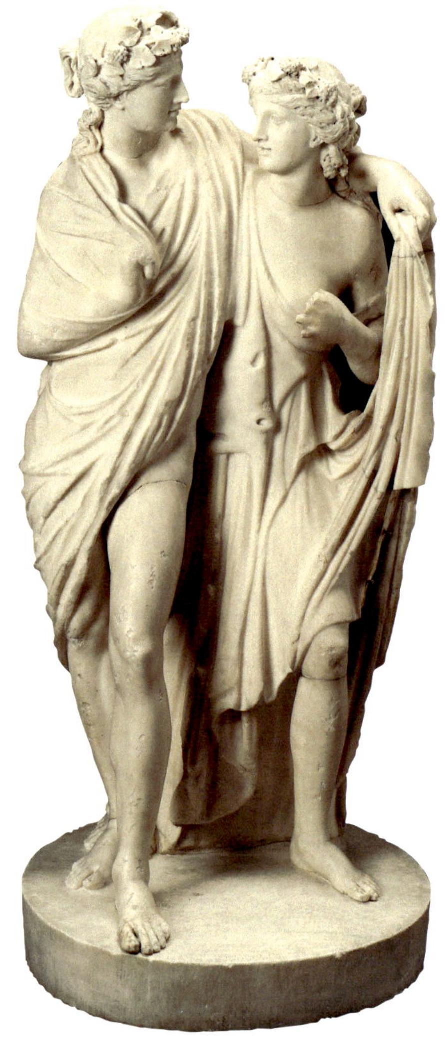

Marble
H. 81 cm (31 7/8 in.)
Gift of Paul E. Manheim 68.770

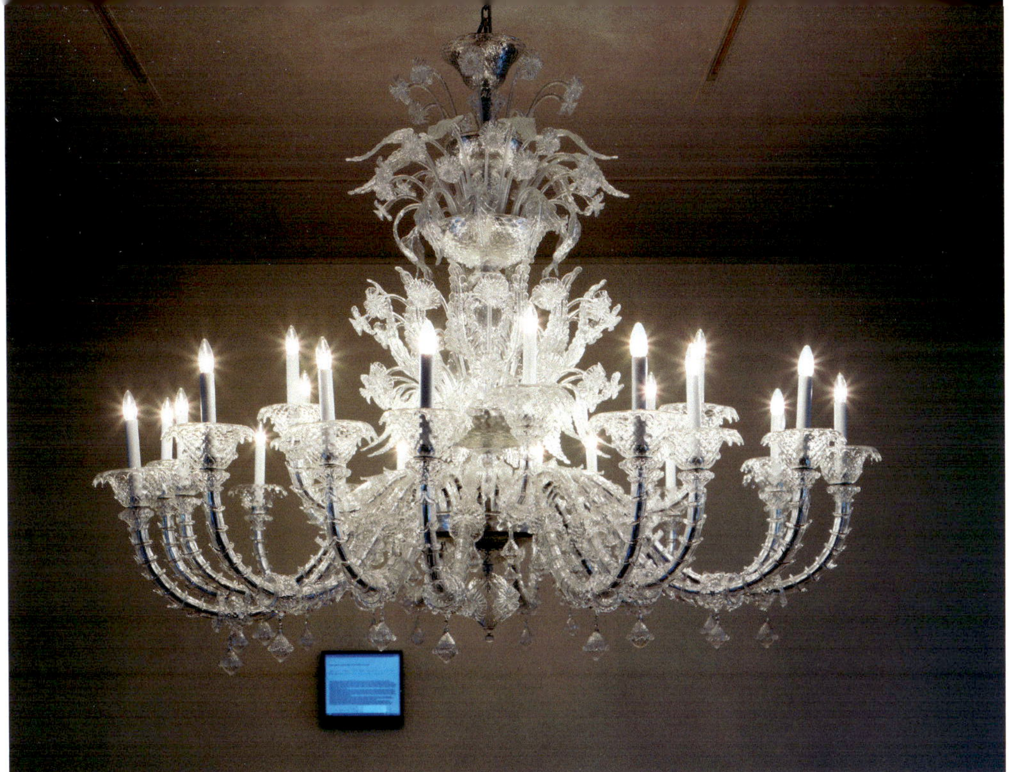

"Flicker" by Ian Sommerville (1959)

Cerith Wyn Evans (British, born in 1958)

2004

"Flicker" by Ian Sommerville (1959) is one in a series of twenty crystal chandeliers, each of which is programmed to flash a different text in Morse code. The texts come from various literary, poetic, theoretical, and scientific genres. A computer monitor mounted on a nearby wall accompanies each chandelier and displays its coded text as dots and dashes along with a translation in plain English. The title of the installation refers to the British mathematician Ian Sommerville's development of a "flicker machine" at the request of the artist Brion Gysin, who intended to create visual impressions on a viewer's closed eyelids using flashing lights.

The computer that houses the Morse-code translation software runs on equipment available when the artist created the work in 2004. As new computer technology develops and old systems become obsolete, different software and hardware may be needed to maintain this work's flickering function. Revealing this work of art to the public will involve activities that call for technical knowledge and expertise in computer maintenance and repair that fall outside art conservators' traditional skill set.

Chandelier, flat-screen monitor, Morse code unit, computer
Variable dimensions
Museum purchase with funds donated by Davis and Carol Noble and Daniel and Judyth Katz 2005.196

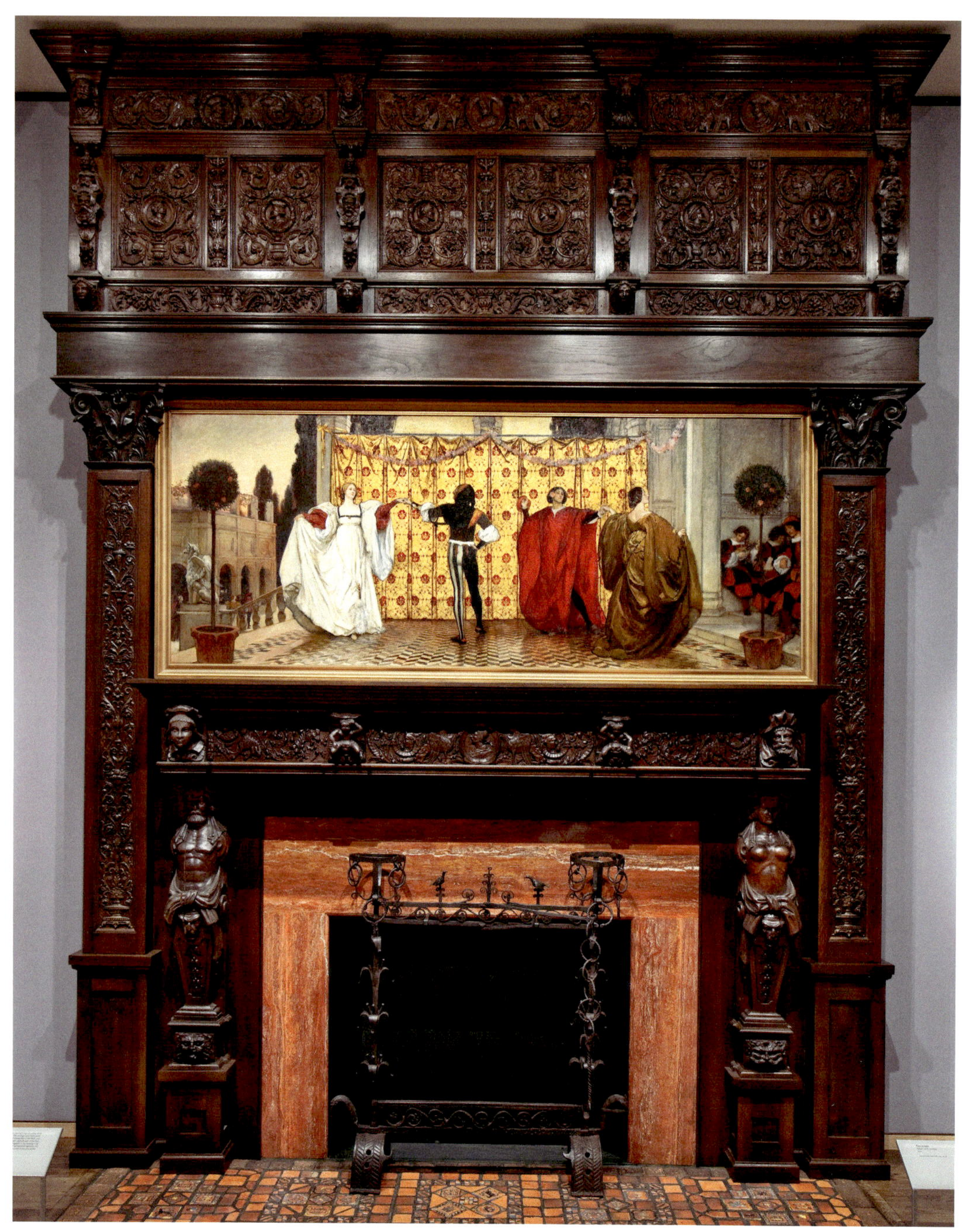

Abbey's painting in a modified Renaissance Revival fireplace surround that emulates its original setting

A Pavane

Edwin Austin Abbey (American, 1852–1911)

1897

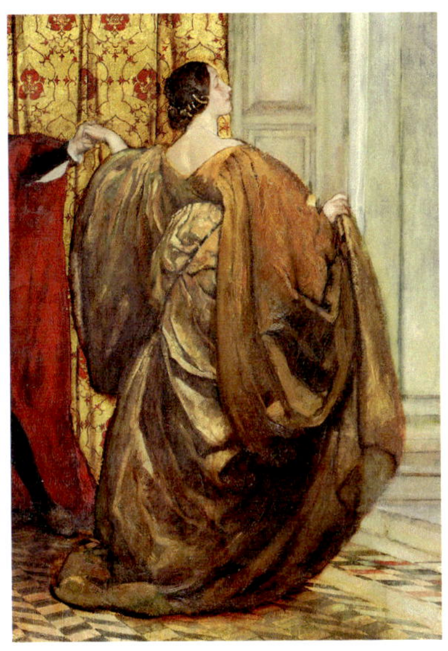

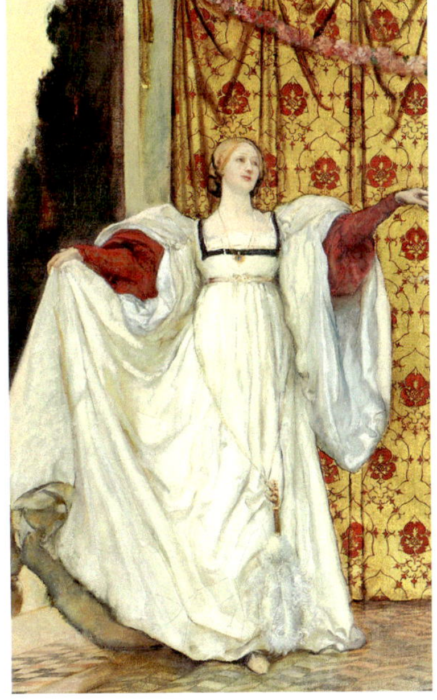

Edwin Abbey, an American illustrator and painter who spent most of his life in England, is best known for mural paintings such as the *Quest and Achievement of the Holy Grail*, completed about 1902 for the book-delivery room at the then newly constructed Boston Public Library. While he was working on this project, Abbey was commissioned by Whitelaw Reid, a prominent New Yorker, to create a painting for the dining room of Reid's apartment in the Renaissance Revival–styled Villard Houses (now part of the New York Palace Hotel). Abbey's painting was to be installed over a fireplace fashioned by the sculptor Augustus Saint-Gaudens, in a room that featured architectural moldings by Stanford White. White was a partner in the architectural firm McKim, Mead, and White, which had designed the Villard Houses. An early photograph shows Abbey's painting in its original Villard Houses setting.

During the planning of new galleries at the Museum of Fine Arts, Boston, conservators, curators, and carpenters collaborated on developing a setting for the painting that emulates its original Renaissance Revival backdrop. When the Museum's building on Huntington Avenue first opened in 1909, it included a meeting room fitted with a late-nineteenth-century Renaissance Revival fireplace, which had been donated to the Museum and had been cut to fit the new space. When the Museum dismantled this meeting room, the old fireplace was saved. With new modifications designed by a furniture and frame conservator, this Renaissance Revival fireplace now serves as the setting for Abbey's painting, closely re-creating the one for which Abbey originally designed his work.

Oil on canvas
101.6 x 261.6 cm (40 x 103 in.)
Bequest of Susan A. D. McKelvey and
Bequest of Kathleen Rothe, by exchange 2004.238

Carousel figure of a greyhound

Charles Looff (American, 1852–1918)

Rhode Island, about 1905–10

before treatment, with a few small cleaned areas

This wooden greyhound was repainted frequently when it was part of a working carousel. When it came to the MFA in 1992, it was chocolate brown except for white lower legs and paws. After cleaning a few small areas on the surface, conservators were quickly able to tell that a considerable amount of colored paint lay below it. Museum scientists therefore took small chips of paint (each a fraction of a millimeter in size) from several areas, set them in resin, and then sanded the blocks of resin so they revealed more than a dozen layers of paint and varnish between the brown surface and the animal's wooden core. The many layers of restoration contained the same binder (oil) as the original paint, which meant that there were no solvents that would rapidly cut through the restorations without potentially attacking the original paint as well. The conservators painstakingly removed the layers one by one, using small amounts of a commercial paint stripper. Even with this meticulous procedure, they could not remove some of the earliest of the restoration layers without stripping the original paint with them. The greyhound therefore now appears in a nearly original color scheme.

Painted wood, glass
137.2 x 38.1 x 185.4 cm (54 x 15 x 73 in.)
Gift of Claire M. and Robert N. Ganz 1992.267

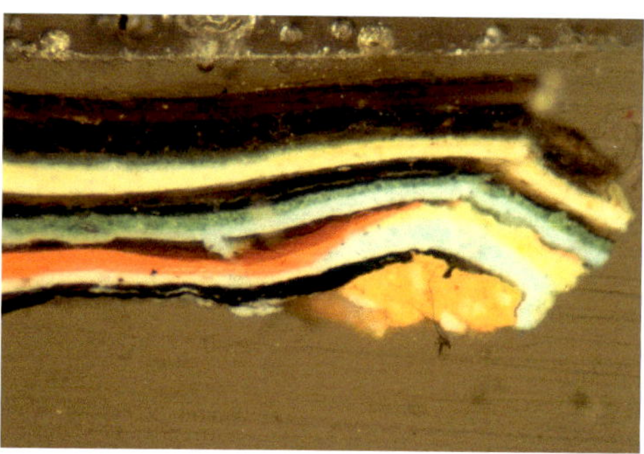

A highly magnified cross section of paint from the greyhound before treatment. The yellow at the bottom is original paint from the edge of the blanket under the saddle, partially covered by original blue and red paint from the adjoining decorative band. Above these are layers of varnish and paint from later restorations, which were removed during treatment.

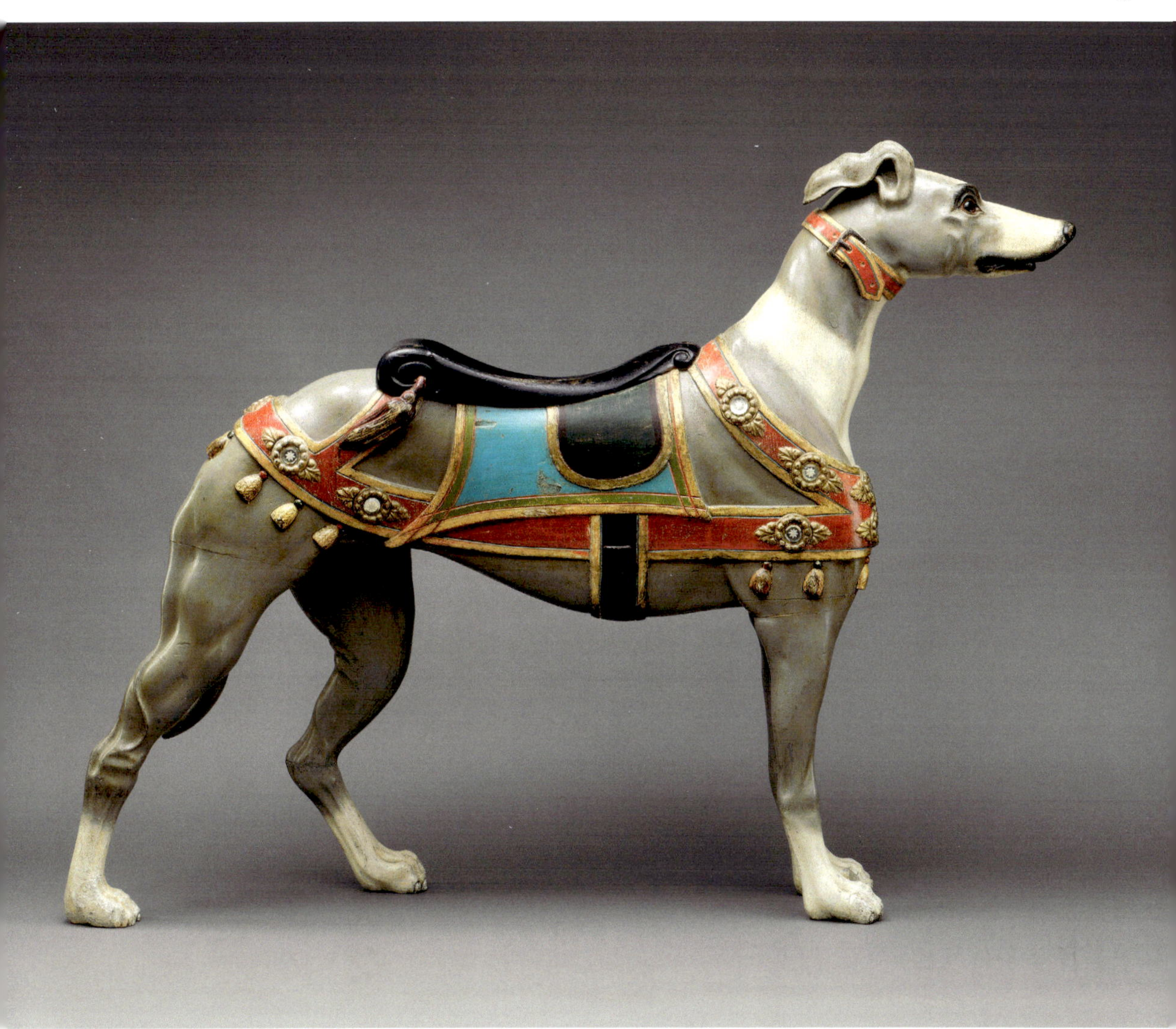

after treatment

Mummy case and mummy of Tabes

Egypt, Third Intermediate Period, early Dynasty 22, 945 B.C.–A.D. 818

Cartonnage, human remains

L. 167 cm (65¾ in.)

Hay Collection—Gift of C. Granville Way 72.4820c

Mummy case and mummy of Nesptah

Egypt, Third Intermediate Period, Dynasty 22, 924–889 B.C.

Cartonnage, human remains

L. 189 cm (74 7/16 in.)

Hay Collection—Gift of C. Granville Way 72.4838a

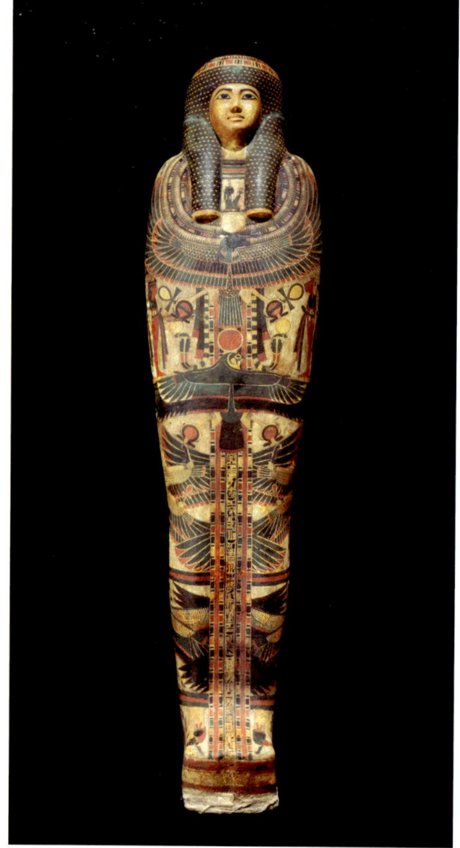

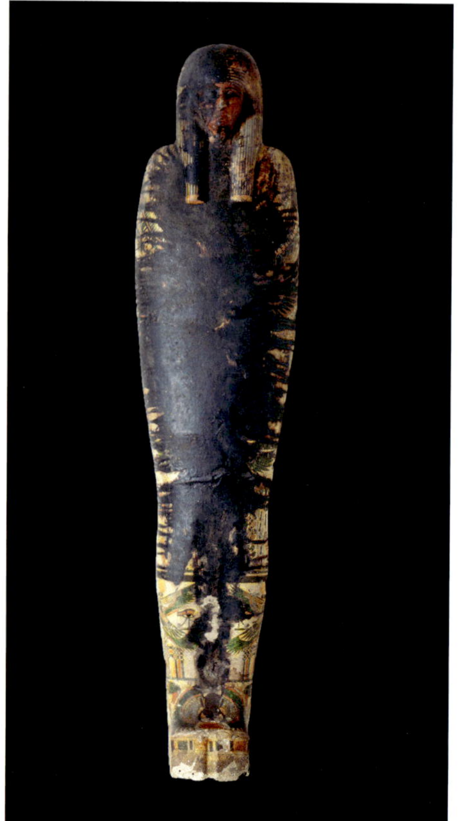

Tabes was the songstress of the god Amen and wife of Nesptah, barber in the temple of Amen. When she and her husband died (presumably some years apart), their bodies were mummified and placed in separate sets of nested coffins for burial. Painters decorated the inner coffins with water-soluble pigments and covered parts of the surface with a varnish of mastic, a natural plant resin. After the mastic varnish dried, ancient Egyptian priests or mourners poured a thick viscous liquid over the inner coffin lid, allowing it to drip down the sides as part of a burial ritual. Scientific analysis has shown that such libation liquids consisted of vegetable oils sometimes mixed with resins or wax. Although the liquid was probably transparent and amber-colored when it was first applied, it turned nearly opaque black as it solidified and aged, completely obscuring the decoration below.

Museum professionals differ in how they think about and treat such coatings. In the case of Tabes's inner coffin, MFA curators decided to have the coating removed to reveal the elaborately painted ritualistic scenes and long vertical inscriptions below. By comparison, the black coating on the coffin of Nesptah was left in place as evidence of the original burial ritual.

Amida, the Buddha of Infinite Light

Japan, Kamakura period, latter half of the 13th century

When it was first made, this gilt wooden sculpture of Amida Buddha shone brightly. Over time, however, much of the gold on its surface turned black from the smoke of incense sticks burned inside the temple. Such patinas are common on sculptures that are the subject of ritual worship. Periodically, temple monks may arrange for old sculptures to be cleaned, regilded, and repainted. In the Museum, however, curators and conservators have decided not to remove the patina unless they can be sure that the original cut-gold surface will not be compromised or that there will be no great discrepancy between cleaned and darkened surfaces. They consider the soot an important part of the object's history.

Japanese cypress with gold and inlaid crystal; joined woodblock construction
H. 79.5 cm (31 5/16 in.)
Special Chinese and Japanese Fund 12.129

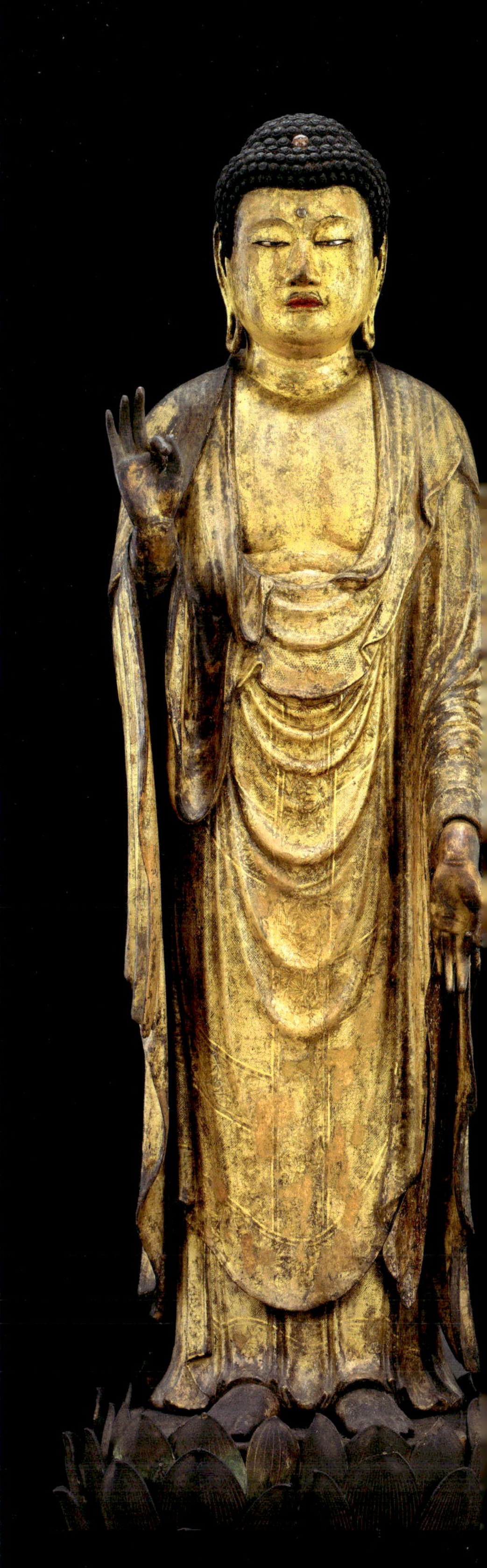

Two Peasant Women in a Meadow

Camille Pissarro

(French, born in the Danish West Indies, 1830–1903)

1893

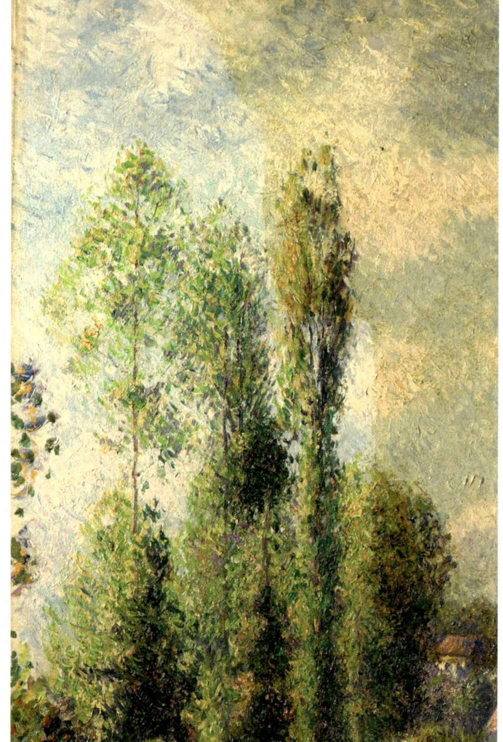

detail, during cleaning

Varnish protects a painting from pollutants and gives its surface a rich, unifying glossiness, deepening the colors and increasing the illusion of depth. Most European and American oil painters working before the late nineteenth century varnished their work for these reasons. Indeed, in France any painting associated with the French Academy had to be varnished to be considered truly finished. However, starting perhaps as early as the 1860s, and certainly by the 1870s, a group of artists later called the Impressionists began to reject many of the Academy's practices, including its signature use of thick varnishes. The Impressionists did not like how varnish altered the complex color relationships and luminous qualities of matte-surface paintings. The group also believed that rejecting the uniformity of the Academy's surfaces distinguished their own work as modern.

The shocking modernity of the Impressionists' matte surfaces was undoubtedly one reason so many of their paintings were later varnished, even though this practice was known to be against the artists' wishes. The idea that paintings needed to be protected with varnish persisted, and dealers believed (perhaps correctly) that the addition of varnish would make the paintings more familiar to their clients and therefore easier to sell. Someone—probably not the artist—varnished this meadow scene some time after Camille Pissarro created it.

Most varnishes used in Pissarro's time were made of natural tree resins dissolved in a solvent such as turpentine, sometimes with the addition of oil. These coatings turned more and more yellow with age, tinting the colors underneath and making them appear increasingly darker and duller. In this case, the thick layers of old varnish turned Pissarro's whites a dingy yellow and the blues green, subtly changing the other colors as well.

Knowing that Pissarro, like his contemporary Claude Monet, rejected varnish after the 1870s (Pissarro even went so far as to inscribe "Please do not varnish this picture" on the back of some of his works), MFA conservators carefully removed the discolored coating on this painting by rolling tiny swabs soaked in a special solvent mixture over the surface. The solvent was specifically created to dissolve the discolored varnish without causing any damage to the paint layer below. This treatment followed Pissarro's original intent by restoring the high-keyed but subtle color relationships. The now-matte impastoed surface, freed from the clogging yellow coating, shimmers with the sensation of hot summer air.

Oil on canvas

93 x 73.2 cm (36 5/8 x 28 13/16 in.)

Deposited by the Trustees of the White Fund, Lawrence, Massachusetts

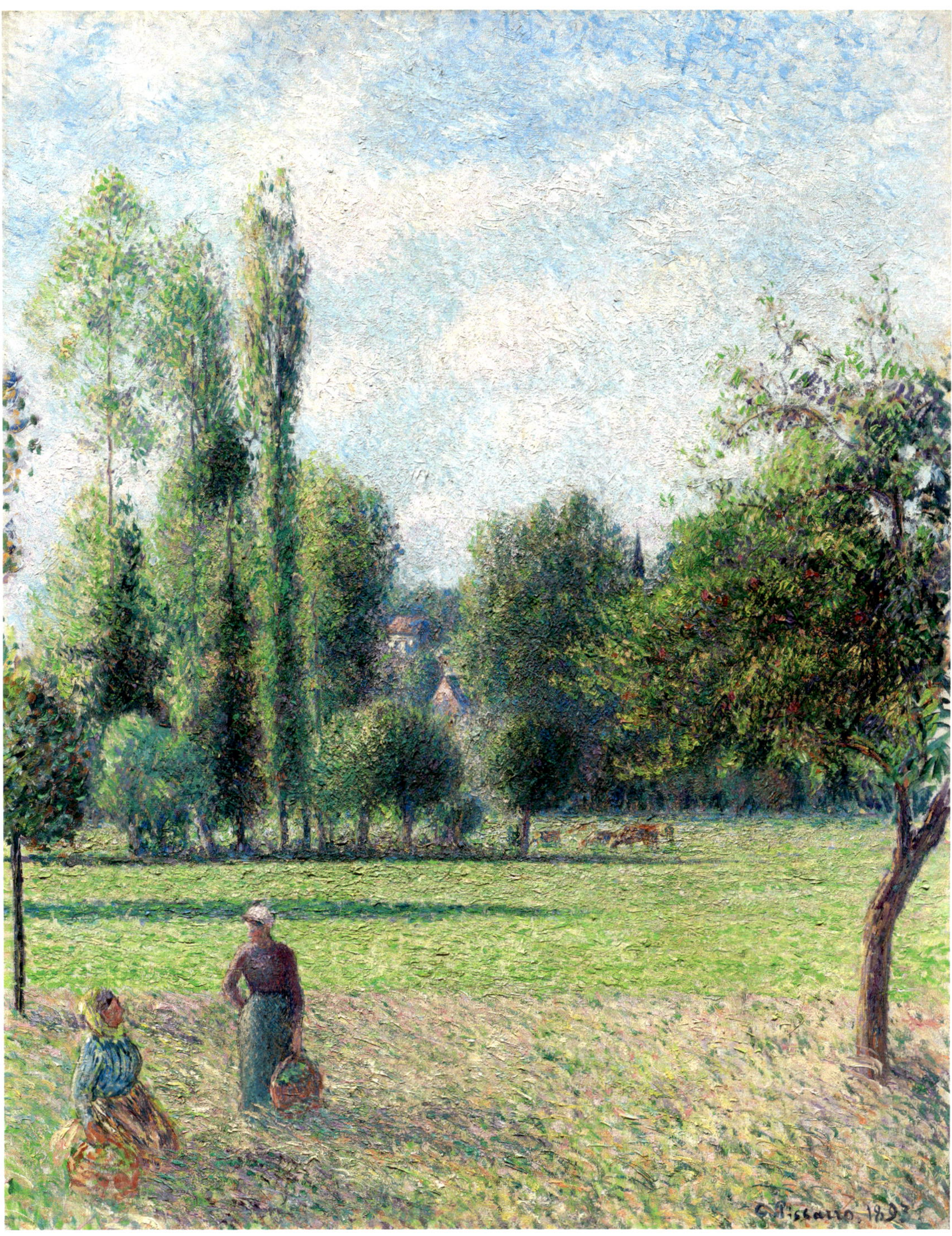

after cleaning

Judith with the Head of Holofernes

Jan Massys (Netherlandish, 1509–1575)

1543

Over the last century, conservation scientists have found means to drastically slow the degradation of natural resin varnishes by adding certain chemicals to them. Scientists have also worked with manufacturers to develop synthetic varnishes that have similar working properties but better aging characteristics than traditional products. With such technological developments and the knowledge that Jan Massys had always intended his work to be varnished, MFA conservators decided to revarnish Massys's image of Judith.

After removing an old (but not original) and discolored natural resin varnish and earlier restorations to the image, the conservators reapplied a thin, clear layer of natural resin varnish over the original areas of paint. The new varnish is very similar in appearance to the coating the picture would have had initially but is much more stable. They then restored the losses in the original paint and coated the entire work with a thin layer of stable synthetic varnish. The natural resin varnish serves to isolate the original painting from the newly applied restorations. If it becomes necessary in the future, the two layers of varnish (with the restoration paint sandwiched between them) can be removed without endangering the original oil paint below.

Oil on panel
102.2 x 75.6 cm (40¼ x 29¾ in.)
Abbott Lawrence Fund and Picture Fund 12.1048

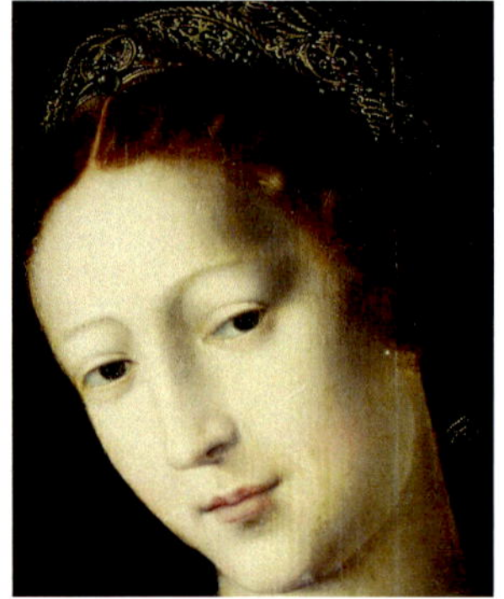

before treatment

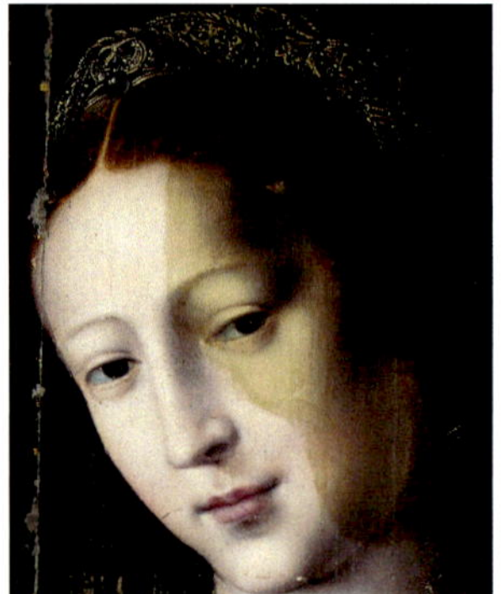

In this detail, the discolored varnish and earlier restorations have been removed from the left side of the face and adjoining background.

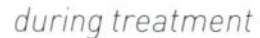

during treatment

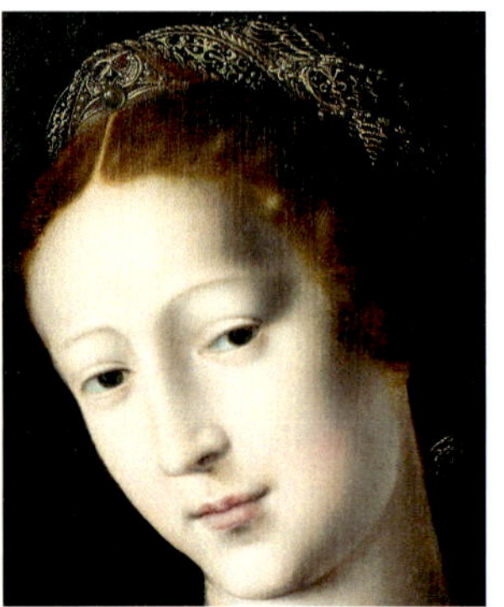

after treatment

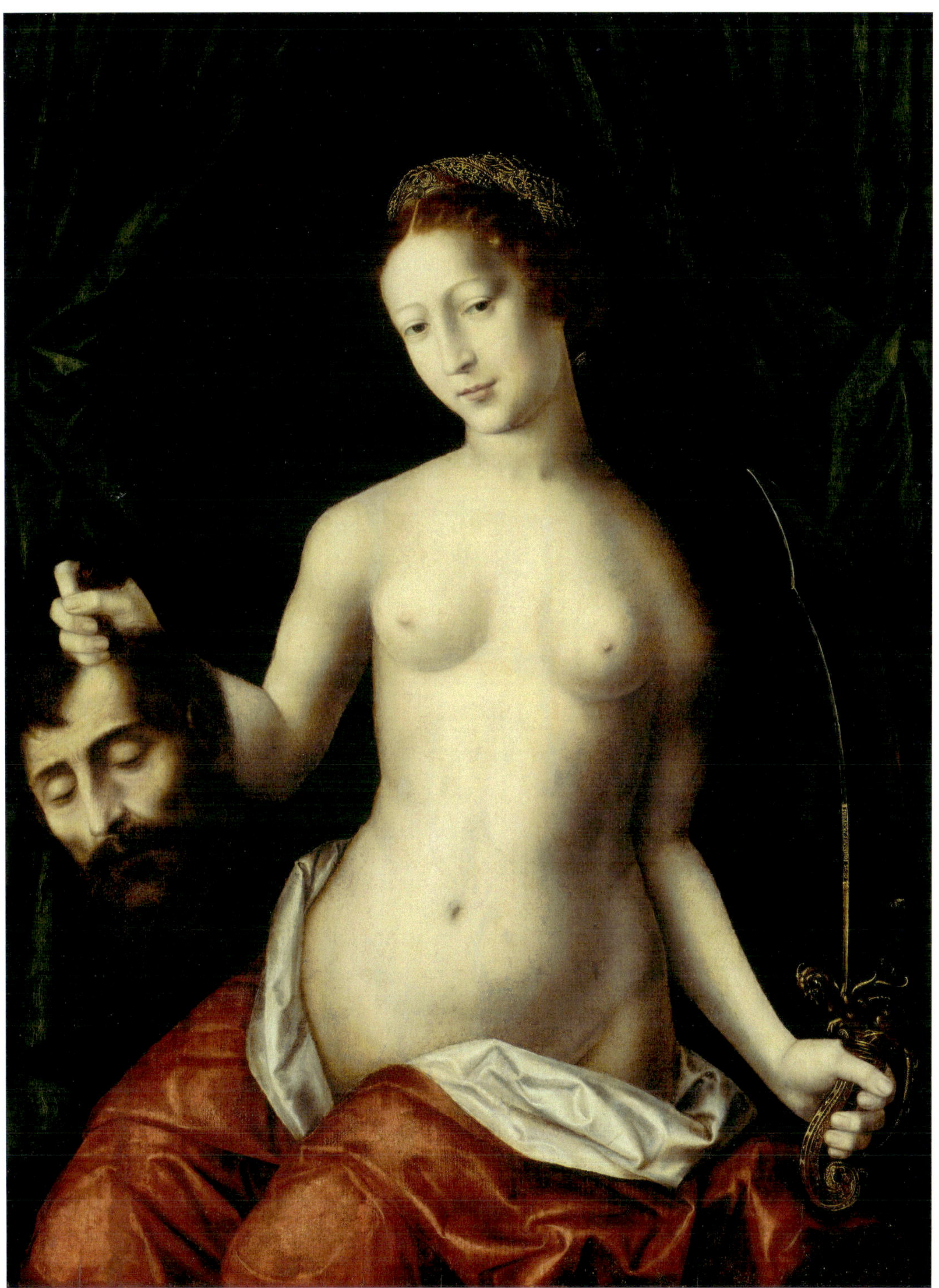

before treatment

Statue of Priapus

Roman Empire, Imperial Period

A.D. 170–240

This ancient marble sculpture was once painted and possibly gilded, but long burial in the ground caused those layers to disappear. Even the marble beneath suffered from contact with groundwater, which is naturally acidic. Disfiguring encrustations from soil and plant roots also formed on the surface. In the past, cleaning marble frequently involved harsh methods that removed not only surface accretions but also some of the unaltered mineral grains below. The challenge to conservators in cleaning this sculpture was to find a method that could effectively remove what was undesirable but cause minimal or no damage to the original surface.

Laser cleaning, one of the newest methodologies available, uses fine laser beams to burn or blast away surface materials. Conservators have a great deal of control over the laser-cleaning process, so dirt can be removed from even very fragile materials such as feathers or ancient textiles. Different types of lasers are now available, and some work better on certain materials than others. Currently, one of the most common applications of laser cleaning is the removal of dark encrustations from white rocks, such as marble or limestone. An infrared laser is often used in such cases because the dark encrustations absorb the radiation heavily, whereas the light-colored rock beneath mostly reflects it. The conservator of this object used an infrared laser to carefully remove some of the gray or black accretions, leaving a surface still slightly discolored by the weathering process. The discoloration is barely noticeable to most Museum visitors.

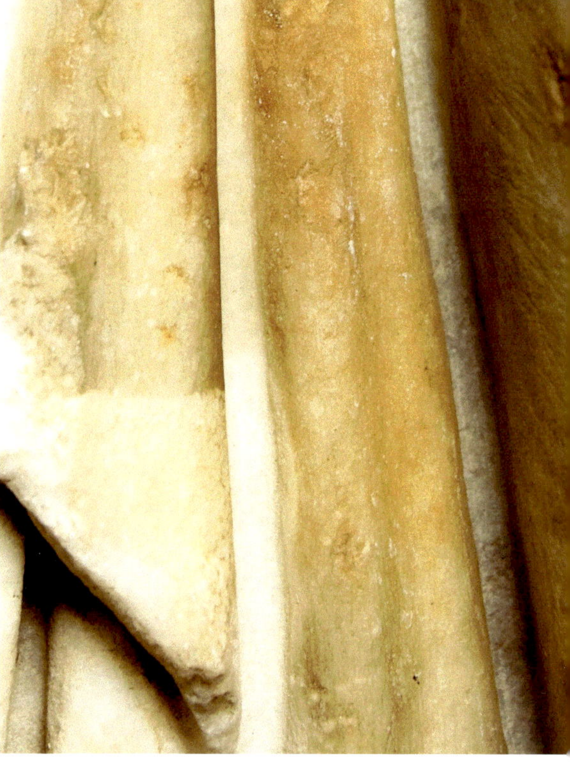

Laser cleaning removed accretions from the folds in the drapery.

Marble

H. 159 cm (62 5/8 in.)

Gift of Fiske Warren and Edward Perry Warren

Res.08.34a

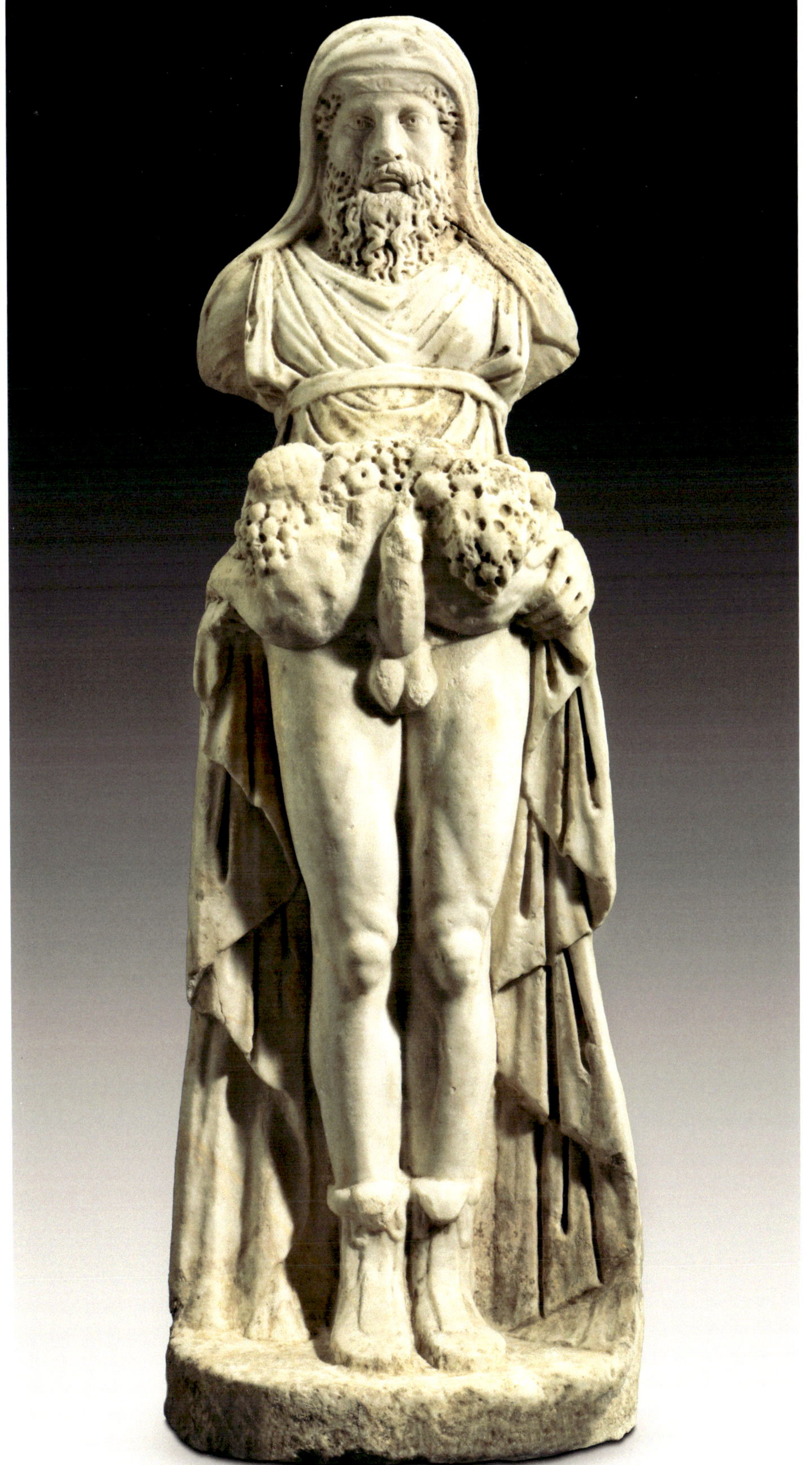

Drinking vessel in the shape of a fist

Anatolian, Hittite New Kingdom, 14th century B.C.

Silver

10 x 15.5 cm (3 15/16 x 6 1/8 in.)

Gift of Landon T. and Lavinia Clay in honor of Malcolm Rogers 2004.2230

Perfume jar in the shape of a female head

Etruscan, Hellenistic Period, 1st half of the 2nd century B.C.

Bronze

H. 10.5 cm (4 1/8 in.)

Henry Lillie Pierce Fund 98.682

Although widely separated in time and place of origin, these two metal vessels shared the fate of having been buried in the ground for a very long while. As a result, both underwent corrosion and became covered with compounds in the process. Uneven gray silver chloride covered the silver Hittite drinking cup; irregular red patches of cuprite and green patches of malachite encrusted the bronze Etruscan perfume jar. This corrosion occurred due to a chemical process called oxidation, in which metal atoms ionize and then combine with other elements from the air or soil to form the corrosion products. Because many metals, such as copper, lead, tin, and silver, are more stable in oxidized forms than in their metallic state, retaining a shiny surface on works of art made of such metals is a challenge.

The silver chloride obscured the detailed decoration on the surface of the Hittite drinking cup, so the conservators removed it completely. They ran an electric current from an external electrode into the object itself and through a solution containing dissolved salts. This process of local electrolysis changed the silver chloride back to silver by replacing electrons that had moved out of the silver atoms during corrosion and then depositing the new silver atoms back onto the object. If carried out over a long enough period, this process, called reduction, leaves behind a clean metal surface.

Because the corrosion products that commonly form on copper alloys in burial environments protect the underlying metal from further deterioration, MFA conservators partly retained the red and green encrustation on the Etruscan bronze. They cleaned away only the corrosion that disfigured the object, using a scalpel. This painstaking procedure was carried out under a microscope to avoid any possible damage to the underlying metal.

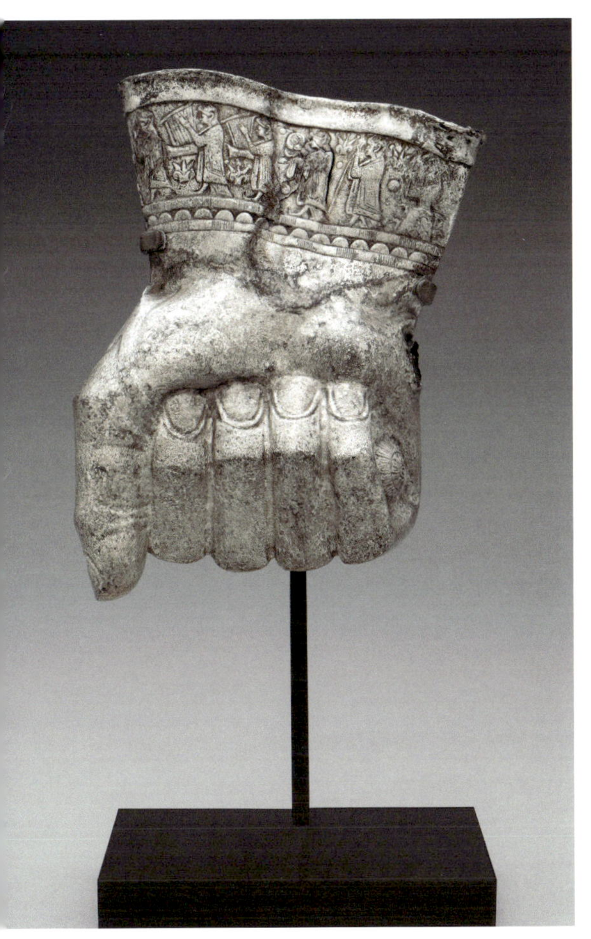

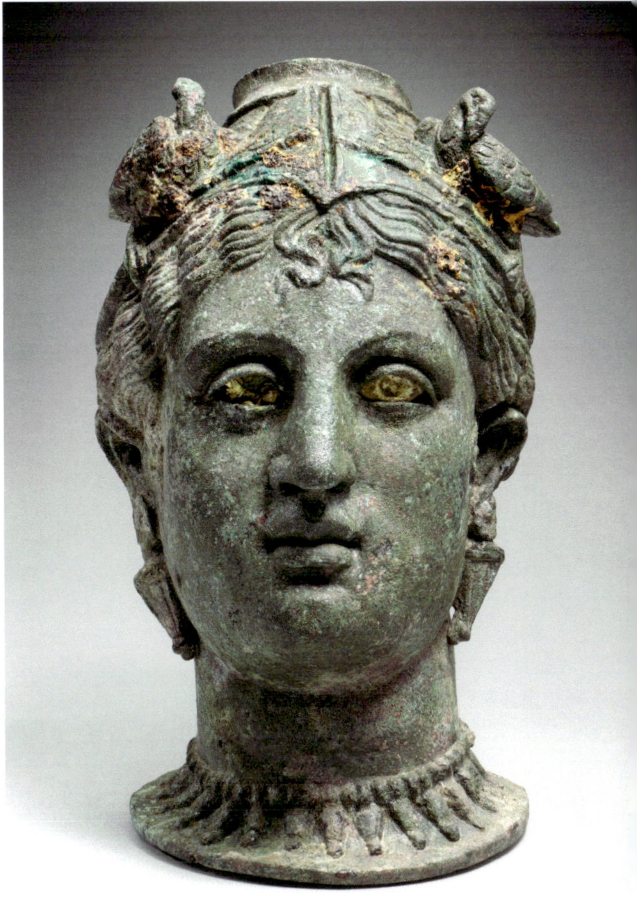

Armoire

The Company of Master Craftsmen for W. and J. Sloane

Queens, New York, 1926–42

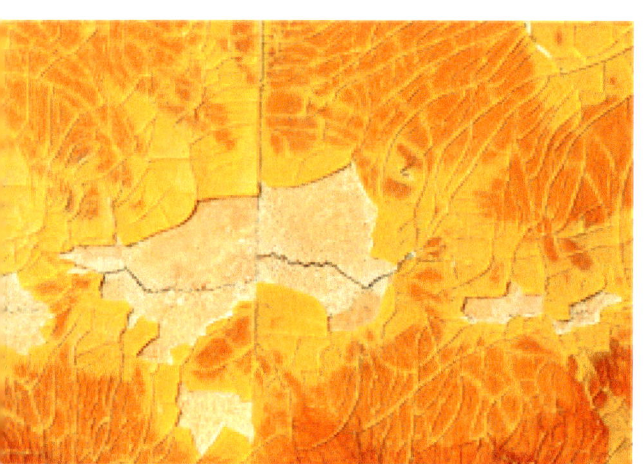

Detail of the armoire's surface before treatment, showing fine cracks and losses of the varnish

This armoire and the bedroom set it comes from feature the early use of cellulose nitrate, a synthetic varnish developed in the 1850s but not available in a formulation suitable for commercial furniture until the late 1920s. Unfortunately, cellulose nitrate discolors and becomes brittle as it ages, so over time, the coating on the armoire turned yellow and opaque, and it was crisscrossed in some places by a fine network of cracks. In some areas the varnish fell off completely. However, the early date and rarity of the original coating make it important to retain the varnish despite these problems.

Conservators used a more stable synthetic resin, a type of acrylic copolymer dissolved in a solvent, to consolidate weakened areas of the original varnish without significantly changing the glossiness of its finish or its color. To provide a consistent overall finish, they tinted a portion of that solution the same color as the aged cellulose nitrate to fill some of the more jarring losses. In the future, the new varnish will not be easy to remove, if it can be removed at all, but the synthetic resin used by the conservators is known to have good aging properties.

Mahogany, lumber-core plywood, cherry, tulipwood, maple, rosewood, brass
134.6 x 92.7 x 52.1 cm (53 x 36½ x 20½ in.)
Gift of Priscilla Cunningham in honor of Charles C. Cunningham Jr. and Thomas L. Cunningham
2004.2200

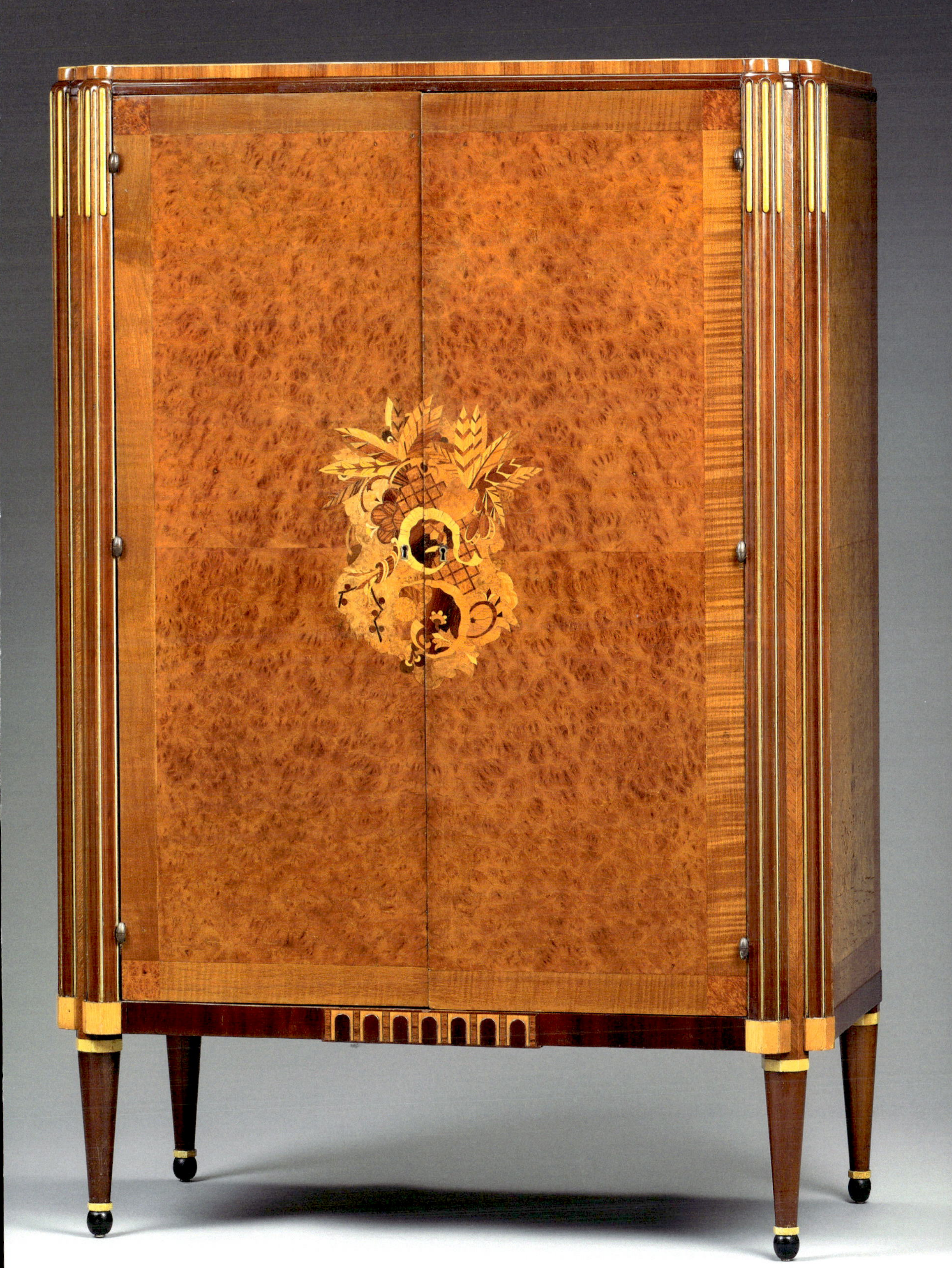

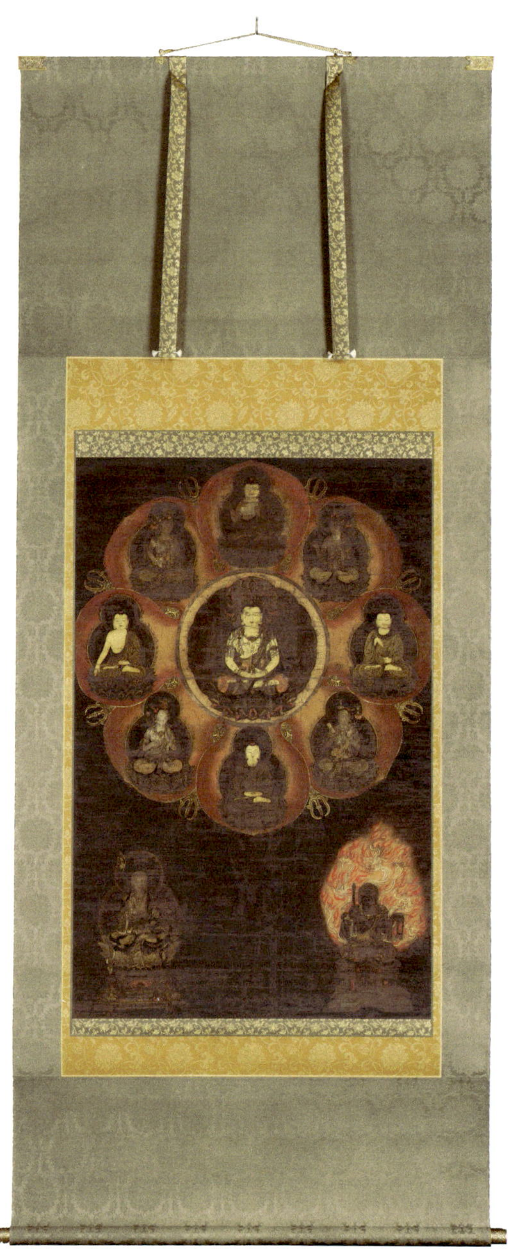

after treatment

Sonsho Mandala

Japan, Kamakura period, 14th century

This Japanese painting was made on silk and mounted as a hanging scroll. Over time, fragments of the silk grew threadbare or fell away from the paper backing to which it was pasted. Conservators traditionally patched such losses with pieces cut from other old paintings, but today they usually replace them with new infilling silks instead. Using new silk allows conservators to better match the weave and color of the original material.

To treat this painting, MFA conservators selected silk that closely matched the weave of the original fabric and had been artificially aged with nuclear radiation before dyeing and painting it to match the color. The radiation made the stiff, new silk as physically weak as the old painting silk so that the repaired painting would roll and hang without any distortions. Finally, the conservators cut the fills to fit the exact shape of the losses and adhered them to the paper lining behind the painting with wheat-starch paste.

Before work on this painting began, the conservators noticed that the body of the small deity at the top is not original. Someone appears to have repainted it on an old patch of repair silk during an earlier restoration, probably to preserve the whole image as an object of religious devotion. Because the old repainting fitted the overall image both aesthetically and iconographically, conservators and curators agreed to inlay the repair back into the painting, together with a misplaced fragment of the chest. Asian paintings conservators today rarely repaint missing areas.

Hanging scroll; ink, color, and gold on silk
90.6 x 56.7 cm (35 11/16 x 22 5/16 in.)
Special Chinese and Japanese Fund 05.200

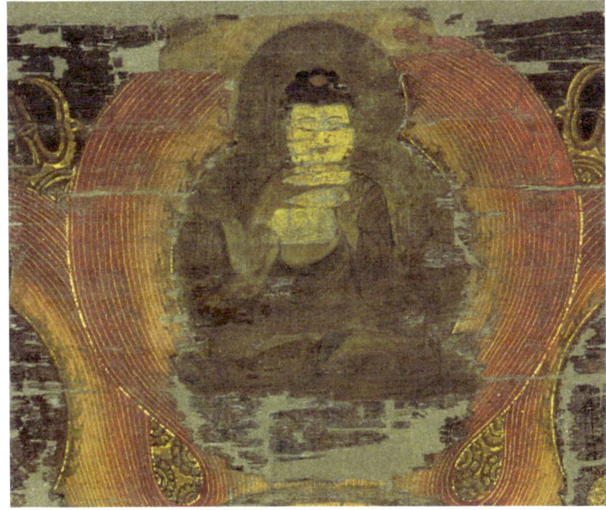

Detail of the small deity from the top of the painting, during treatment. In an earlier restoration, new fabric had been placed in the area of loss and painted to make the figure appear whole.

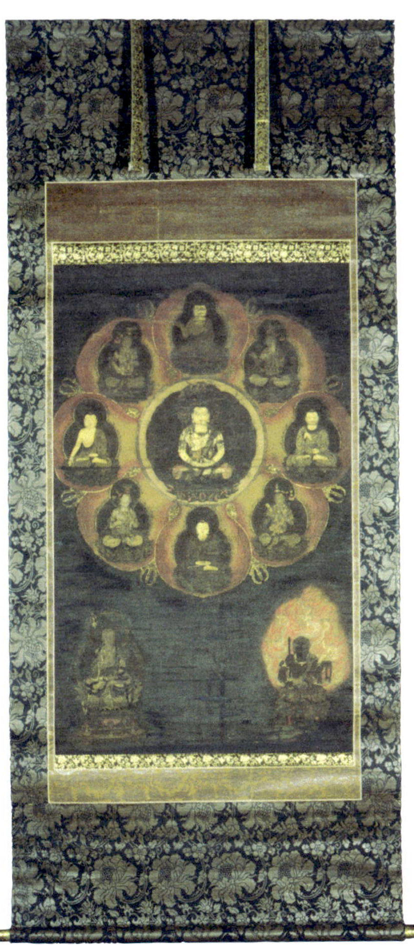

before treatment

Mrs. Richard Patteshall (Martha Woody) and Child

Attributed to Thomas Smith (American, about 1650–1691)

1679

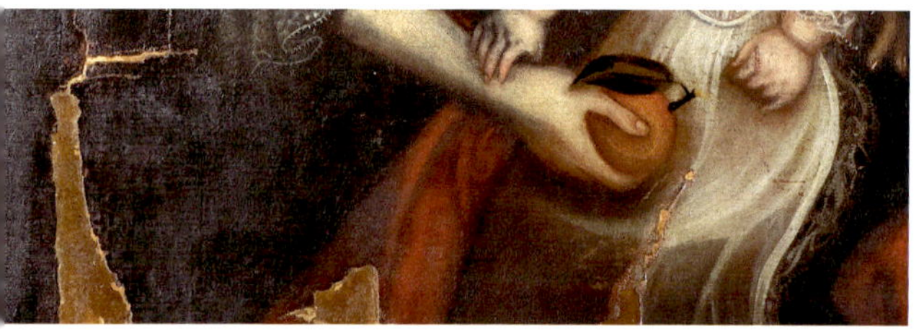

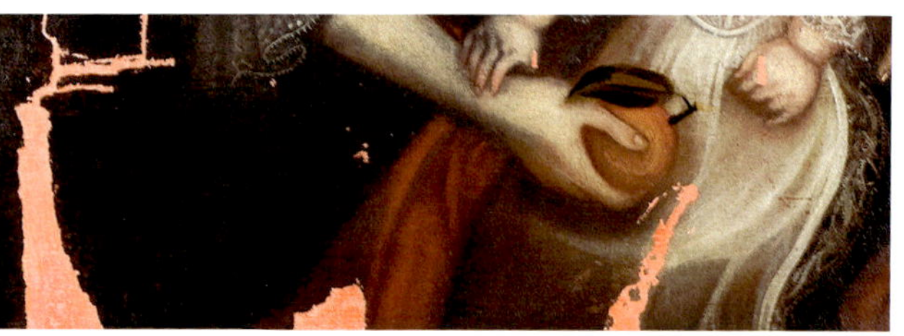

top: after cleaning, before inserts were placed into the losses
above: during treatment, with tinted fills in place

Martha Patteshall was the great-grandmother of Paul Revere. This arresting portrait of her with a child became damaged early in its history. Despite the fact that seventeenth-century colonial New England paintings are exceedingly rare and only a few images of a mother and her child survive from that era, several tears, areas of lost paint, and lost pieces of canvas made it impractical for the Museum to display this painting for many years.

To repair the damage, Museum conservators attached a second lining to the back of an earlier lining and inserted small pieces of new canvas to fill areas of loss, removing old repairs in the process. They chose the new canvas with an eye toward closely matching the weave texture of the original. Once the new pieces were in place, they dripped a liquid fill onto those areas and slowly built up the recessed surfaces until they reached the level of the paint around them. Finally the conservators tinted the fill material pink (the color of the original ground layer), scratched lines into the surface to replicate the painting's irregular network of cracks, and painted in the fills to closely match surrounding paint. The painting is now prominently displayed as an icon of New England's early artistic heritage, and visitors to the Museum are able to appreciate the striking sense of volume and depth conveyed by the artist and recovered by talented paintings conservators.

Oil on canvas
113.7 x 90.8 cm (44¾ x 35¾ in.)
Gift of Isabella Halsted 1994.253

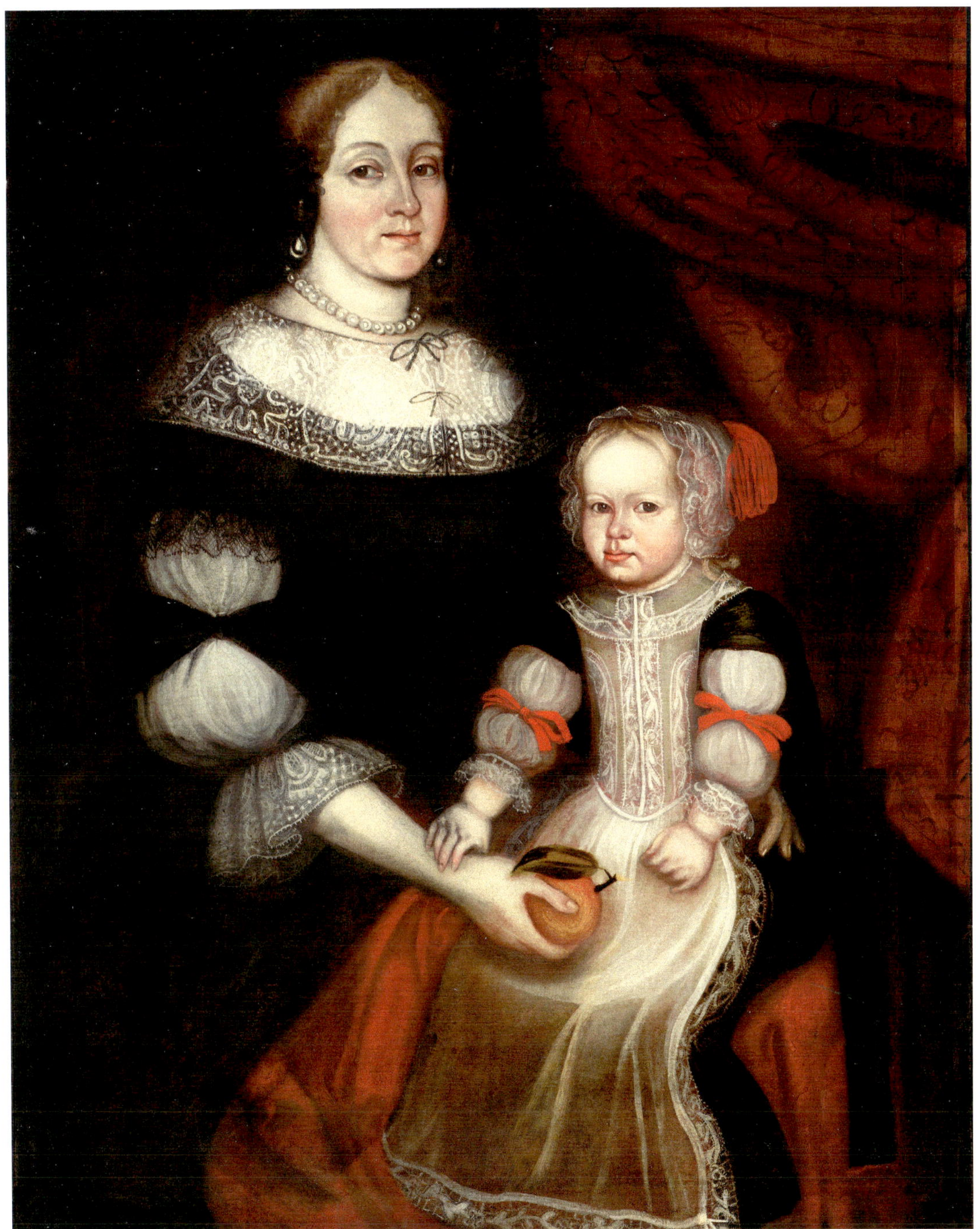

after treatment

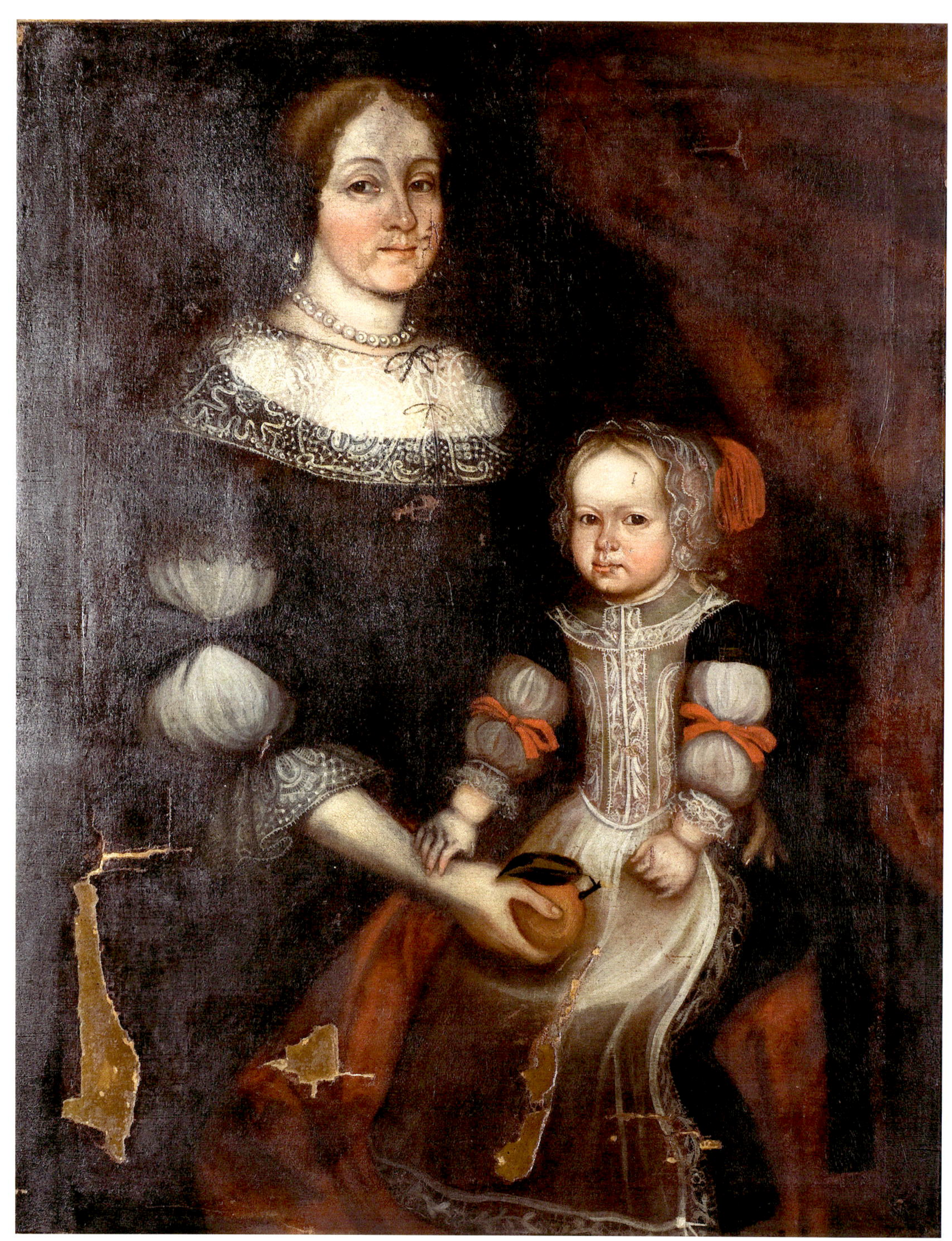

after cleaning, before inserts were placed into the losses

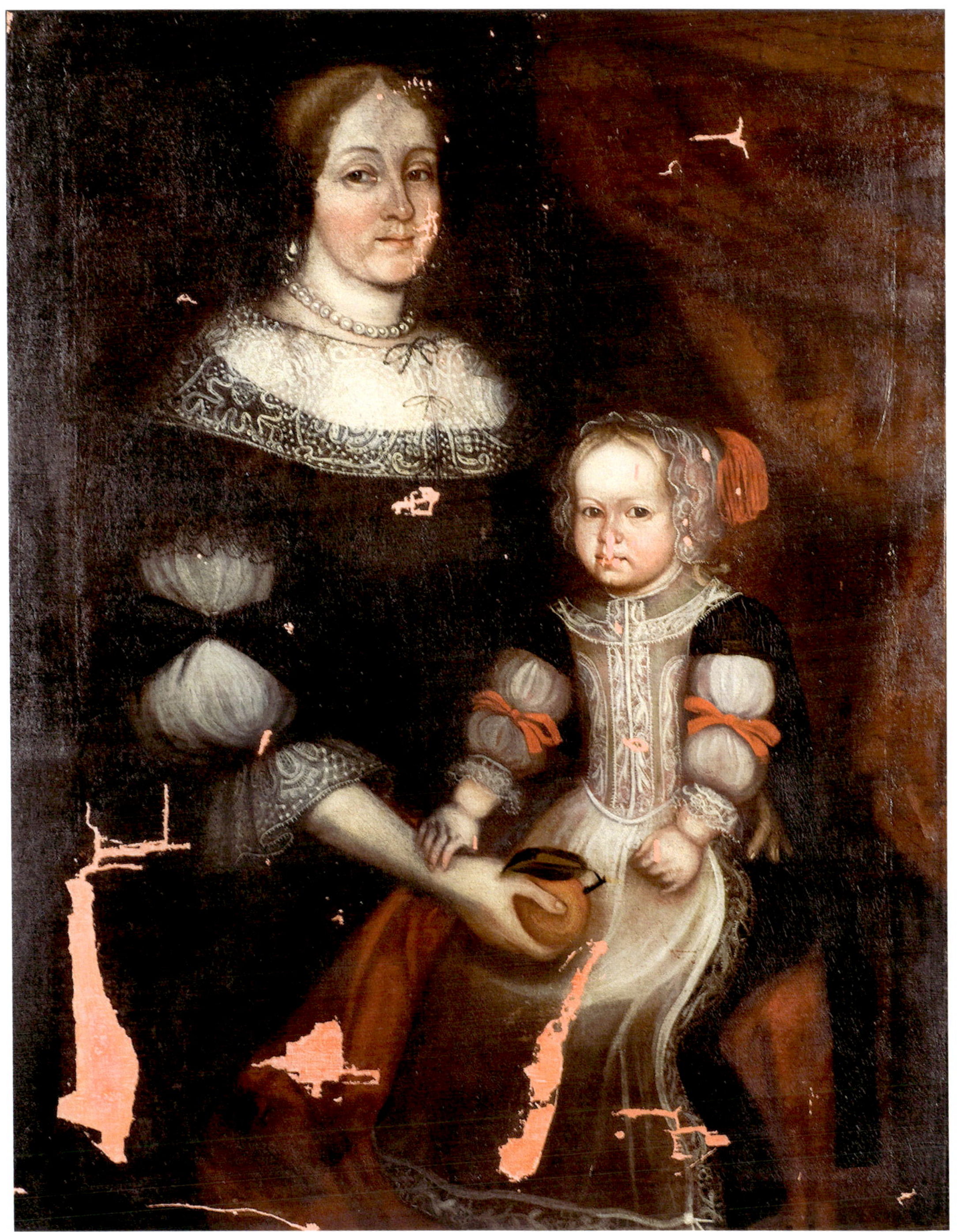

during treatment, with tinted fills in place

Pleasure Boats on the Sumida River under Shin-Ōhashi Bridge

Chōbunsai Eishi (Japanese, 1756–1829)

About 1792

Japanese woodblock prints were created in multiples for a mass market, so many impressions of a particular design may survive. The vibrant colors of this impression of Chōbunsai Eishi's print have changed very little since it was made in about 1792, but the lower right corner was lost due to insect damage. Fortunately, the Museum has another impression of the same image in better structural condition.

Conservators collaborated with digital-imaging specialists to use the second impression for an innovative repair of the damaged one. First they digitally photographed the lower right corner of the intact print at high resolution, precisely capturing the black outlines of the waves and the texture of the paper. After printing the digital image on archival-quality paper with stable, colorfast inks, they carefully carved out a fill from the digital reproduction to match the damaged area and adhered it in its proper place on the corner of the first print. Finally, they adjusted the color by hand with watercolors. Because the new digital technology was able to capture the subtle three-dimensional texture of the original printing on paper, and because the handwork of the conservators was so skilled, visitors to the Museum will be able to appreciate the artist's original composition without disruption.

Woodblock print pentaptych
ink and color on paper
38.5 x 126 cm (15 13/16 x 49 5/8 in.)
William Sturgis Bigelow Collection
11.14118, 11.21179–82

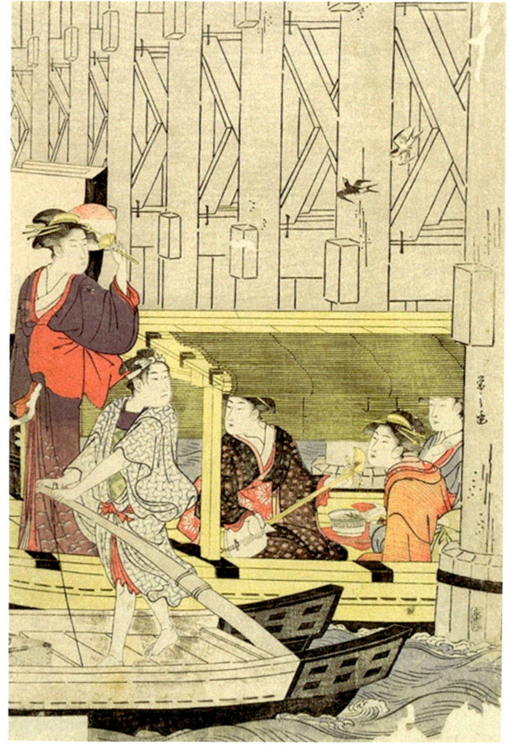

before treatment

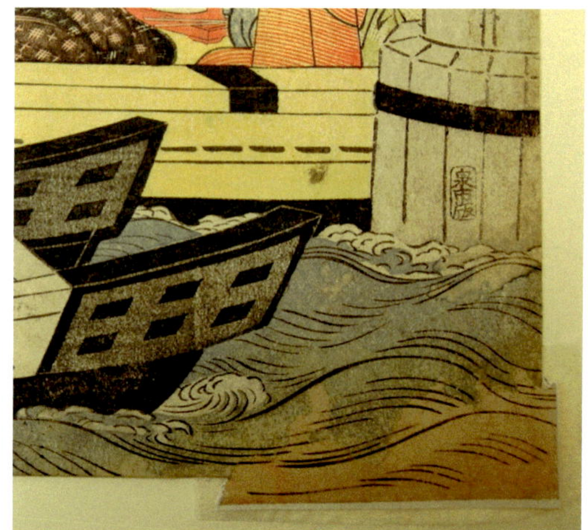

Detail of the lower right corner of the print during treatment, with new fill in place but not yet tinted or trimmed

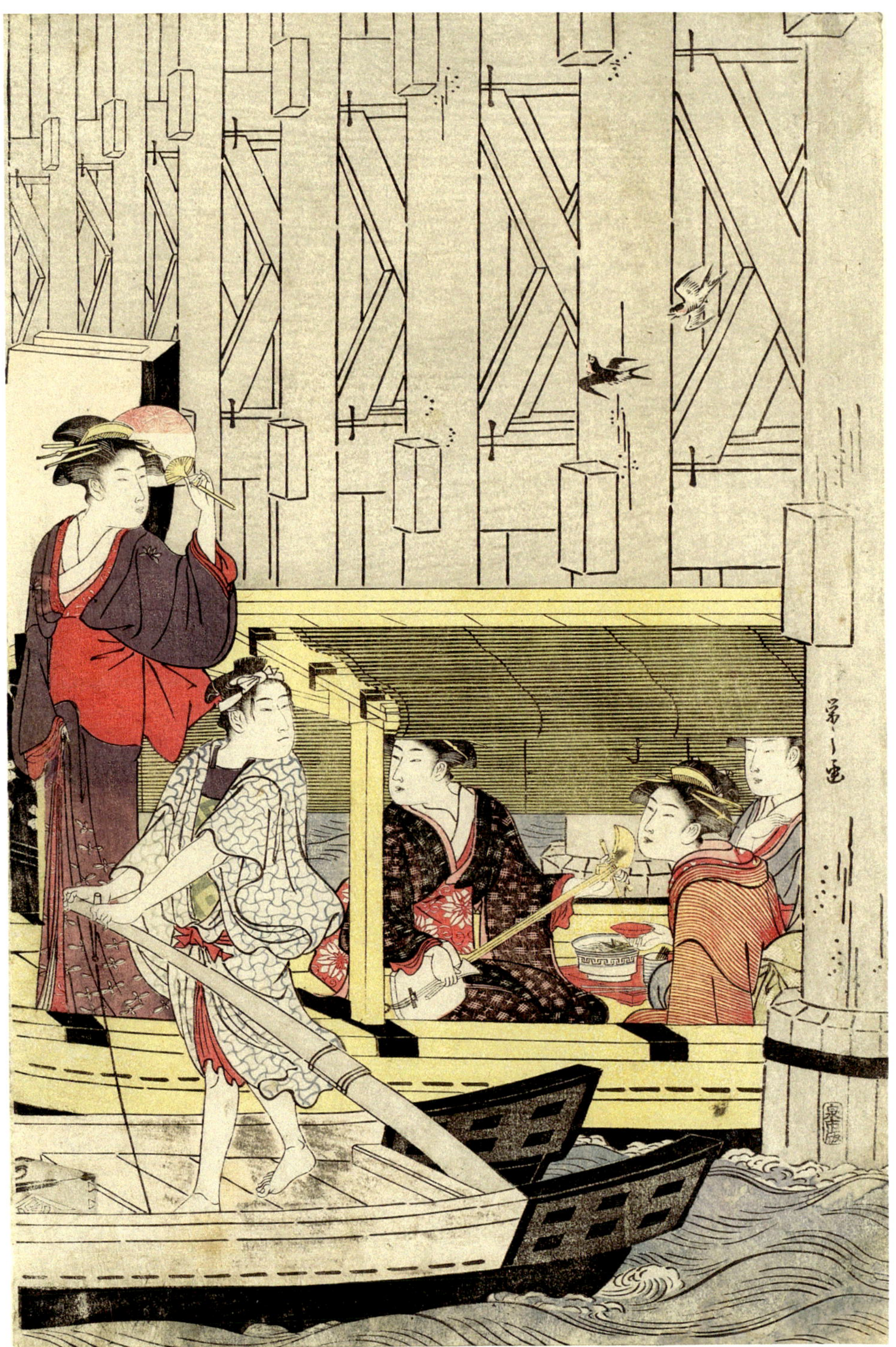

after treatment

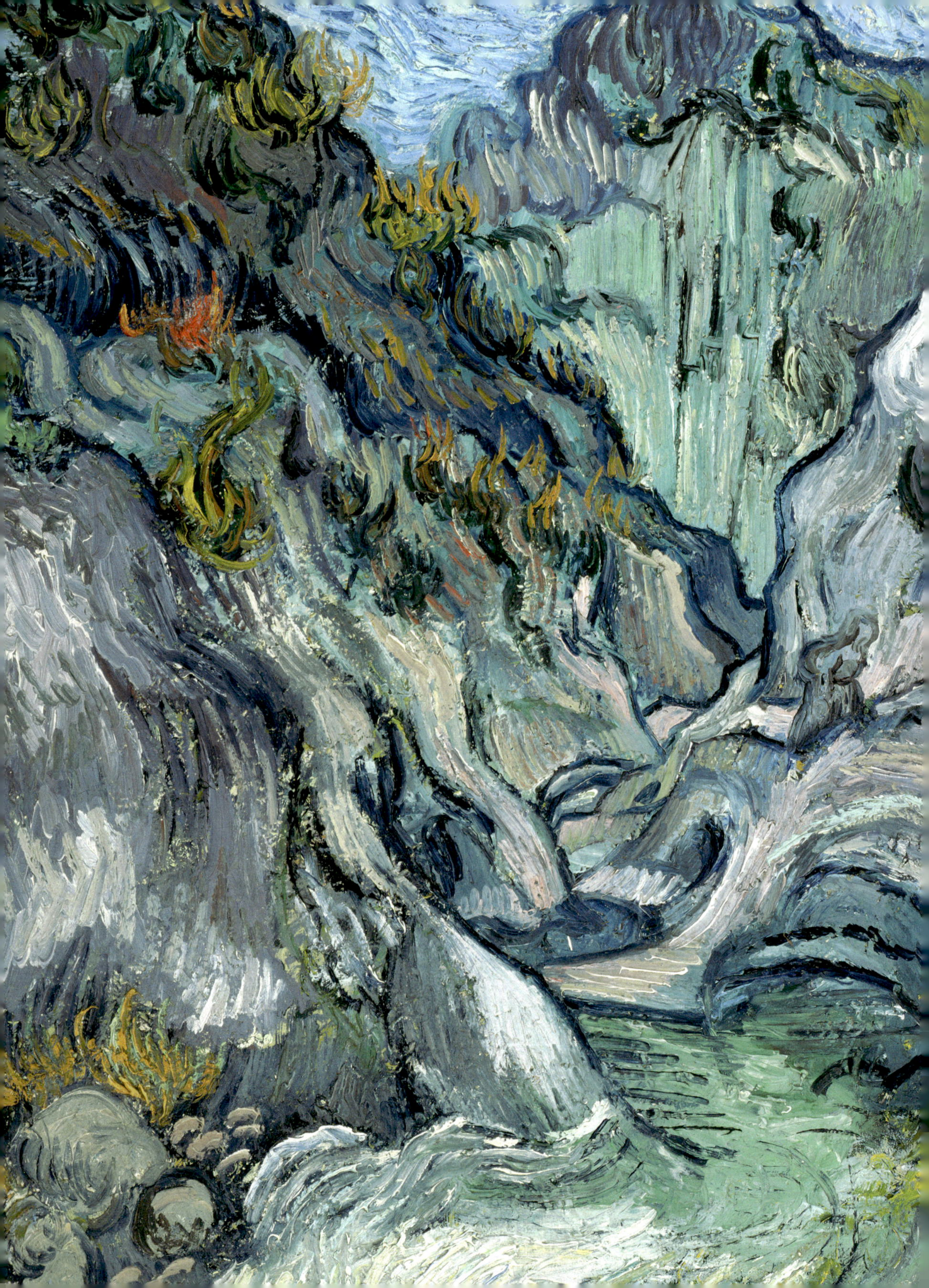

2 INVESTIGATING materials and techniques

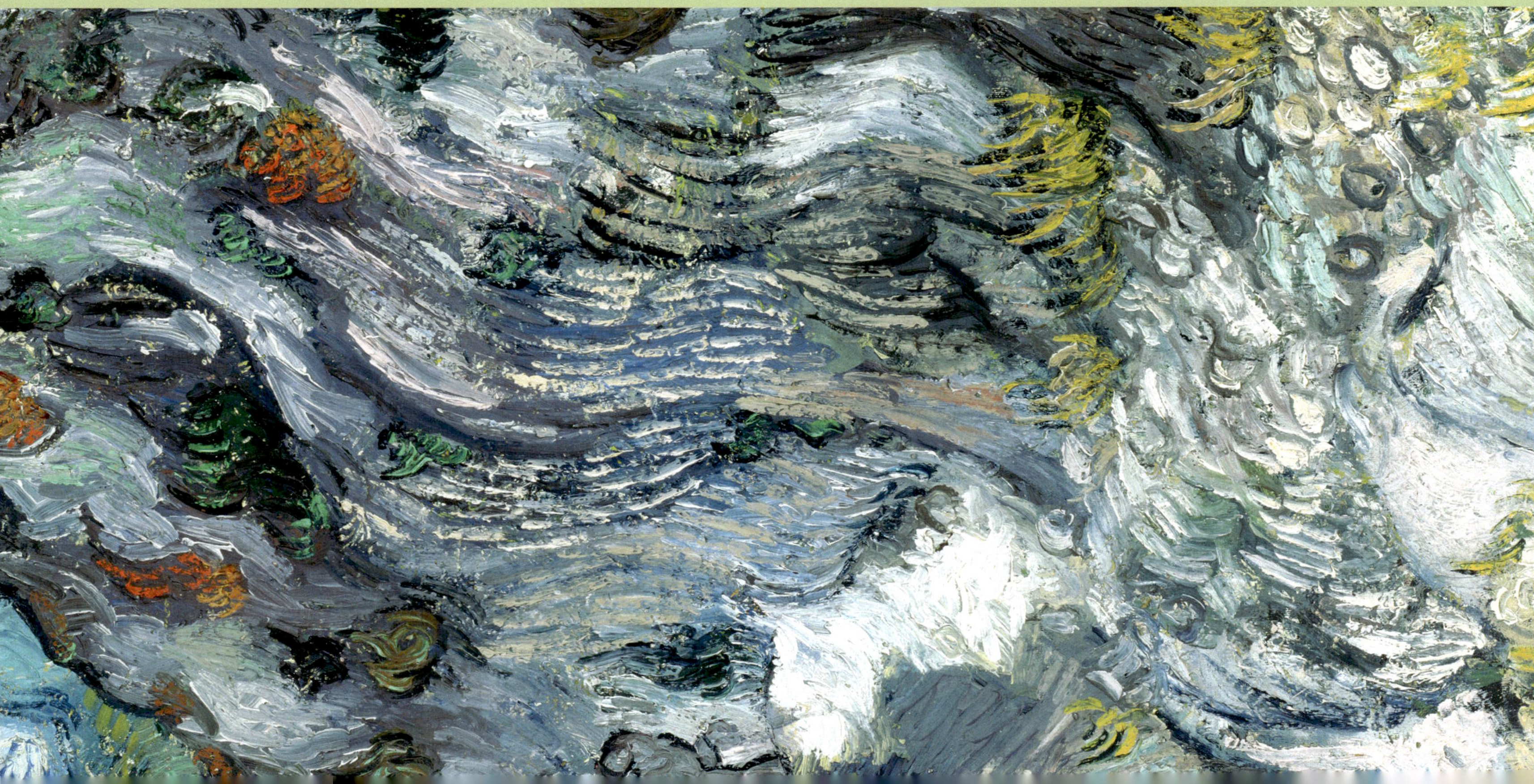

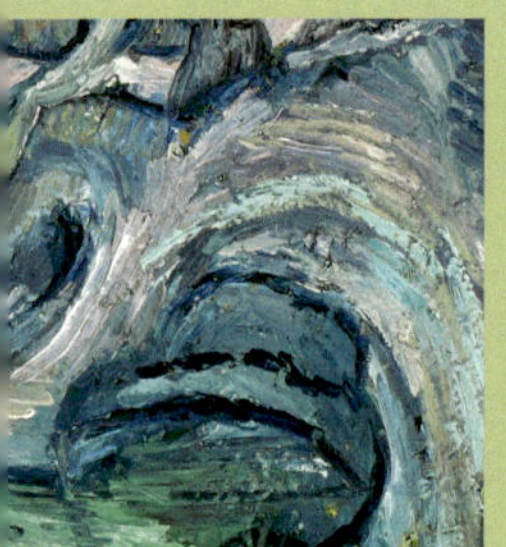
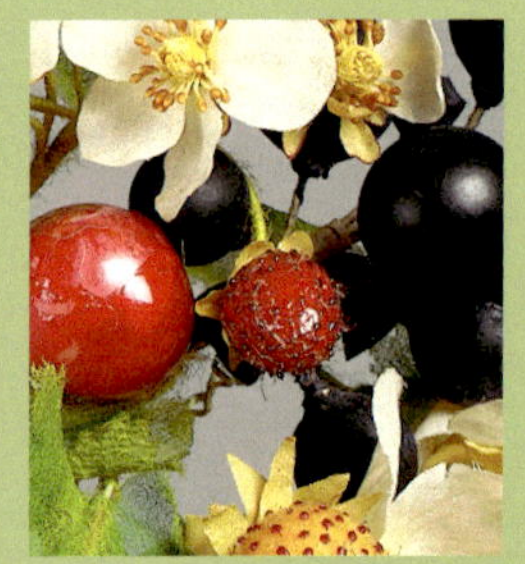
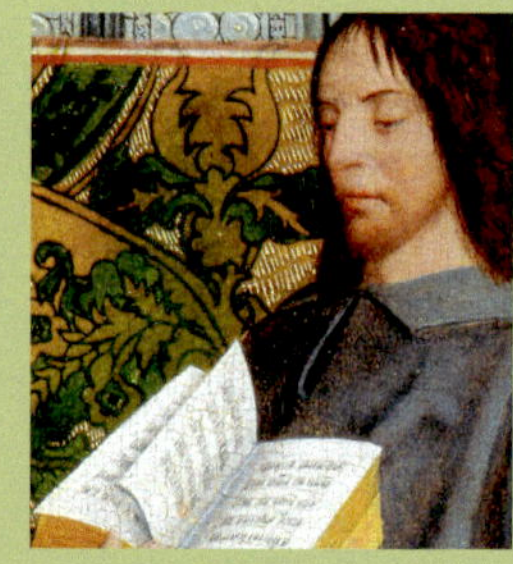
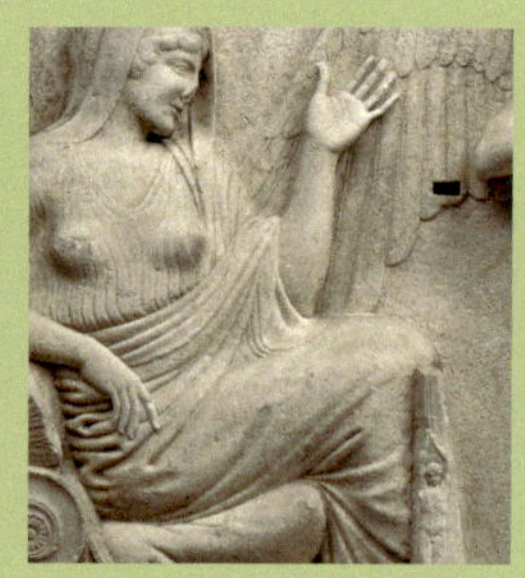
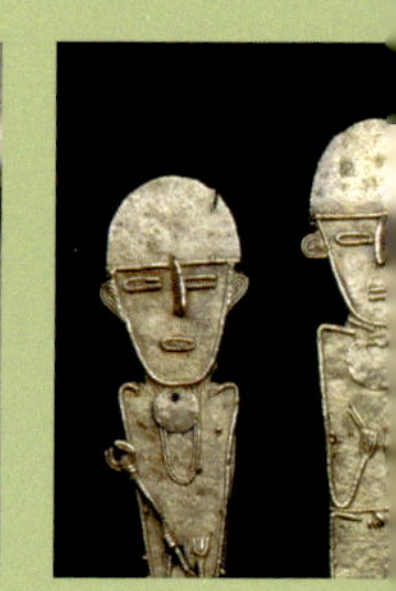

Investigating Materials and Techniques

Artists choose their materials for many different reasons. Sometimes an artist may choose certain materials for their physical or chemical properties. A sculptor, for example, may select a particular stone from among all available stones because it can be most easily worked into a desired form. At other times an artist may select materials because they have properties associated with a meaning or value. In medieval Europe, painters prized the color blue not only because the materials used to make it were costly and rare but also because it suggested majesty through its association with the sky. They often used it in religious paintings, reserving the most precious of blues, which came from lapis lazuli, for the most important central figure.

Conservators and conservation scientists investigate the materials and techniques with which objects are made, using the sophisticated analytical tools of modern science and materials research. One practical goal of materials analysis is to enable conservators to better diagnose an object's condition and thus make plans for more effective treatment. Since materials can change in appearance over time, such research can also provide clues to how a work of art once looked. Although conservators cannot exactly recapture the original appearance, they are able to make highly educated decisions about how to restore an object if they identify the materials from which it was made and fully understand their properties.

Scientific investigation can also help uncover features hidden from ordinary view. In a painting, brushstrokes, preliminary drawings, or underlying changes in composition may all come to light through investigative processes, such as X-radiography and infrared reflectography. X-rays, for example, revealed an entirely different painting underneath Vincent van Gogh's *Ravine*. The artist made creative choices when executing the new painting because he had to work over an earlier composition.

Materials analysis can also be a crucial means of determining authenticity, complementing stylistic analysis and other traditional tools of the art historian or connoisseur. For instance, radiocarbon dating can determine the age of plant- or animal-based materials, such as wood, textiles, or ivory; and thermoluminescence dating can provide information about when a ceramic object was last fired. In the best of circumstances both techniques may offer proof that a genuinely antique object is not a modern forgery. These scientific techniques are now commonly used to study the origins of works of art in many museums.

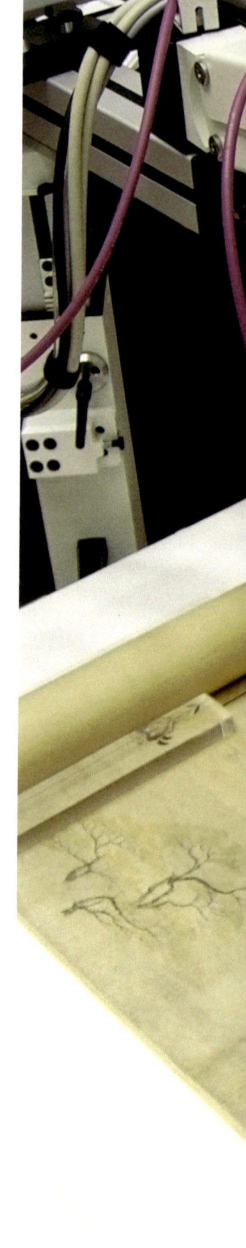

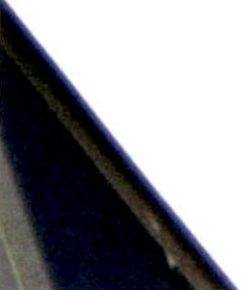

fig 8. **An X-ray fluorescence spectrometer is used to analyze pigments on a Japanese scroll**

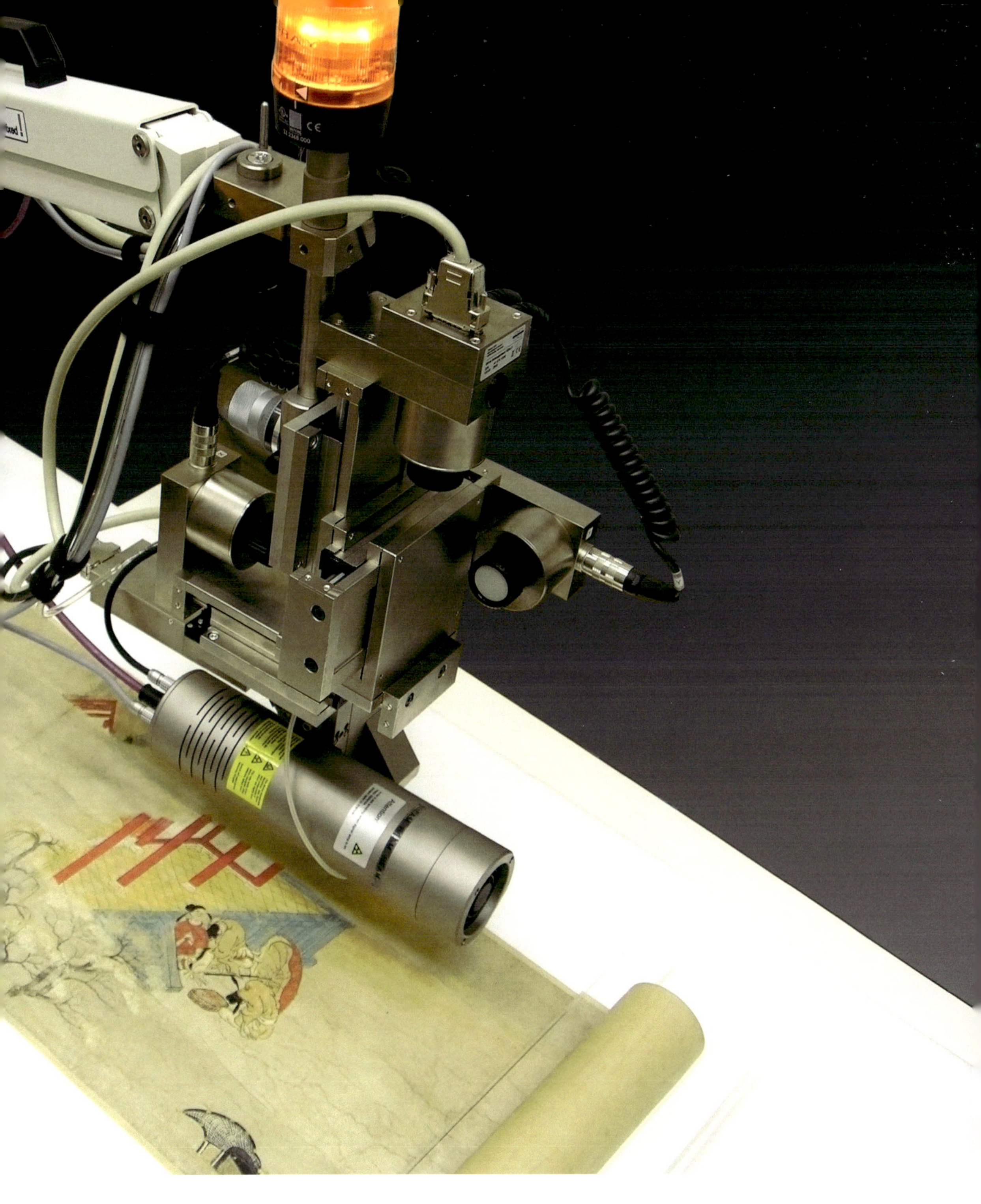

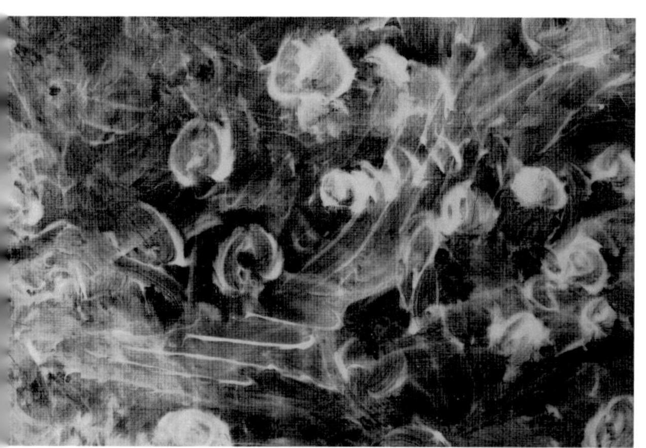

detail of x-ray of Ravine

Ravine

Vincent van Gogh

(Dutch, worked in France, 1853–1890)

1889

Vincent van Gogh created a number of paintings during a two-month stay at an asylum in Saint-Rémy-de-Provence in 1889. He sent drawings and descriptions of his work to his brother Theo, with whom he often shared details about his creations. Over much of his life, Vincent wrote several letters each month to his brother, sharing news about his current work, his feelings and insecurities, and his views about the art of his friends. Curators have long suspected that a drawing of wild vegetation now in the Van Gogh Museum in Amsterdam was such a record, but until recently they knew of no painting that corresponded to the drawing. That painting was recently found beneath the surface of the MFA's *Ravine*.

When *Ravine* is placed under raking light, one can see (even with the naked eye) the edges of thick, circular brushstrokes that are not related to the depicted scene. MFA conservators X-rayed the painting in order to see these strokes more clearly and to prove the presence of another image below *Ravine*'s surface. By comparing photographs and X-rays of the MFA's painting with the Van Gogh Museum's drawing, they were able to show a close correspondence between the works. The circular brushstrokes first seen under raking light appear to form some of the abundant flowers in the underlying composition.

Van Gogh occasionally reused his canvases, either out of impatience or for the sake of economy as he waited for new supplies to arrive from Theo. In this case, he did not scrape down his first painting of wild vegetation; nor did he cover it with primer before setting out to paint *Ravine*. Instead, he sketched out his new composition with charcoal on top of the earlier painting, and then applied new paint directly on top

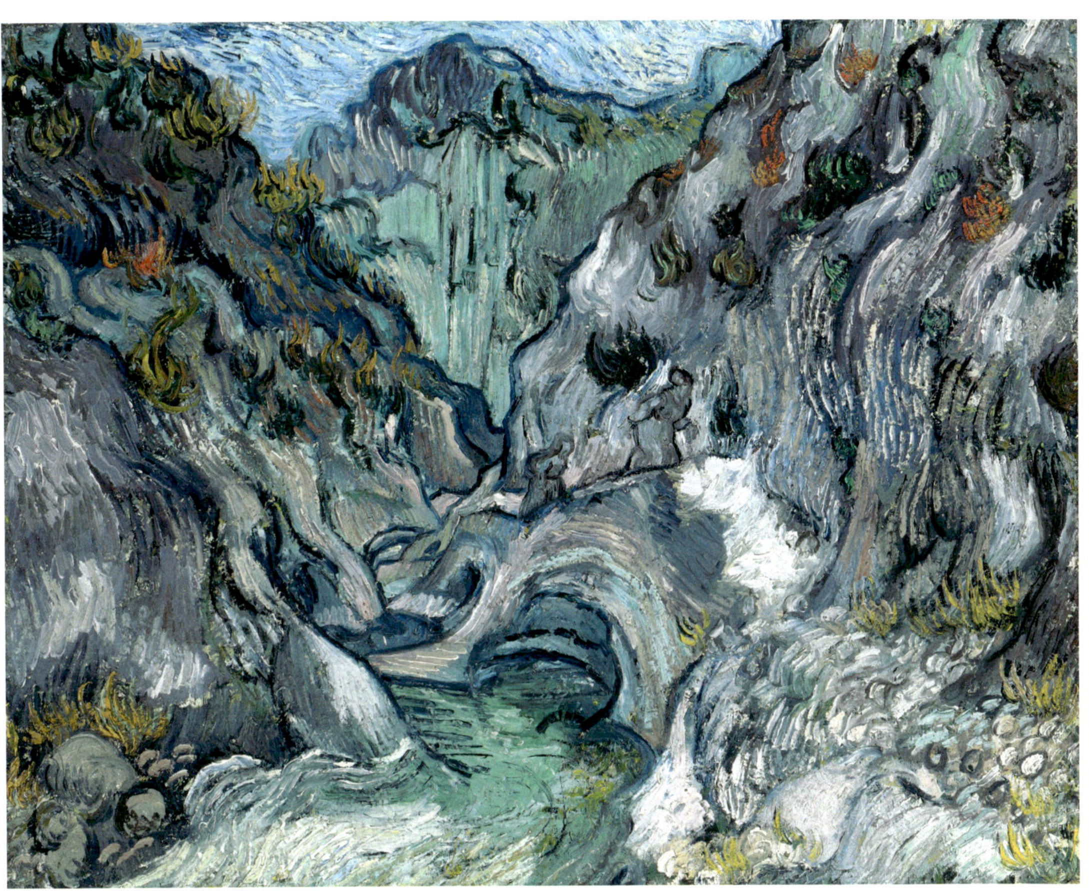

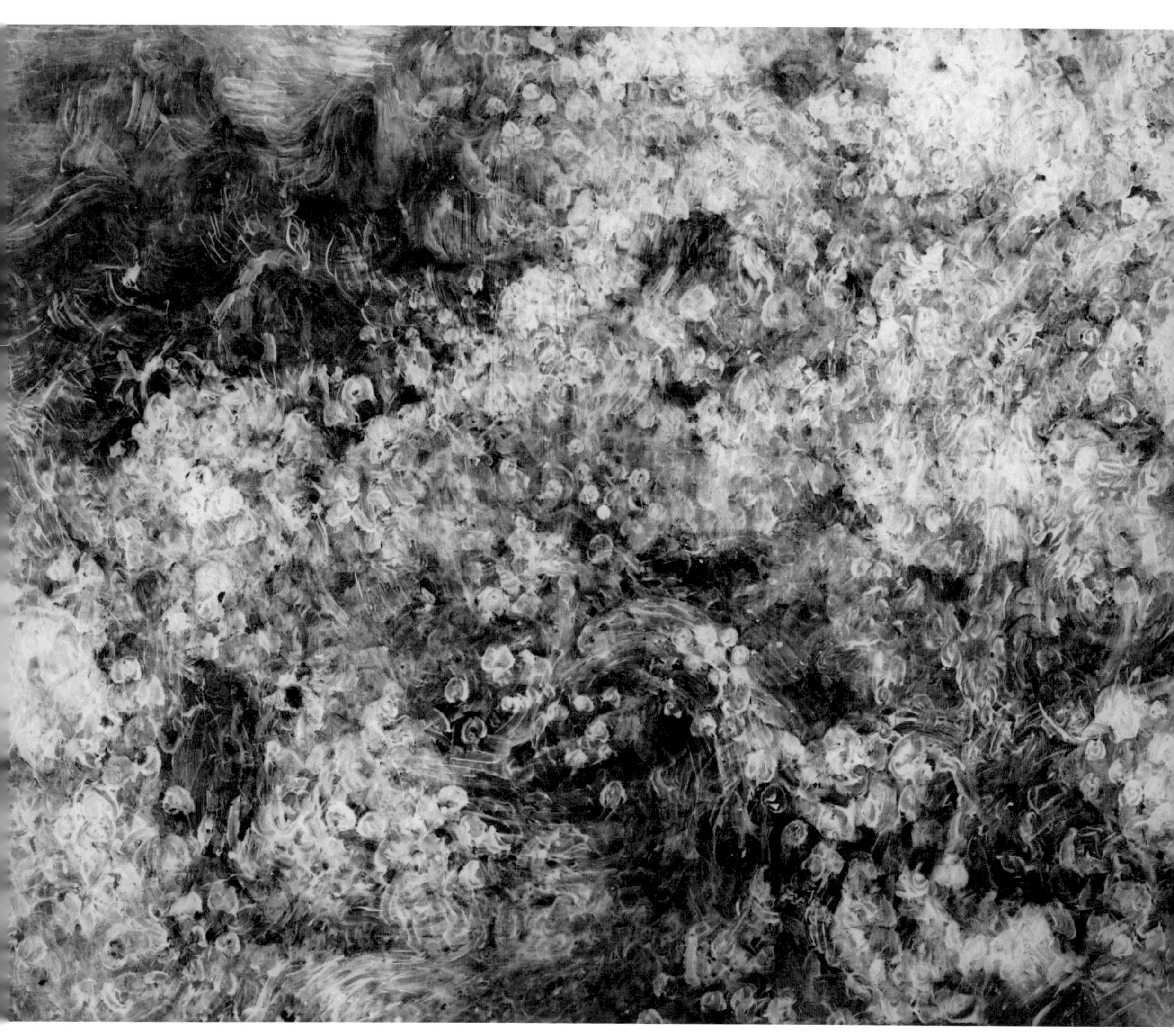

X-ray showing features of both *Ravine* and the painting of wild vegetation underneath

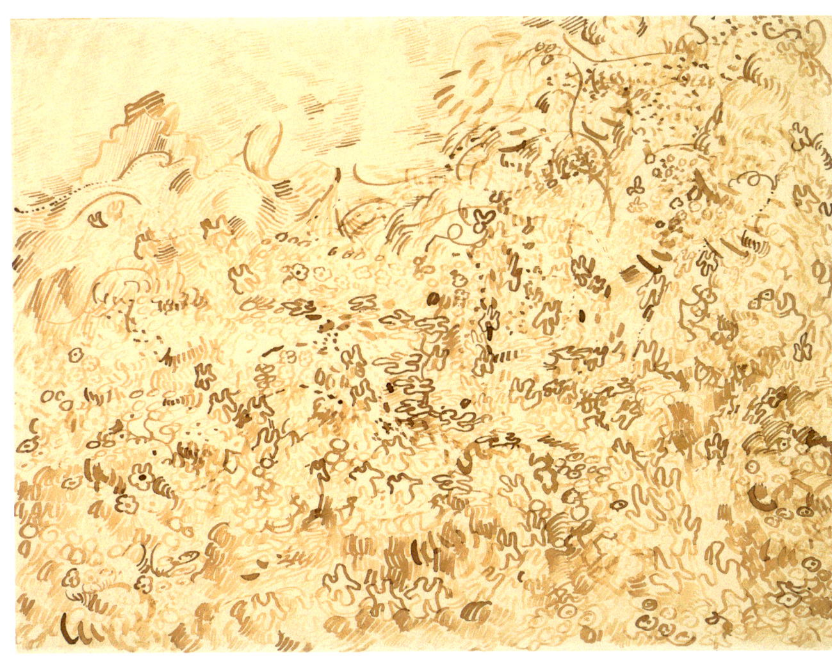

This drawing by van Gogh, sent by the artist to his brother in Paris, records the painting underneath the surface of *Ravine*. *Van Gogh Museum Amsterdam (Vincent Van Gogh Foundation)*

of the old. The irregular surface of the earlier painting must have interfered to some extent with the fresh brushstrokes, but he used that interference to his advantage. In several areas, he painted over only the top edges of earlier strokes, leaving the rest exposed below and making them part of his new composition. Van Gogh must have liked the results, because he painted a close copy of *Ravine* two months later.

Oil on canvas
73 x 91.7 cm (28 3/4 x 36 1/8 in.)
Bequest of Keith McLeod 52.1524

Three-sided relief

Greek, Classical Period, about 450–440 B.C.

This marble relief was purportedly found in the Ludovisi Quarter of Rome in 1894. Most Classical-art specialists assume that it once ornamented a long, rectangular altar. They identify the figures on the sides as worshipers of the divinity to which the altar was devoted. The boy with wings in the center is the Greek god Eros weighing souls. He once held a set of scales, which was probably made of marble and was held in place at the three large holes in his chest and wings. Edward Warren, an American collector living in England, purchased the relief shortly after its discovery and promptly had its front and sides cleaned with a razor blade.

Scholars have long noted that the quality of the relief's carving is low compared with that of an otherwise closely related sculpture known as the Ludovisi relief (now in Rome). The style and unusual shape of the MFA object have even led some to argue that it was made in the late nineteenth century, shortly before its supposed excavation. In the 1960s, scientists at the MFA concluded that the object was of ancient origin. Their primary evidence came from material on the back of the relief. Using a microscope to examine cross-section samples mounted on glass slides and polished until they were thin enough to be transparent (a type of sample known as a thin section), they observed a well-adhered layer on the stone surface that looked much like material observed on ancient marble sculptures buried in soil for many centuries.

In the late 1980s, archaeologists in northern Italy excavated fragments of Archaic Greek marble sculpture similar to the MFA's relief. This event put most concerns about the clumsy sculptural style to rest, but questions about when the carving had been made remained. MFA scientists, conservators, and curators therefore undertook a new study of the sculpture. The study team focused again on the inside of the relief, but this time new technology, the scanning electron microscope, allowed the researchers not only to visualize the deteriorated layers but also to identify their chemical composition. The scanning electron microscope showed that the underlying marble, which consists mainly of the mineral dolomite, has a dense, fine-grained layer of calcium carbonate adhering to it. In places, the calcite surface layer has eaten into the marble along the grain. This kind of weathering on dolomitic marble closely resembles a phenomenon geologists describe for such marble buried in certain types of soil. The natural process occurs over an extended period and is impossible to reproduce quickly by artificial means. Although still not proof of the relief's antiquity, these findings are more conclusive than the earlier study and better confirm the sculpture's authenticity.

Dolomitic marble from the Greek island of Thasos
82 x 161 cm (32 5/16 x 63 3/8 in.)
Henry Lillie Pierce Fund 08.205

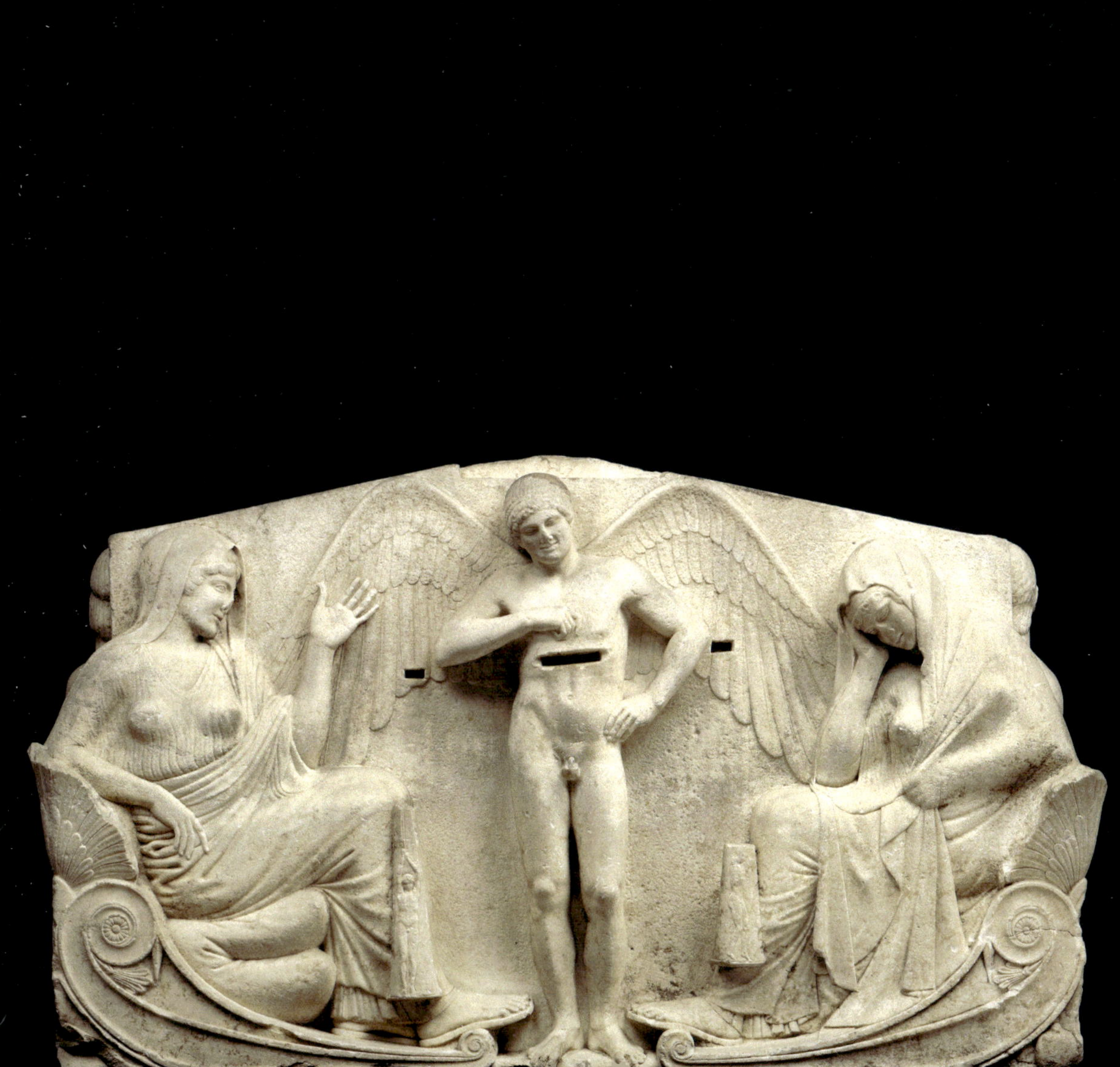

Crucified Christ

Germany or Austria, 11th century

This polychrome sculpture is a rare early example of a monumental crucified Christ figure. Unfortunately, because there are few surviving objects with which it might be compared, its precise geographic origins and dating are difficult to determine with certainty. In 2008 MFA conservators, curators, and scientists collaborated with German specialists in medieval polychromed wood sculpture to study this figure. All aspects of the materials and techniques used to make it, including the wood and how it was cut, trimmed, and joined, as well as the many layers of paint, were important to the research. Because this sculpture had been an object of devotion for centuries, it had been restored more than once in the past. The nature of those restorations also required investigation.

The scientists took small slivers of the wood and studied them microscopically, looking for characteristic features of specific wood types, and discovered that the figure is made of willow. They also took paint samples from two dozen areas selected for the likelihood that they had hidden layers of the object's earliest paint. By making cross sections from the samples, they were able to examine them with optical and scanning electron microscopy, plus other lab techniques, to identify the number of paint layers and the specific pigments in each sample. Meanwhile, conservators carefully studied the surface of the sculpture itself with a type of microscope doctors use to aid surgical procedures. The examination was crucial for correlating information from a few scattered and tiny samples to the many square feet of paint that cover the entire sculpture.

X-rays revealed how the artist put the sculpture together. The figure's body and the base were carved from a single giant piece of wood, a quarter of a tree trunk at least six feet in diameter when whole. The

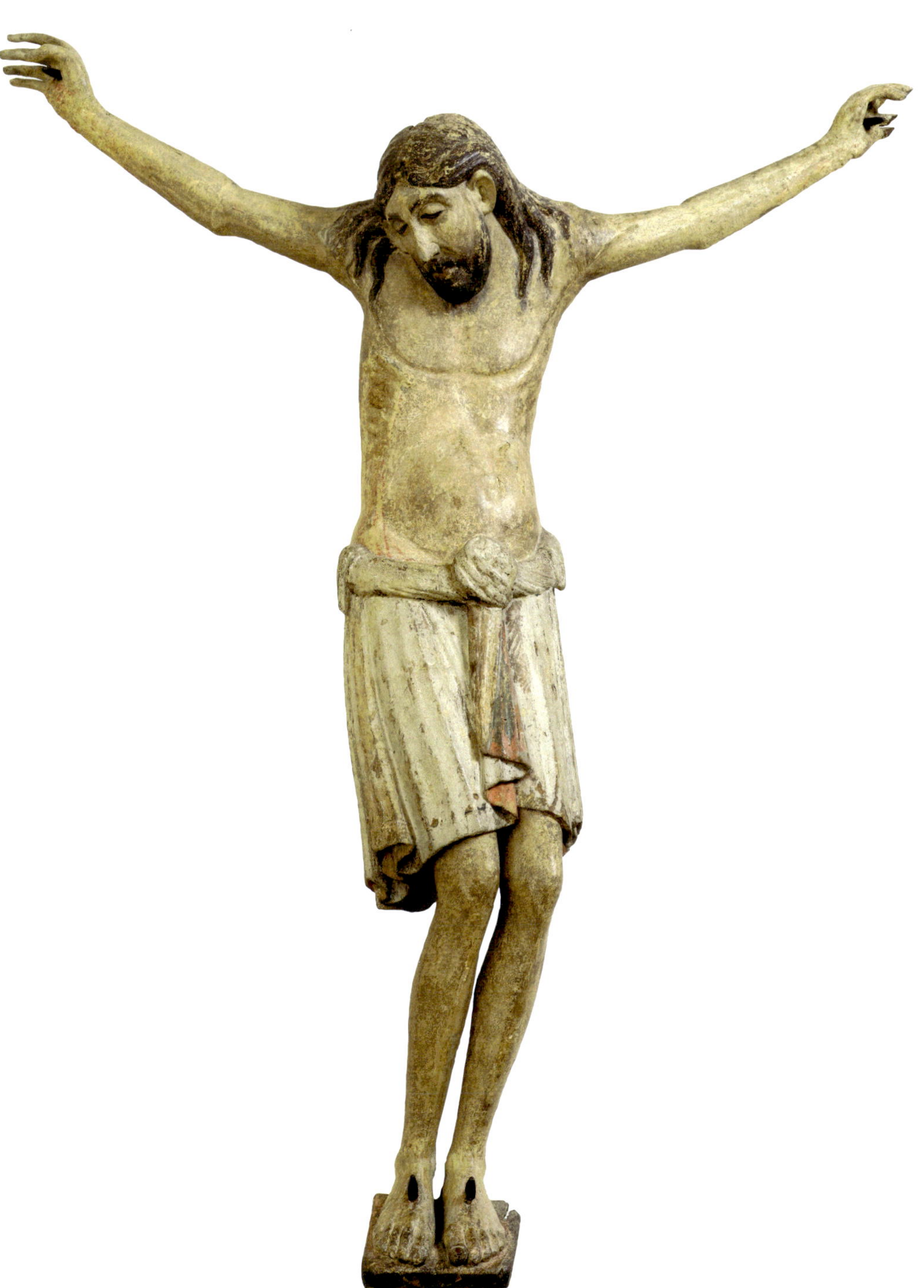

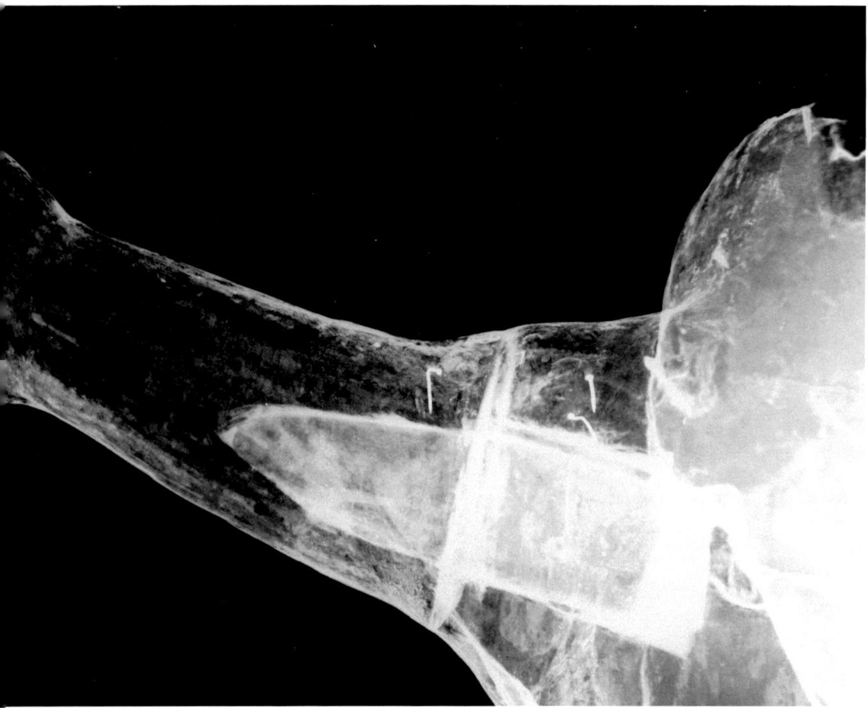
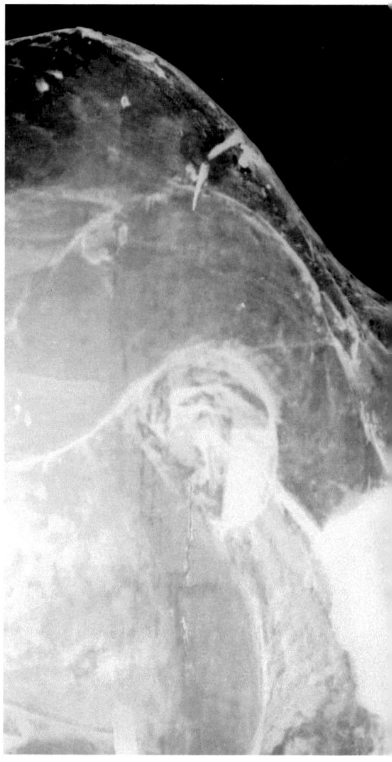

X-rays of the sculpture's upper body, showing large tapered dowels used to attach the arms to the torso

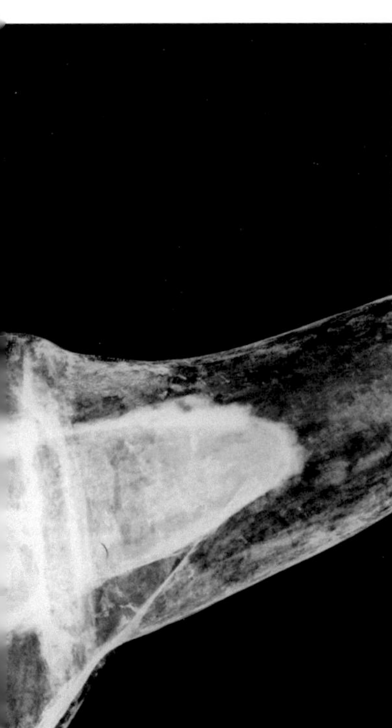

shape of the original trunk may have dictated certain characteristics of the figure, such as the manner in which the head is angled. The sculptor carved the arms separately, also from willow, and attached them to the body with large, tapered wooden dowels. Sometime later, someone cut off the support under Christ's feet and hollowed out the back and head. The figure wore a crown at one time, and it may have even been lashed to the now-missing cross.

The painted surface we see today, and even some of the carving, is not original. Parts of the sculpture were repainted in the thirteenth century. Significant areas were reworked at the end of the fourteenth century; for example, the ribs were carved more deeply, and a wound accentuated with drips of bright red pigment was added in Christ's side. These changes transformed the sculpture from a relatively peaceful figure to a more dramatic one, perhaps in response to new ideas about how the crucified Christ should be represented. The new image stresses his humanity and elicits empathetic responses from the viewer. Although the sculpture has been repainted many times since, for the most part it is this vision of Christ on the cross that we see today.

Except for Museum records documenting that conservators removed the arms and reattached them in the 1920s, and that they consolidated flaking paint repeatedly over the years, there is little evidence of the sculpture's having received any modern restoration treatments. Careful investigative research by curators, conservators, and scientists has given us a better sense of how the sculpture came to look the way it does now and how its original appearance may have differed. The new information has yet to solve all questions about the sculpture's origins, but study on this subject continues.

Willow with polychromy

From top of head to bottom of base under feet: 180 cm (70⅞ in.)

1951 Purchase Fund 51.1405

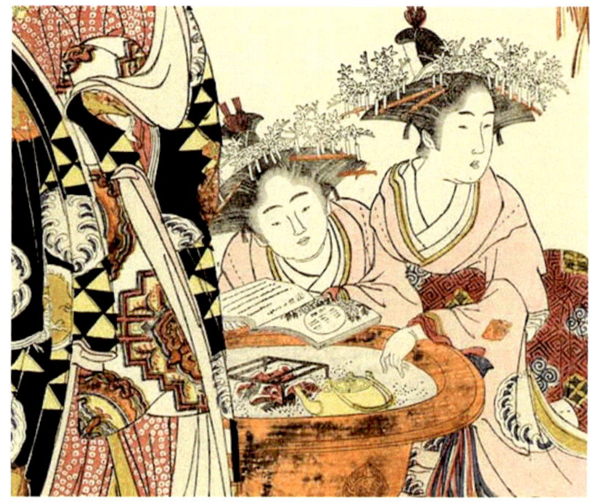

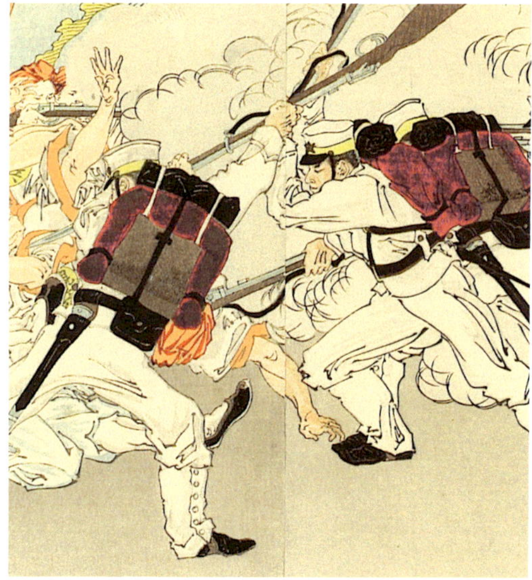

New Beauties of the Yoshiwara in the Mirror of Their Own Script

Kitao Masanobu (Japanese, 1761–1816)

1784

Woodblock printed book; ink and color on paper

38 x 25.7 cm (15 x 10.1 in.)

Source unidentified 2006.1341

Great Victory for Our Troops at the Fall of Asan

Migita Toshihide (Japanese, 1863–1925)

1894

Woodblock print; ink and color on paper

Vertical ōban triptych: 35.9 x 71.7 cm (14⅛ x 28¼ in.)

Jean S. and Frederic A. Sharf Collection 2000.434a–c

Thanks to conservation research on the stability of colorants and pigments used in Japanese woodblock prints, conservators today are well versed in the adverse effects of time or environment on such materials. However, sometimes what might seem to be an environmental change may be original to the work of art, intentionally created by the maker rather than an accident of time. Distinguishing between the two can be difficult. A conservator's knowledge of historical studio practice and the particular artist's intentions, as well as of current research about the possible environmental causes of a perceived change, is crucial for determining whether or not a particular print should receive treatment.

These two works, one by Kitao Masanobu and the other by Migita Toshihide, nearly straddle the heyday of color woodblock print production in Japan from the eighteenth to the twentieth centuries.The brazier in the lower right of Masanobu's print of courtesans was originally all red, but the pigment discolored over time. Red lead changes to a deep brown when exposed to acids or to a dense metallic black when exposed to sulfur-containing gases. By the time Toshihide created his battle scene more than one hundred years later, artists and printers may have intentionally discolored red lead in imitation of and appreciation for the effects of time they saw in early prints like Masanobu's.

Toshihide or his printer created the dark black we see in the red areas of the Japanese flag and the soldiers' backpacks by first printing a layer of bright red synthetic color (a pigment not available in Japan in Masanobu's time), and then printing a layer of intentionally blackened red lead pigment on top of it. The purposely discolored area has a metallic quality that differs from the duller discoloration of red lead naturally exposed to acids or sulfur-containing gases.

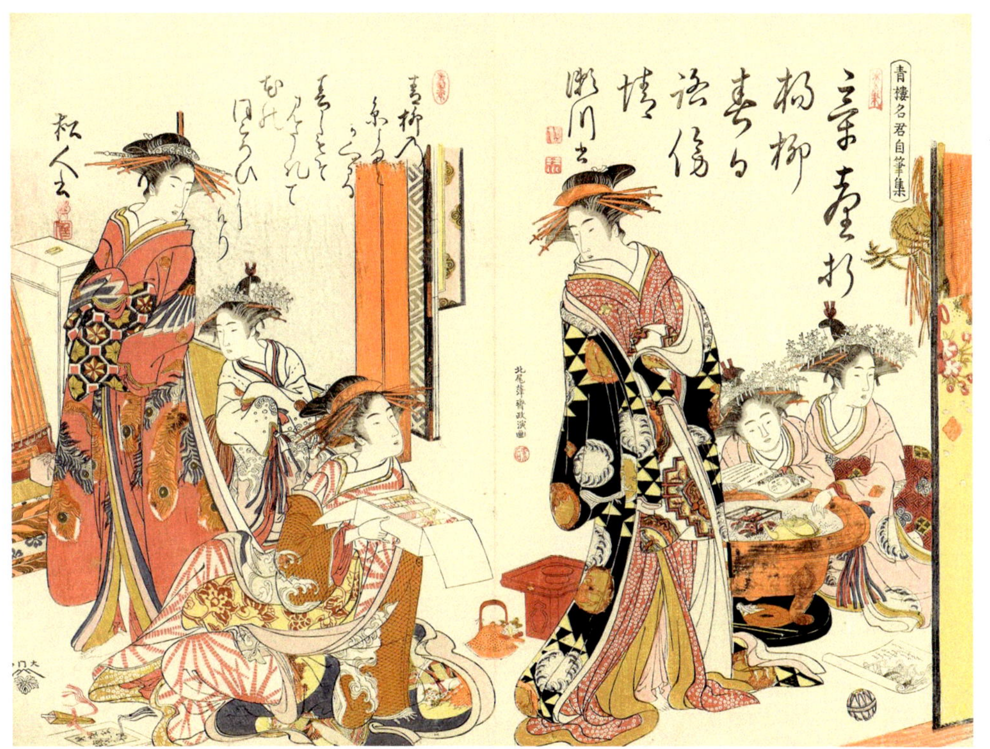
青樓名君自筆集

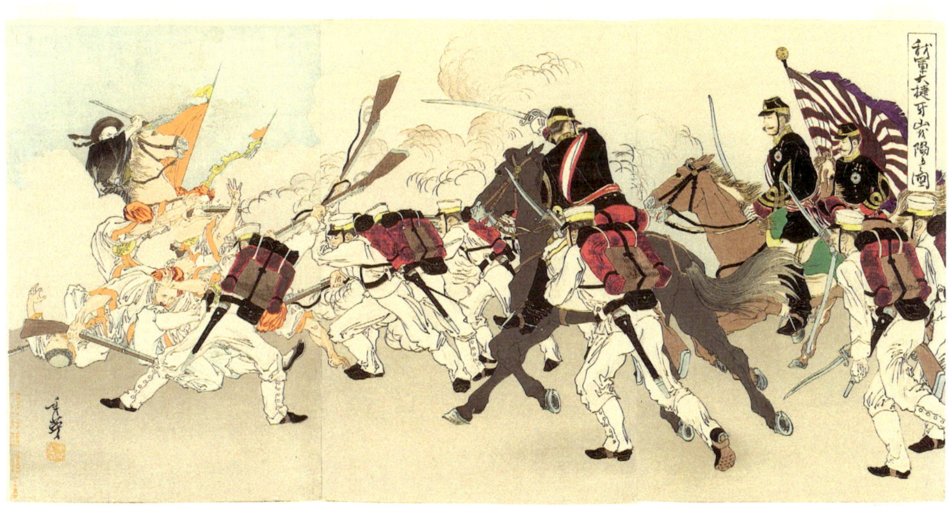

Votive effigies

Muisca culture

Central highlands, Colombia, 1100–1550

The ancient Muisca people of Colombia's central highlands created beautiful and meticulously crafted golden objects, such as these votive effigies called *tunjos*. Representing warriors, religious practitioners, women holding infants, animals, and personal implements, tunjos were symbolic offerings for maintaining the balance of the universe. Although objects like these appear to be made of pure gold, in fact artisans in Central and South America used many different techniques to work metal alloys made of gold, silver, and copper. When scientists at the MFA undertook a study to determine the composition of this group of ritual objects, they were surprised to find that they were not all made in the same way.

By first analyzing the figures with X-ray fluorescence, then taking samples and analyzing them with a scanning electron microscope, the scientists were able to determine that several of the figures have thin, almost pure gold layers on their surfaces. The Muisca artists achieved those layers with the ancient process of depletion gilding, which produces a thin layer of gold on the surface of objects made of a gold-copper alloy called *tumbaga*. Current theories about depletion gilding suggest that the artists heated a suitable object in a mineral- or plant-based acid solution, dissolving the copper from the tumbaga surface and leaving a layer of gold. After cleaning and polishing the work, the artist could repeat the process until he or she achieved a desired color. The scanning electron microscopy showed that some of the figures were immersed for a long time or multiple times, producing a thick layer of gold. Other figures were immersed briefly, producing extremely thin layers. Some figures were not treated with acid at all. The analysis also made it possible to identify the composition of the

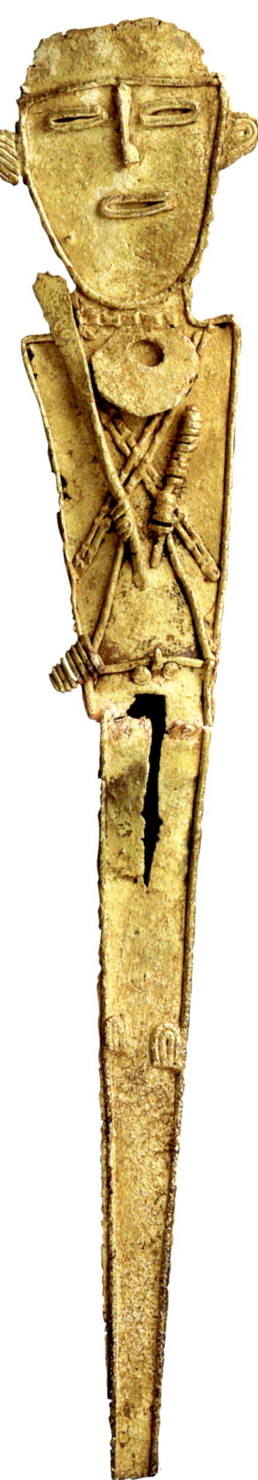

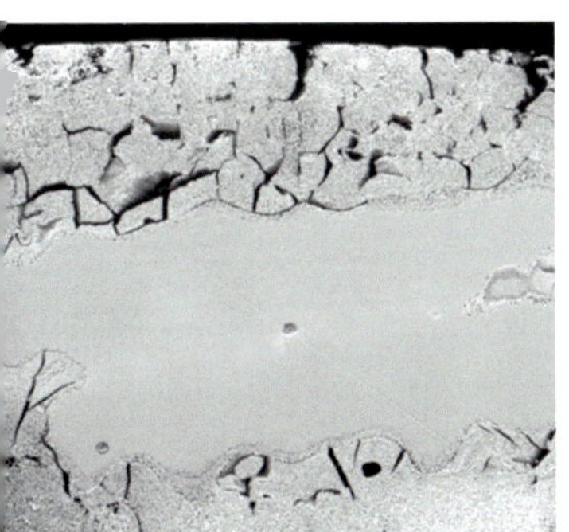

A highly magnified cross section of the metal (1 mm thick) from an effigy. The image, made by a scanning electron microscope, shows the spongelike, gold-enriched surfaces at top and bottom.

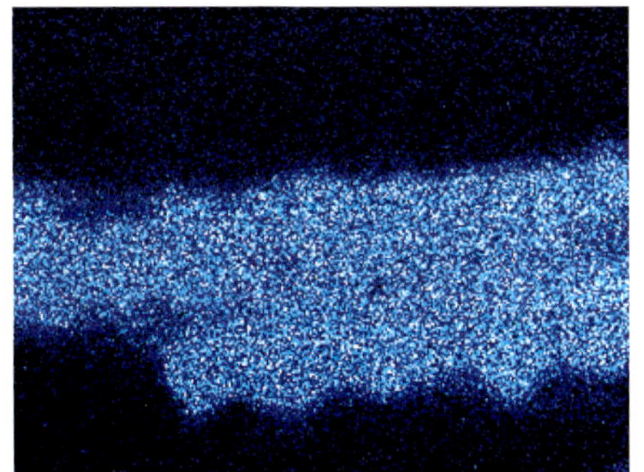

X-ray map showing the distribution of copper in the cross section. A considerable amount of copper is present in the interior of the metal but virtually absent from the surface.

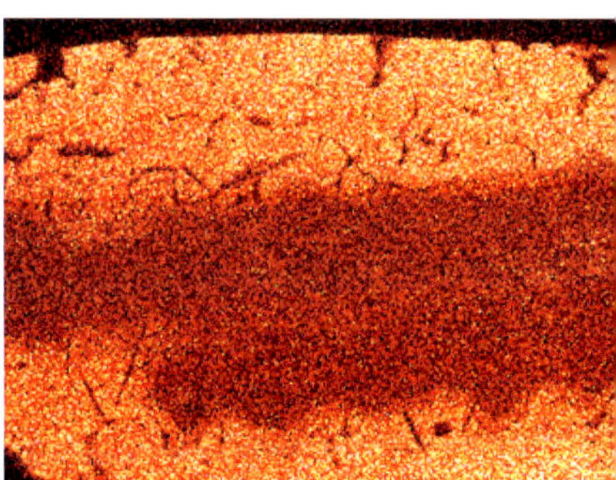

X-ray map showing the distribution of gold in the cross section. Little gold is found in the interior while high concentrations of it are present on the surface.

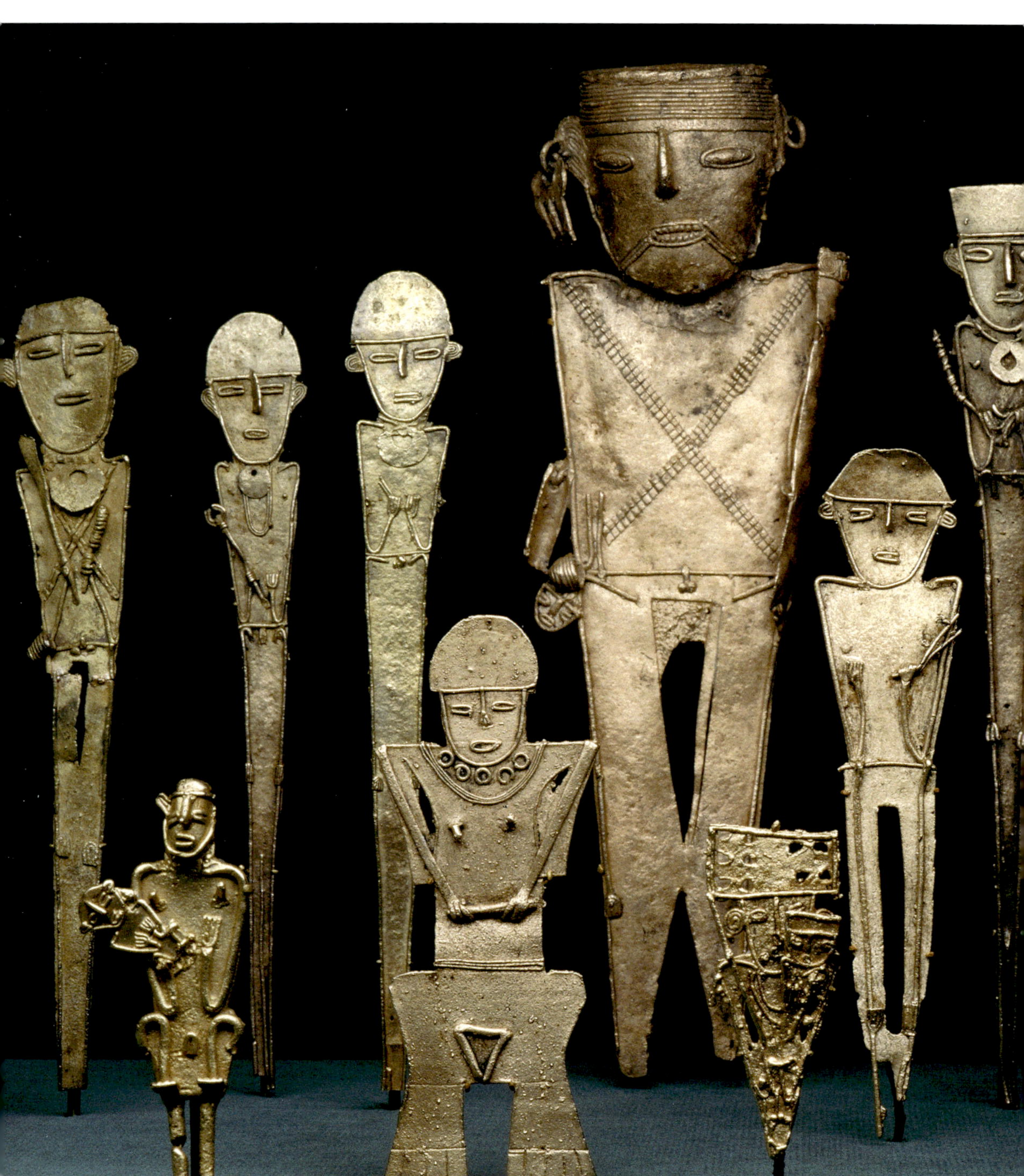

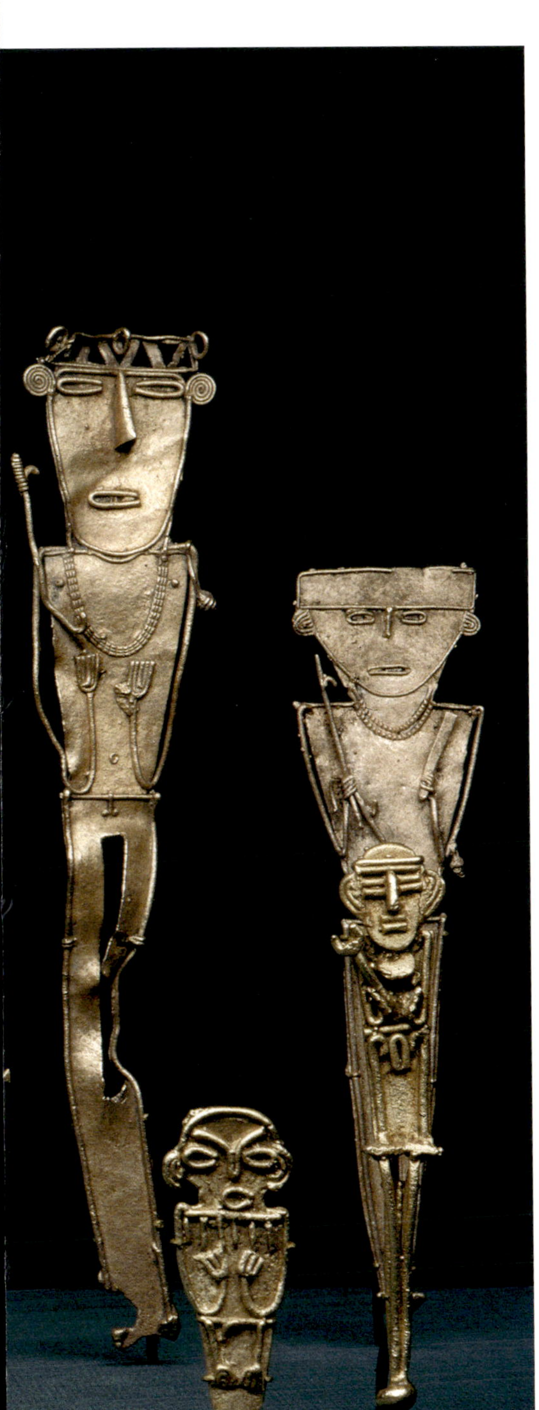

tumbaga from which each of the objects was cast. Some figures were found to be made of nearly pure gold.

The research leaves open the question of why the Muisca artists varied their techniques to make such similar ritual objects. Perhaps they favored the gold-copper alloy because it melts at a much lower temperature than either pure copper or pure gold, or because depletion gilding achieved a desired color without large quantities of gold, which was an imported commodity.

Gold and copper alloy
The effigies range in height from 4.4 cm (1¾ in.) to 21.0 cm (8¼ in.)
Gifts of Landon T. Clay 1975.65, 1975.39, 1975.76, 1975.37, 1975.38, 1975.67, 1975.51, 1975.79, 1975.44, 1975.41, 1975.115, 1975.48, 1975.88, 1975.43, 1975.78

Woman's headdress

Made in France and worn in the United States, mid-19th century

Headdresses with artificial fruit and flowers were popular among the socialites of 1850s Paris. This lusciously naturalistic example, decorated with artificial cherries, strawberries, grapes, plums, flower blossoms, and coral, was worn by women of the Lamb family of Boston. Scion Annie Lawrence Roche most likely commissioned it when she lived in France from 1850 to 1853.

Because this headdress is an early example of such a decorative item of dress, conservators and scientists collaborated to carefully investigate its materials. Study under a stereobinocular microscope showed conservators that each element was handmade, built up from smaller elements and constructed in fantastic ways from simple substances. These substances appeared to be natural. To confirm this, scientists took complex samples from the headdress and applied many analytical techniques to fully identify and characterize all the materials used to make it.

Analysis began with Fourier transform infrared spectroscopy, which provided general information on pigments, binders, and adhesives. Following this, the scientists used gas chromatography/mass spectrometry to provide details on the specific nature of the binders and adhesives.

The investigation showed that the flower petals and leaves consist of pieces of dyed, painted fabric stiffened with starch. The blueberries are thin, colorless glass globes tinted with a mixture of beeswax, an inorganic pigment called ultramarine blue, and an organic red dye. The coral was made from a tinted layer of gum arabic, a plant gum that was also used to make commercial watercolor paints at that time. All of these materials are fragile, and some, such as the starch and gum, are highly susceptible to dissolving in water, so the conservators had to choose their treatment materials carefully. If such a fashion had been popular twenty or thirty years later, the fruit and flowers could well have been made of commercial plastics and synthetic dyes.

Wire, silk, cotton, gum arabic, starch, beeswax, pigments, glass, and gelatin
53 cm (20⅞ in.)
Gift in memory of Mrs. Horatio Appleton Lamb 51.360

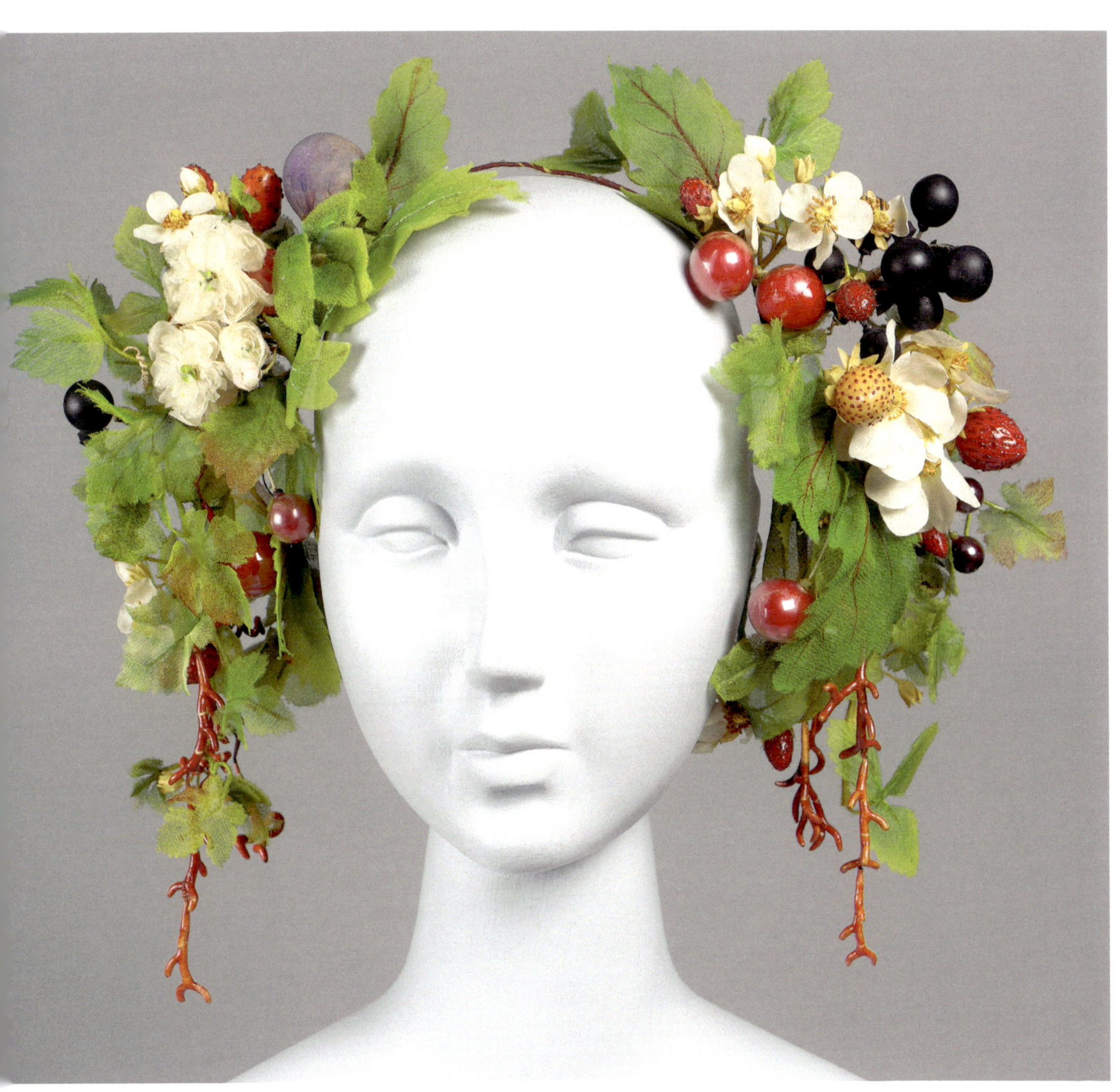

Banded textile fragment with birds and inscriptions

Persian, northern Iran near Rayy, Seljuk Dynasty, 11th or 12th century

Silk

70 x 96 cm (27 9/16 x 37 13/16 in.)

Denman Waldo Ross Collection 31.402a–c

Modern-day forgery of a Buyid silk

Persian, Iran, 1930 or later

Silk

24 x 64 cm (9 7/16 x 25 3/16 in.)

Gift of Mrs. Edward Jackson Holmes 59.173

During the 1920s and 1930s, a number of silk fragments came to light that were said to have been excavated at Rayy, a site in northern Iran that was part of the Persian Empire during the Buyid and Seljuk dynasties. By the 1940s, many textiles identified as Buyid entered private and museum collections, causing controversy over the textiles' origins and dating. Some scholars regarded them as genuine creations of the tenth to twelfth centuries, and others saw them as fakes. More recently, after much study and analysis, scholars have argued that the earliest fragments to surface are genuine, and that the later so-called discoveries are forgeries made in response to the high demand for the genuine ones. Most of the fragments have inscriptions, but only a few correspond with the type of inscriptions typically found on authentic Buyid artifacts. Also troubling is the condition of many fragments, which seems too good for archaeological textiles that are supposed to be eight or nine centuries old.

In 1992 scientists carried out radiocarbon analysis to clarify the dating for seventeen of the Buyid textiles. First developed in the 1940s, radiocarbon dating can determine the age of old materials that originated from plants or animals. Radiocarbon, also known as carbon 14, is created in the earth's upper atmosphere through a reaction of the sun's cosmic radiation with nitrogen gas and is incorporated by all materials that contain carbon, including living plants and animals. Knowing the amount of radiocarbon relative to the total amount of carbon (most of which is not radioactive) in a living thing and the rate at which radiocarbon decays, scientists can calculate the length of time that has passed since the material died. In this way, they can determine the age of an artifact. Textiles, wood, ivory, bone, and many other organic materials can, in principle, be dated by this technique.

The 1992 study found that four tested fragments have radiocarbon dates consistent with their proposed medieval origins. A smaller group of fragments was dated to the fourteenth through seventeenth centuries, and the remainder to sometime between the mid-seventeenth century and the present. Although the MFA's textiles were not included in the radiocarbon analyses, a comparison of their weaves, inscriptions, and other characteristics with those included in the 1992 research suggests that fragment 31.402 is an authentic medieval textile, but that fragment 59.173 is probably a forgery made in modern times.

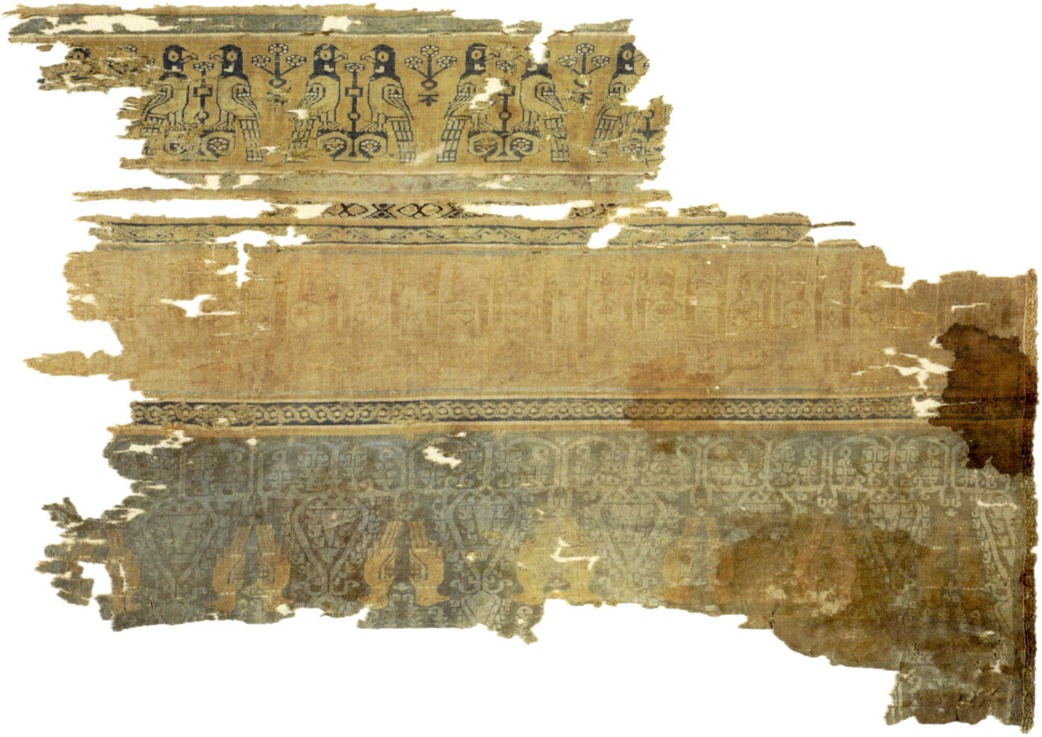

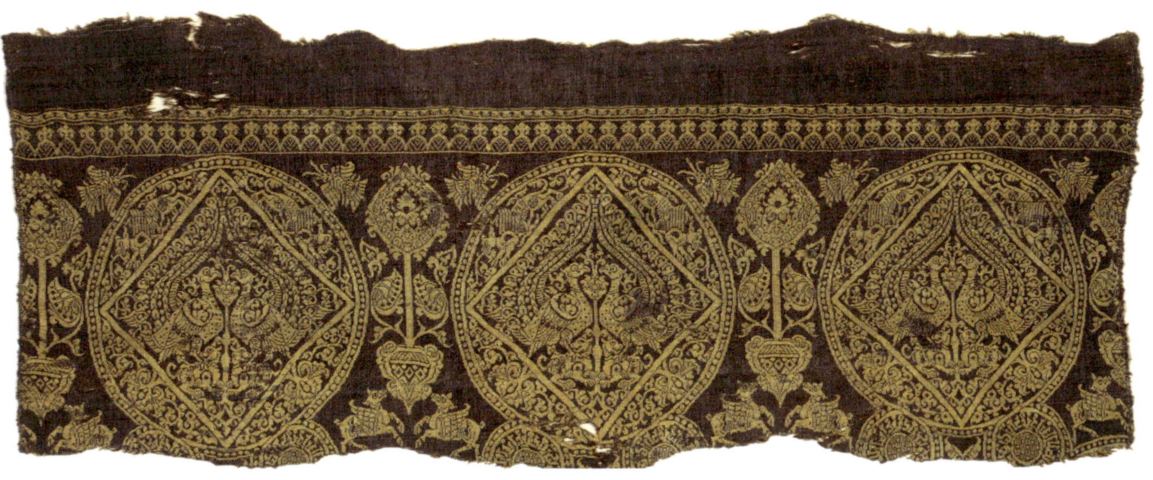

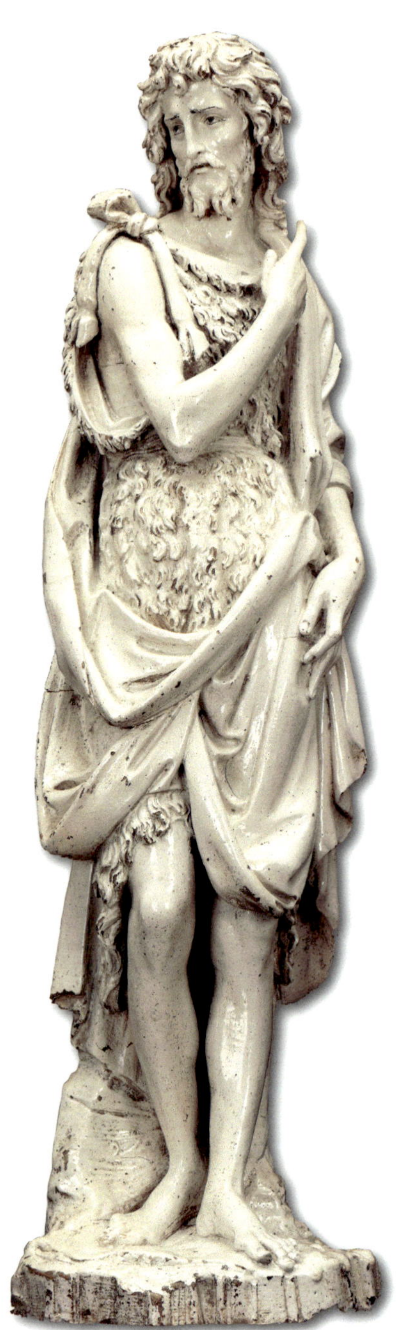

Saint John the Baptist

Giovanni Francesco Rustici (Italian, 1474–1554)

About 1505–15

When this sculpture came into the Museum's collection in 1950, it was in poor condition and was attributed to the della Robbia family. It remained in storage, unpublished, for more than fifty years. As part of preparations for an exhibition of Italian Renaissance sculpture in 2007, conservators, scientists, and curators undertook new research and treatment for this object.

First conservators had to remove thick accumulations of dirt and several layers of aged paint and varnish before what remained of the original sculpture could be studied and appreciated. They also removed a gesturing index finger and an oversize goat's leg attached to the skin Saint John wears over his shoulder. Both were clumsy restorations of lost original parts.

X-rays showed that the figure was built from the bottom up in three major sections. Seams between the sections, visible even to the naked eye across the neck and up the chest, may represent days of work in succession (where the drier clay of one day's work met the more damp clay of the next day). Both the head and the torso are hollow. The sculptor probably wrapped flattened balls of clay around rags or paper, which he removed before firing. He needed to keep the thickness of the clay consistent over the entire figure so it would fire evenly and not be too heavy.

Taking small chips of the fired clay body of the sculpture as well as of the glaze that covers it, Museum scientists prepared cross sections for X-ray fluorescence analysis in a scanning electron microscope. The results allowed them to determine the sculpture's chemical composition. Its base material contains a fair amount of calcium carbonate and a very low amount of iron. The glaze is rich in lead and tin, with small quantities of copper and iron. The metallic elements created the glaze's off-white color when fired. The slight tint allowed the artist to emphasize the play of light and shadow across the complex figure in a way that would have been more difficult with a brighter or more reflective white glaze, and in fact the glaze used here differs from the famed white glaze of the della Robbias. Moreover, copper has never been found in any della Robbia glaze tested to date.

Better able to understand these qualities of style and manufacture, curators attributed the work to the Florentine sculptor Giovanni Francesco Rustici. As previously noted by Museum curators, the MFA's Saint John resembles the central figure in Rustici's bronze group on the Baptistery in Florence. The Renaissance chronicler Giorgio Vasari noted Rustici's close relationship with Leonardo da Vinci, who was staying in Rustici's house during some of the time that Rustici was working on the Bapistery commission. To prepare the sculpture for the exhibition, conservators reconstructed the missing finger and the goat's leg, working with curators to design parts that were appropriate in scale and style for art of the period in general and representations of Saint John the Baptist and other works by Rustici in particular.

Glazed terra-cotta

100.3 x 33 x 26.7 cm (39½ x 13 x 10½ in.)

Gift of Mrs. Solomon R. Guggenheim 50.2624

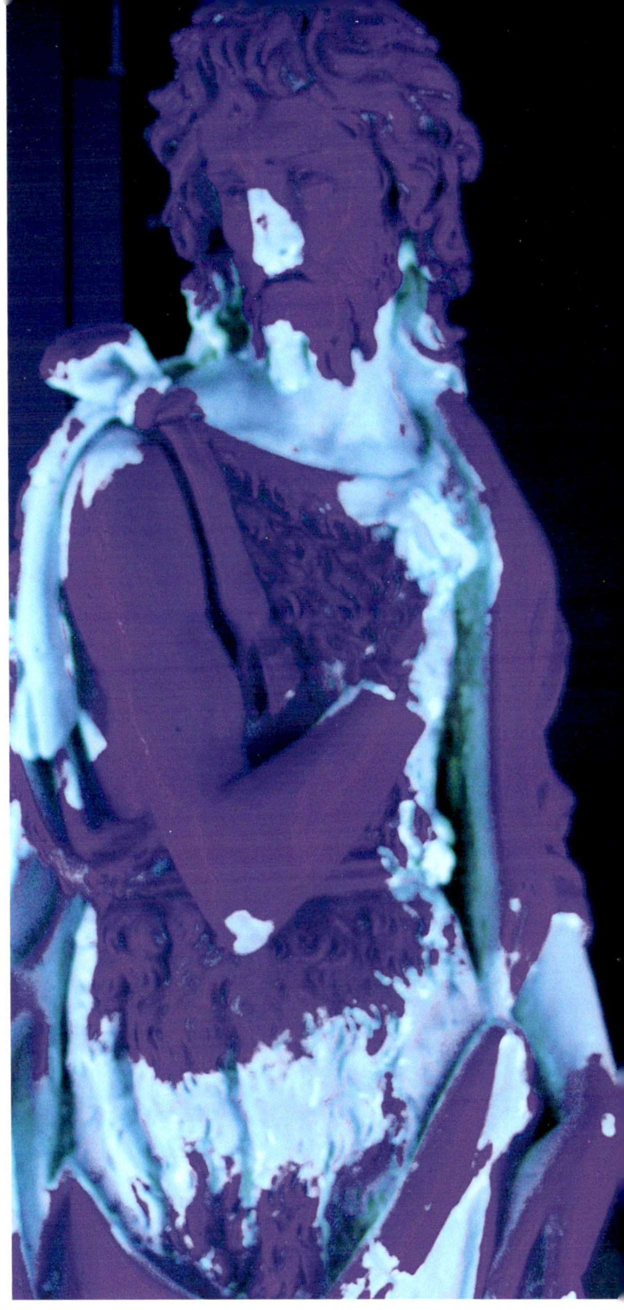

Detail, under ultraviolet radiation. The right hand has been detached, and the fluorescent areas indicate old fills from previous restorations.

Saints Matthias and Matthew

Master of the Holy Kinship

(German, working last quarter of the 15th century)

1475–99

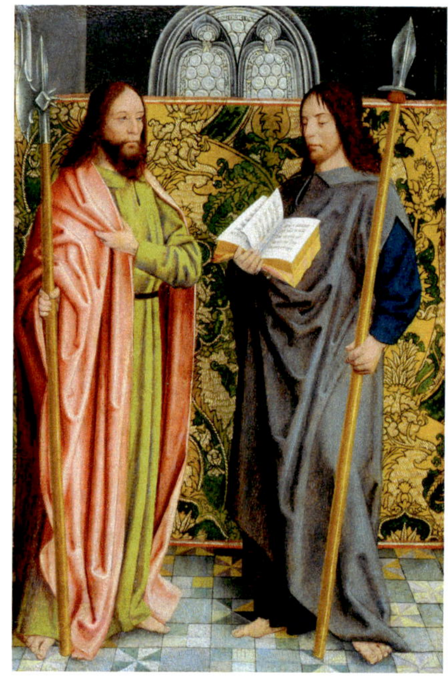

This painting and more than a dozen others produced in Cologne, Germany, at the end of the fifteenth century are attributed to an unidentified artist traditionally called the Master of the Holy Kinship, named after an altarpiece depicting this subject. However, art historians now believe that they were created by a workshop that employed many artists, not just a single master. Medieval and early Renaissance European paintings were usually executed on wood panels covered with a white ground layer of paint. One or more artists drew the design for the painting on that white layer in charcoal, black ink, or thin dark paint. Many artists were then called on to apply colored paints on top of the drawing, completely obscuring it in the process. Assignments for different areas were probably made according to ability and seniority within the workshop.

Identifying the different hands that worked on the paintings and determining how the artists operated together in the workshop setting are part of the Museum's ongoing investigative efforts. Infrared reflectography, an imaging technique developed in the late 1960s, helps researchers by allowing them to see what lies beneath a painting's surface. The technique uses reflected infrared energy, which makes most pigments more transparent than when viewed with regular light. Because black pigments are notable exceptions to this rule, the technique allows researchers to see black underdrawings.

Conservators used infrared reflectography to see the underdrawing of this painting. As in other works attributed to the Master of the Holy Kinship, the figures in the underdrawing are outlined in black paint, which was apparently applied with a brush. Areas of shading are indicated by short dark lines. There appears to have been more than one drawing campaign, with the last one applied in darker paint to reinforce or change certain parts of the design.

One unusual feature of this painting and a number of others attributed to this master is the set of color notations in the underdrawing layer. Although the work of other medieval painters sometimes contains such notations, the practice does not appear to have been very common. There are two notations in the underdrawing of the saint at the left: to the right of his left thumb is a loosely formed letter "g," which may have been shorthand for *grün* (German for green), and just to the left of the same hand is "zot," which corresponds to *rot* (red). These notes told the artists of the workshop which colors the master intended for different areas of the painting.

Oil on panel

48 x 32.4 cm (18 7/8 x 12 3/4 in.)

Denman Waldo Ross Collection 07.646

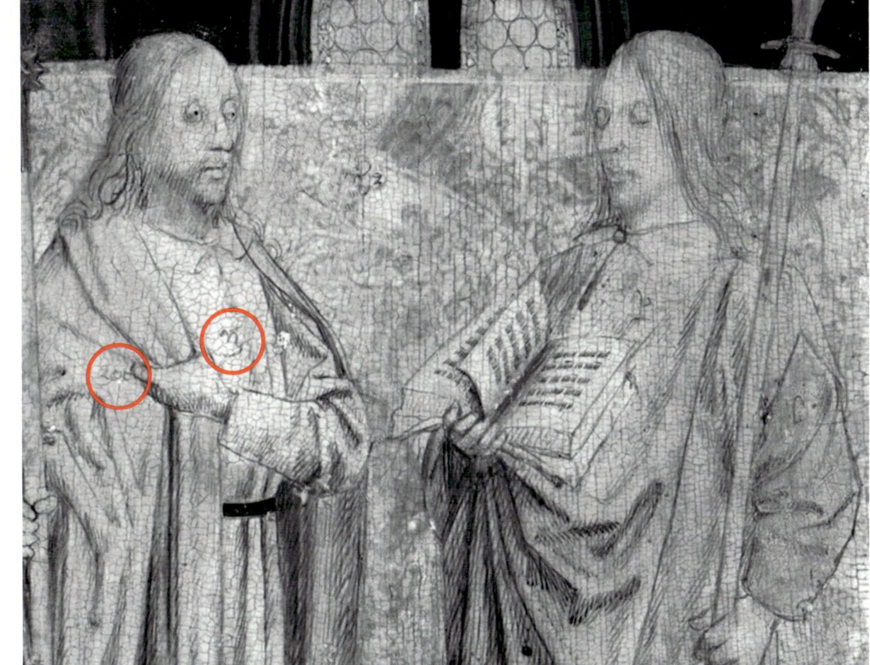

The infrared reflectograph of the upper part of the painting shows the artist's underdrawing, including several color notations. Two notes may be seen on either side of the left hand of the saint on the left: "zot" for *rot* (red) and "g" for *grün* (green).

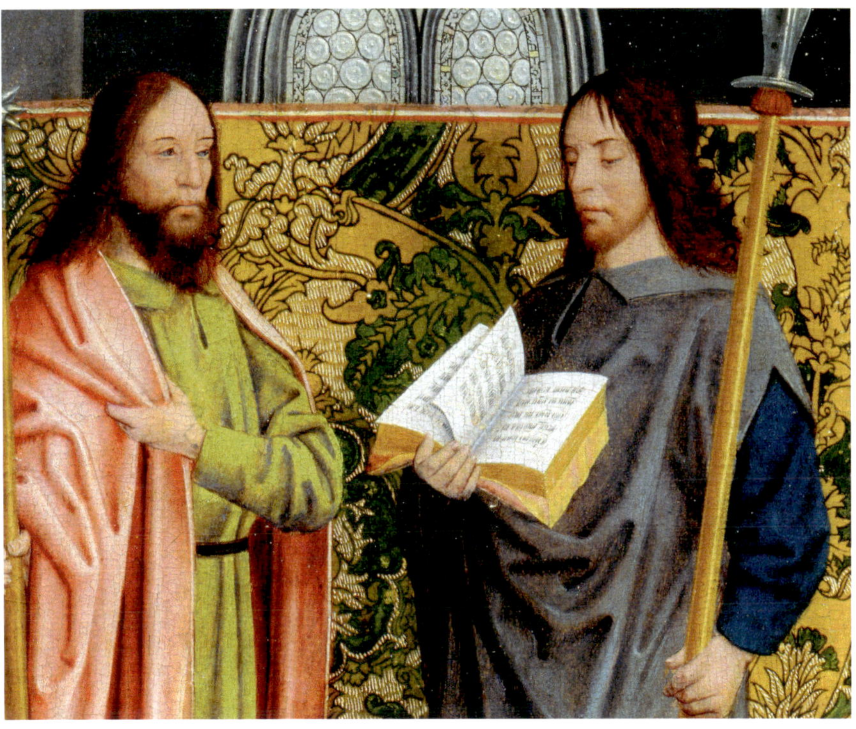

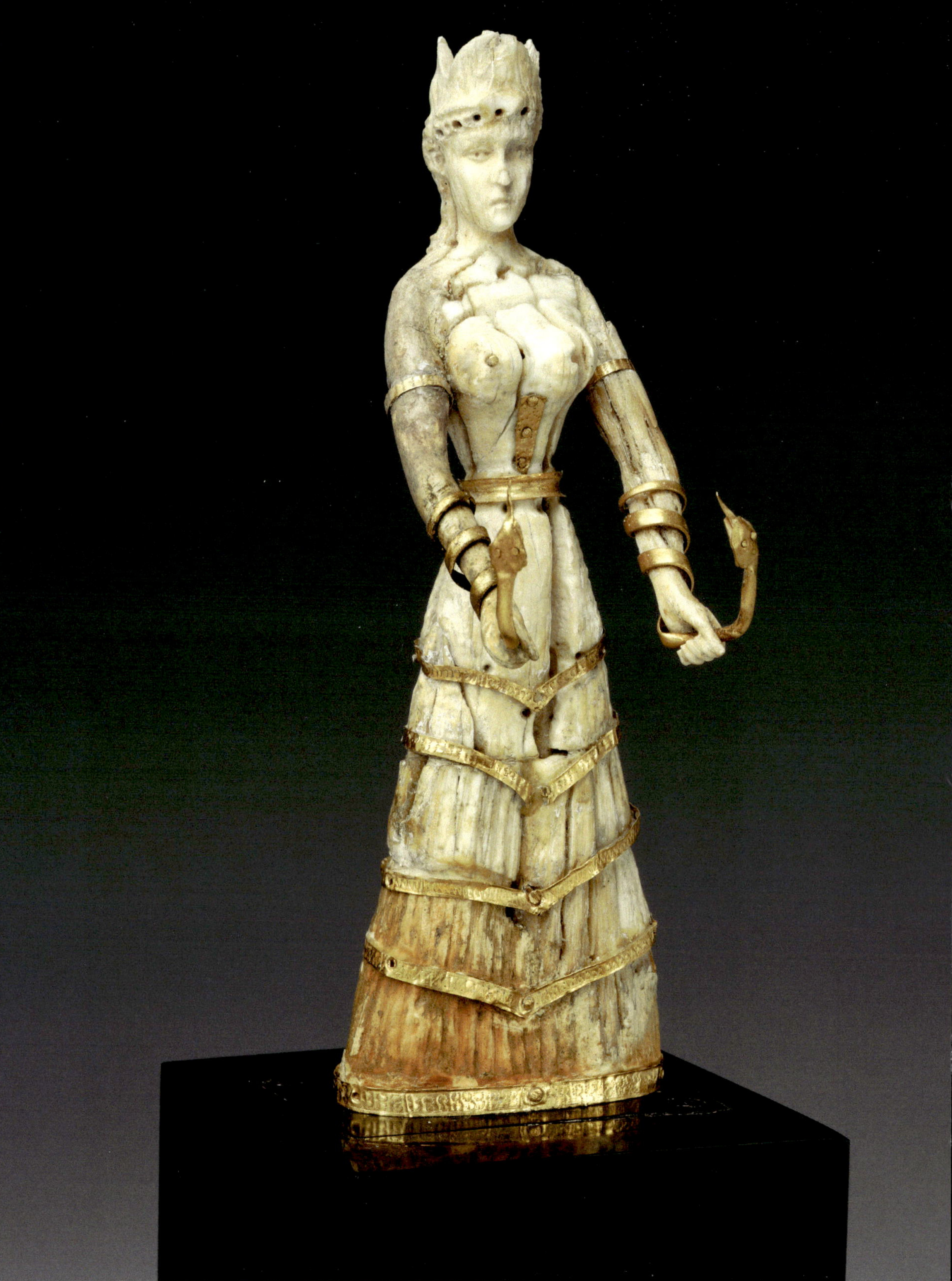

Statue of a snake goddess

Early Aegean, Minoan, Bronze Age, about 1600–1500 B.C. or early 20th century

At the turn of the last century, archaeological excavations on Crete, off the coast of Greece, led to an international fashion for anything attributed to the ancient Minoan civilization, which once dominated the island. Some scholars have argued that this fashion fostered the market for fake Minoan objects, which found their way into major museum collections; some objects may even have been placed at archaeological sites to reinforce an impression of their authenticity. This small ivory and gold figure has been declared one of the best treasures and worst forgeries in the MFA's collection at different times in its history. Investigative scientific research has been able to shed only partial light on the matter.

The Museum acquired the figure in 1914, only a few years after excavations at Knossos, the Minoan capital city, had begun. It was regarded as one of the most valuable artifacts in the collection for many years and was featured in numerous popular and scholarly publications as an authentic Minoan object. But conflicting stories as to exactly where the figure came from and how it got to Boston have haunted it from its first days in the Museum. All that we know for certain is that it arrived in many pieces. There are no records of the earliest restoration work that made it whole.

Arthur Evans, the excavator of the Minoan capital of Knossos, postulated that the sculpture might have come from a site where other ivory fragments had been found, but none of the site's excavation records describes a find that matches any part of this figure. Evans believed the MFA's object to be authentic but argued that it had been illegally removed by some of his workmen. In part because of the lack of records about its source, some scholars questioned its authenticity.

Today, radiocarbon analysis can be used to date objects made of ivory (because it is the product of a living creature), but this sculpture has been treated twice with a wax that cannot be completely removed and that interferes with such testing. For this reason, MFA scientists have not sampled the sculpture for such analysis. The numerous pieces of gold attached to the figure cannot be directly dated either. Gold from the ground often contains silver and a tiny amount of copper. The gold on the snake goddess contains no silver and about 6 percent of copper, so it must have been made by mixing pure gold with copper. At the moment, there are no known examples of such an alloy from the Bronze Age, so some experts have declared this statue a forgery. However, museum scientists worldwide have not analyzed a large enough quantity of Bronze Age gold to determine conclusively that such an alloy did not exist at that time. And even if the gold decoration is a modern product, it is possible that someone applied it to a real Minoan ivory figure. For the moment, the object carries dates of both 1600–1500 B.C. and early twentieth century to reflect its uncertain status. Even if not authentic, the statue is an important reminder of America's early-twentieth-century fascination with the newly discovered ancient Minoan culture.

Gold, ivory
H. 16.1 cm (6 5/16 in.)
Gift of Mrs. W. Scott Fitz 14.863

The Nativity

Jacopo Tintoretto (Italian, about 1518–1594)

Late 1550s, reworked 1570s

This large painting of Christ's nativity was an enigma when it came into the MFA's collection in 1946. Although it was traditionally attributed to the Venetian Renaissance master Jacopo Tintoretto or to his son Domenico, curators have long noted evidence of at least two different hands at work in it: one more skilled in the central figures of Mary on the left and Saint Anne and a shepherd on the right; the other less so in the background scenes of the upper corners. Dating the central figures has also been problematic because their styles do not easily fit into a particular period of Tintoretto's career. The Virgin most closely resembles a figure in a painting by the master from the late 1550s, but the shepherd corresponds to figures in paintings from the 1560s and even 1570s. It is possible that Tintoretto began the painting in the 1550s and repainted parts of it much later. There are also peculiarities in the way that the nativity is depicted; in a scene that demands the attention of all to be on the Christ child, why is the shepherd on the right staring upward, apparently at nothing? Four separate recorded conservation treatments to the painting (three of them since it was acquired by the MFA) suggest that the donor and the MFA's curators and conservators remained uncertain about the true nature of the painting's condition and intended appearance for more than half a century.

Curators and conservators studied the painting again in preparation for a recent exhibition. A complete set of X-rays of the entire painting, an examination with infrared reflectography, and a number of paint cross sections examined under a microscope proved that the painting's canvas support consists of five main pieces sewn together vertically, with one additional piece sewn diagonally on the lower left corner. The left side of the piece with Mary and the right side of the piece with Saint Anne were the tacking edges of an earlier painting—both show holes from the nails that would have held the canvas to the wooden frame on which it had been stretched. Judging by their style, these two pieces were part of an earlier painting from the late 1550s, probably a heavenly vision of Christ on the cross amid clouds. At some point in the 1570s, the crucifixion scene was cut in half vertically and horizontally. The upper part of the original painting was discarded or reused for another painting. A new piece of canvas was added between the two vertical fragments. In addition, new canvas was added at the far left and right. Thus, the figures that had been mourning Christ's fate on the cross were incorporated into the new nativity scene. In the context of the crucifixion, the upward-looking shepherd makes more sense—he was originally a much younger man looking up at Christ on the cross. In the X-ray, we can see that a second male figure stood to the left of the Virgin. He also gazed up and toward the crucified figure. This figure was completely covered by later layers of paint. The added pieces of canvas were painted to remake the painting as a nativity scene. The quality of the painting in these pieces suggests that Tintoretto himself did not do any of the work; he must have delegated it to assistants.

That Tintoretto's studio reused materials, including canvas scraps sewn together for supports and palette scrapings recycled as priming layers, has been well documented; but it is only with technical investigations that we could know how they were combined to create this particularly complicated work, employing completely finished sections of an earlier painting. This is an extreme case of Renaissance recycling with little, if any, precedent.

Oil on canvas

155.6 x 358.1 cm (61¼ x 141 in.)

Gift of Quincy A. Shaw 46.1430

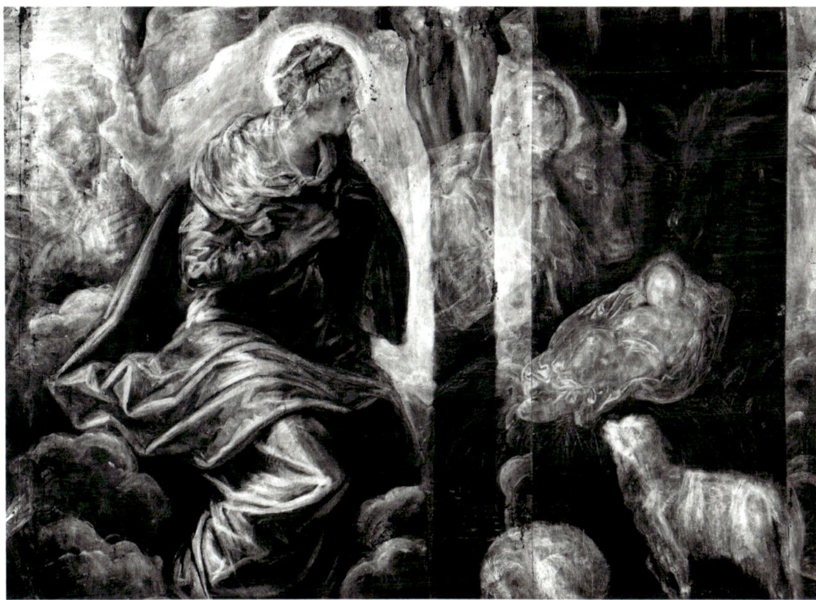

X-ray, detail

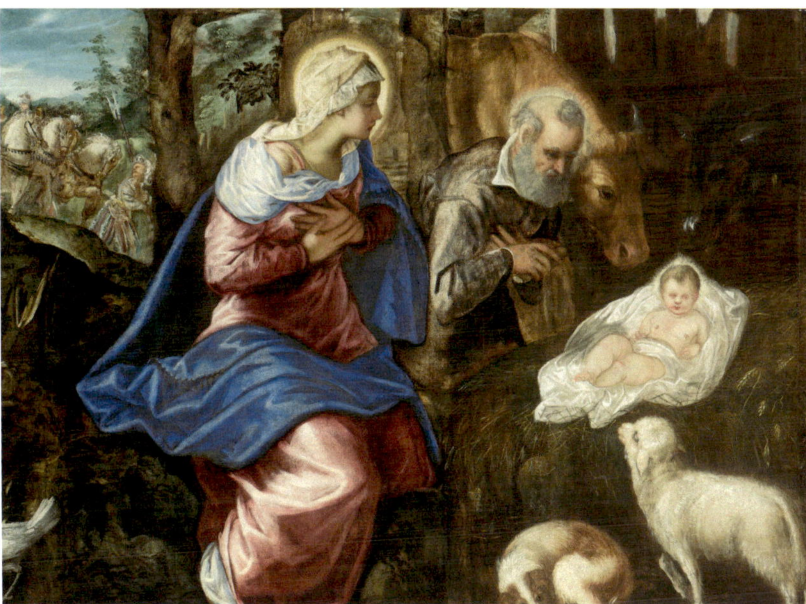

after treatment, detail

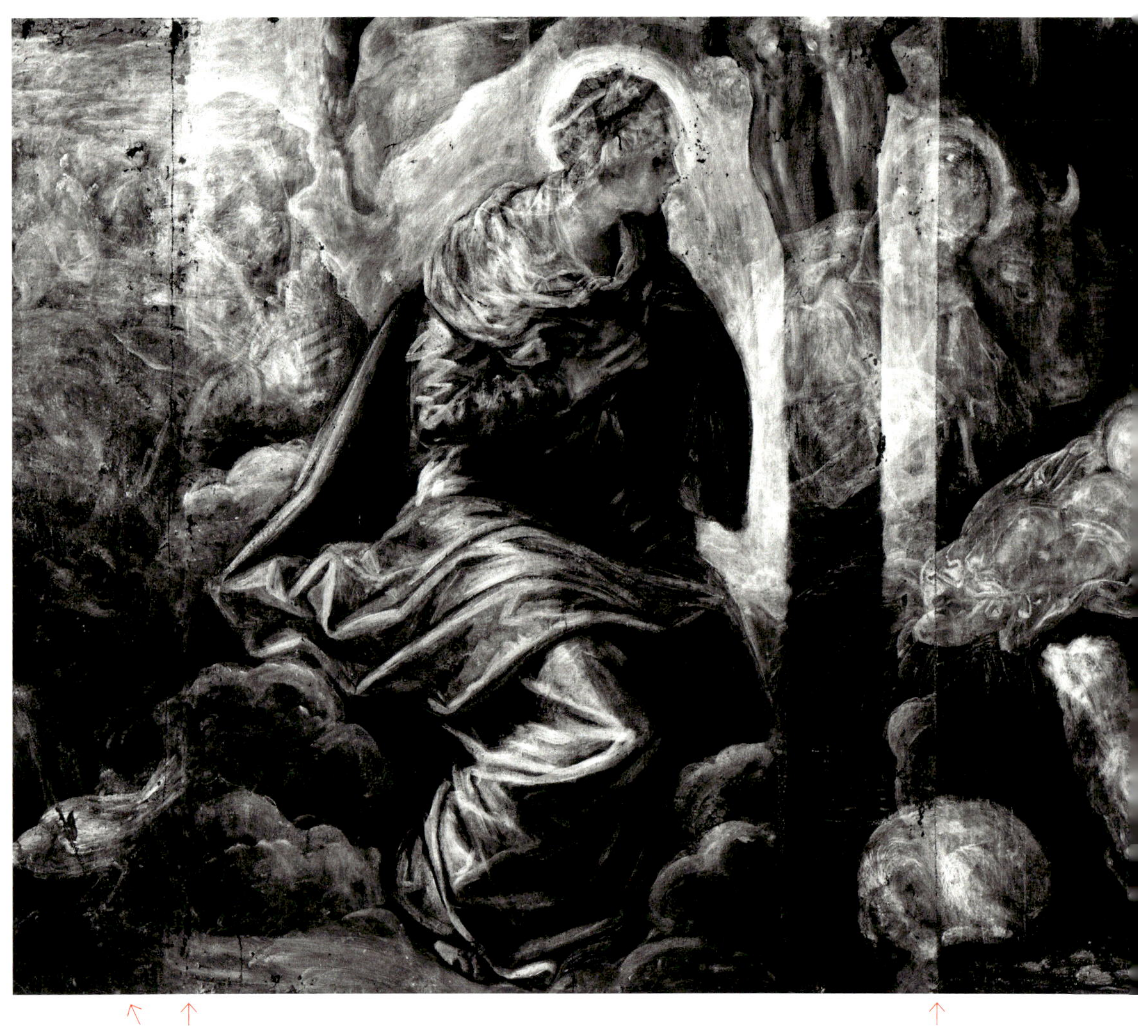

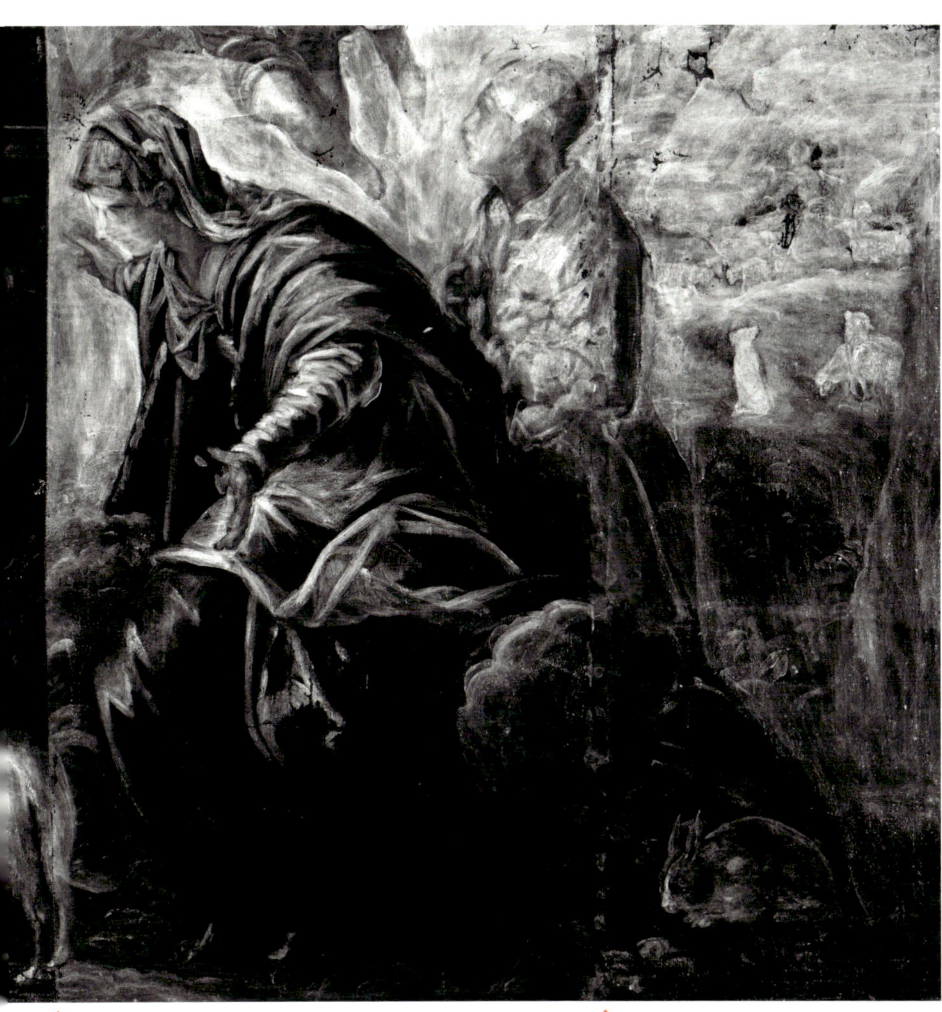

An X-ray shows how *The Nativity* was made from parts of another painting. The arrows point to the seams between pieces of canvas.

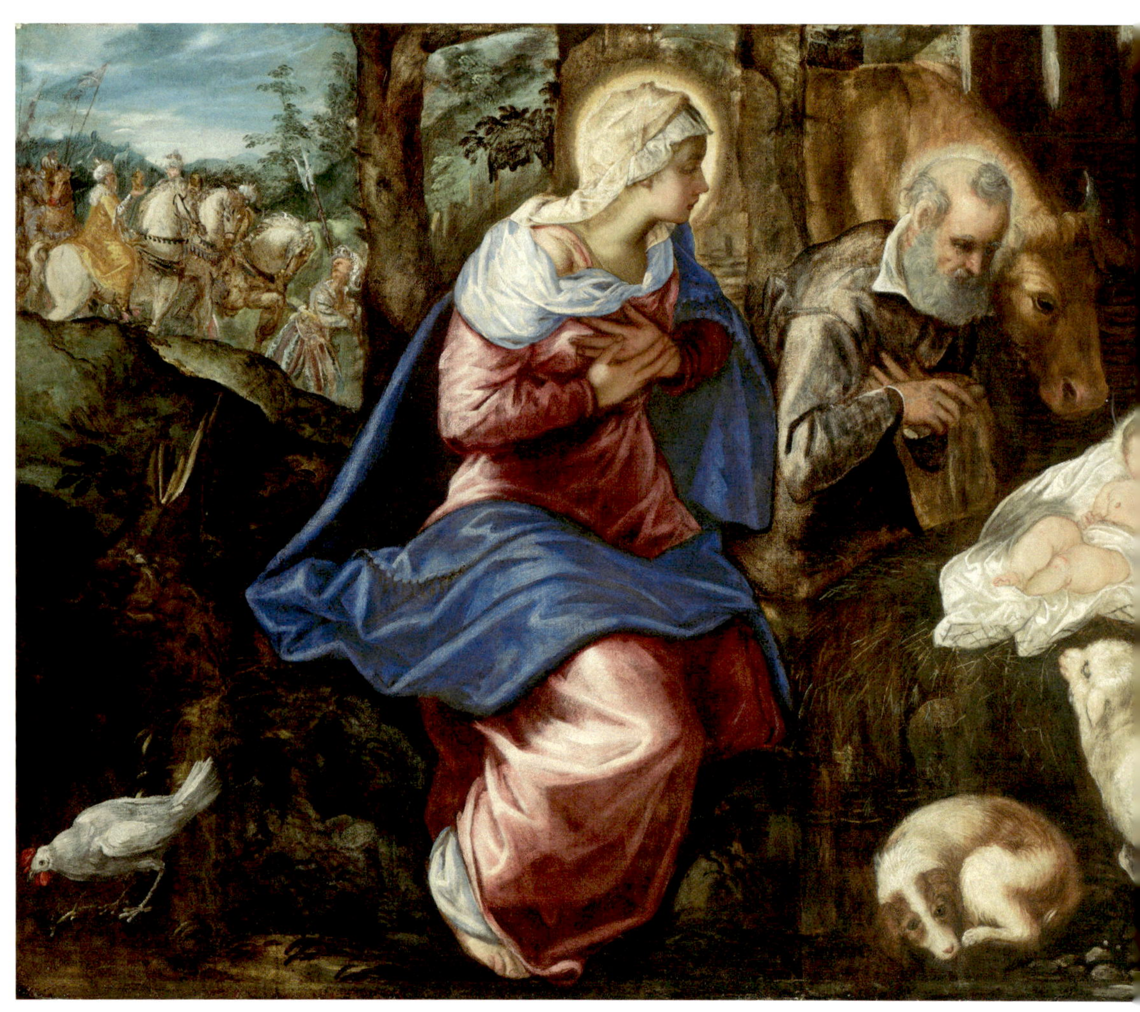

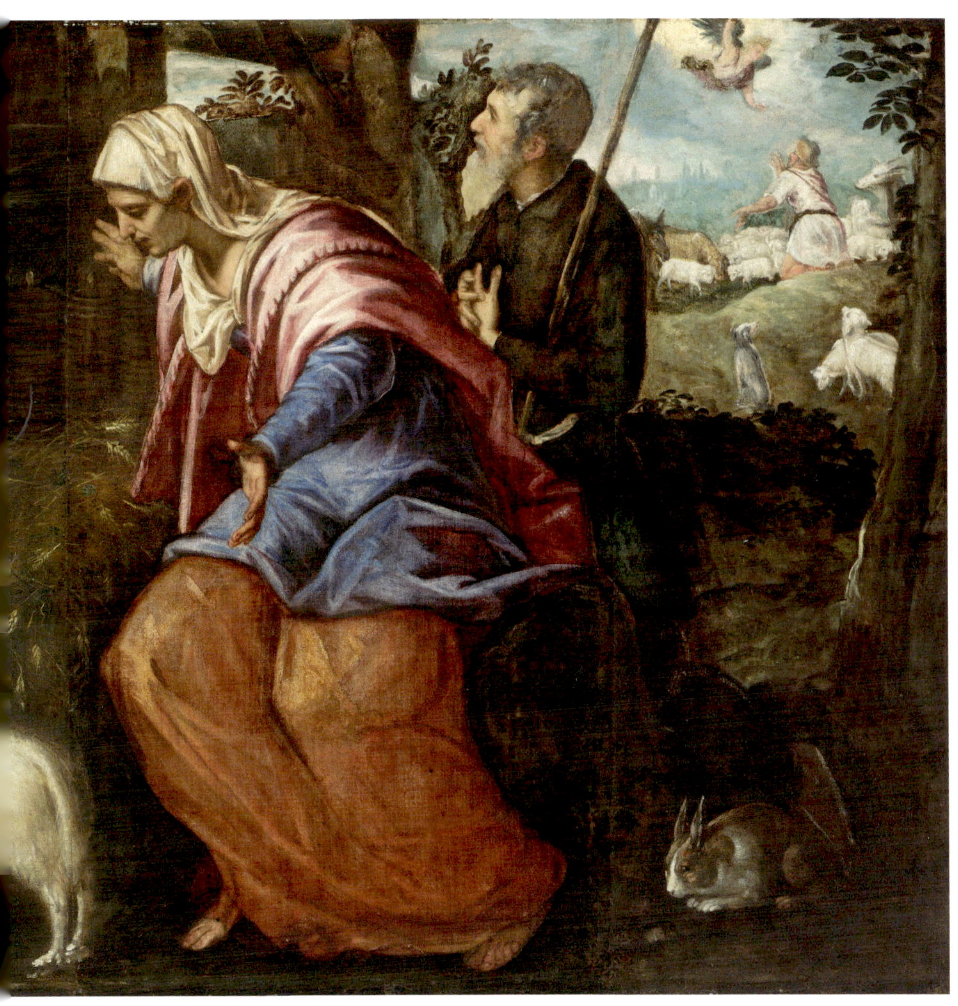

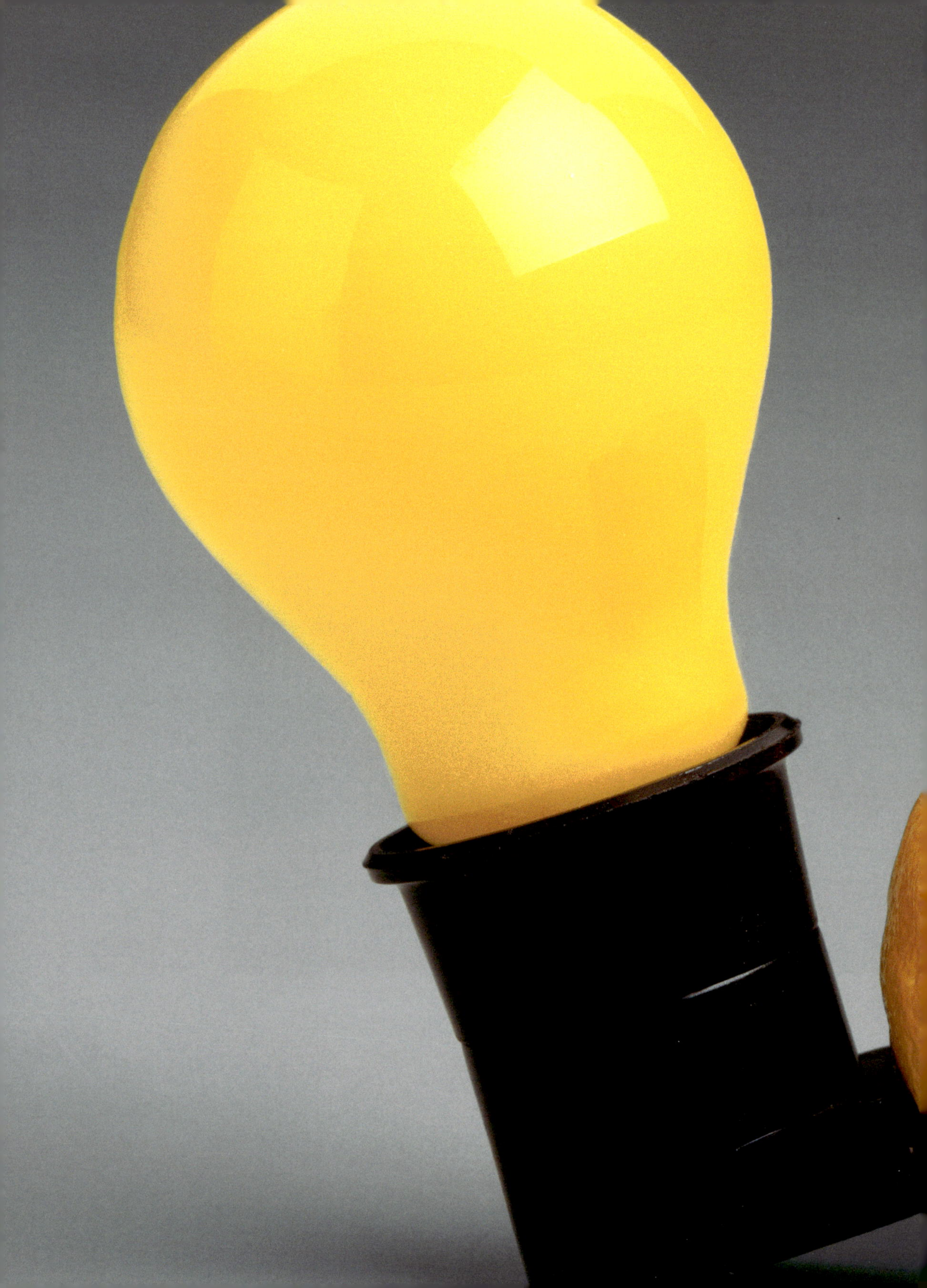

3 PRESERVING art for the future

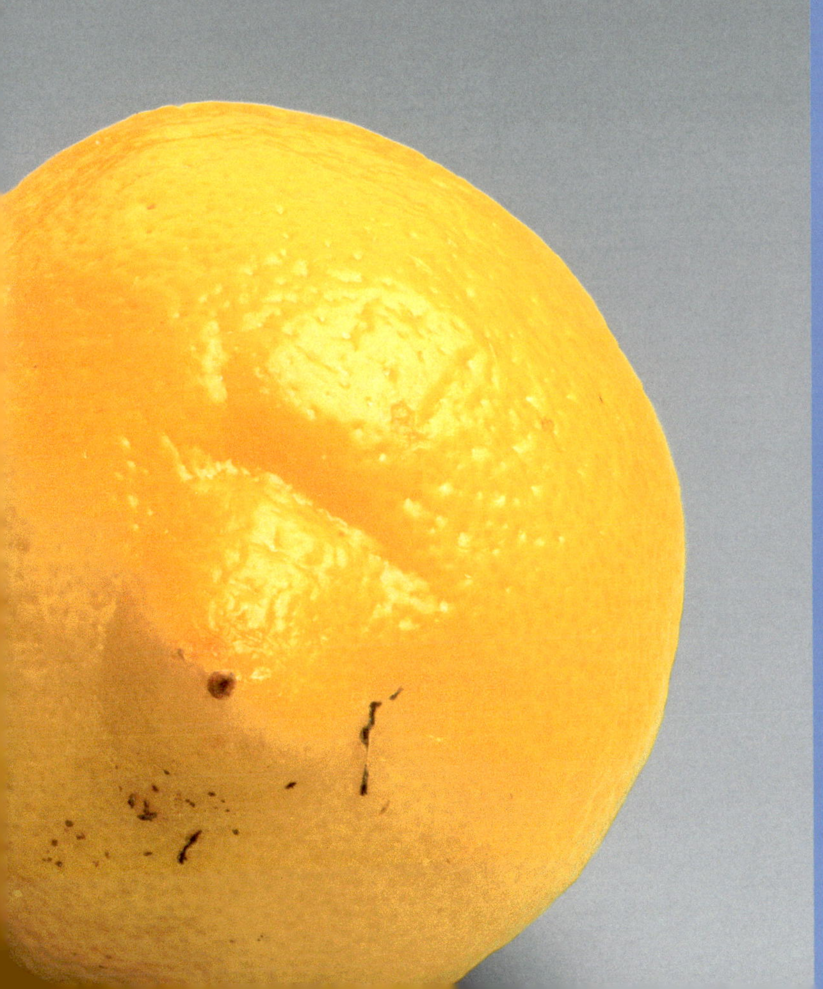

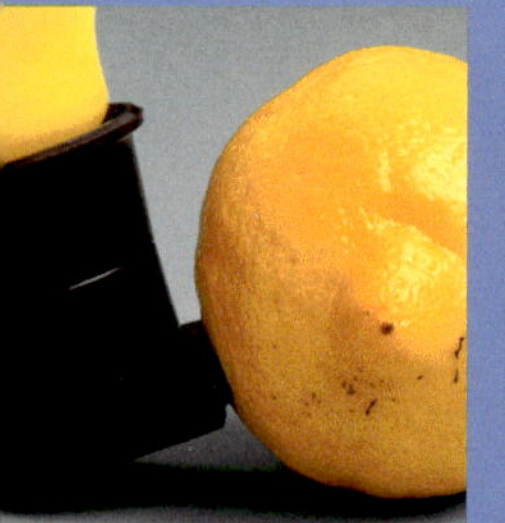
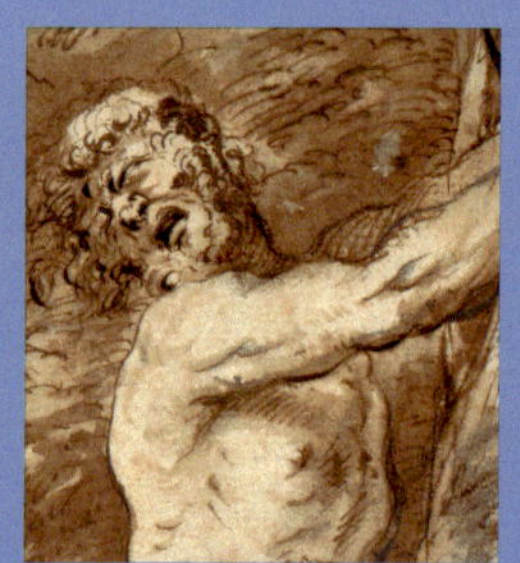
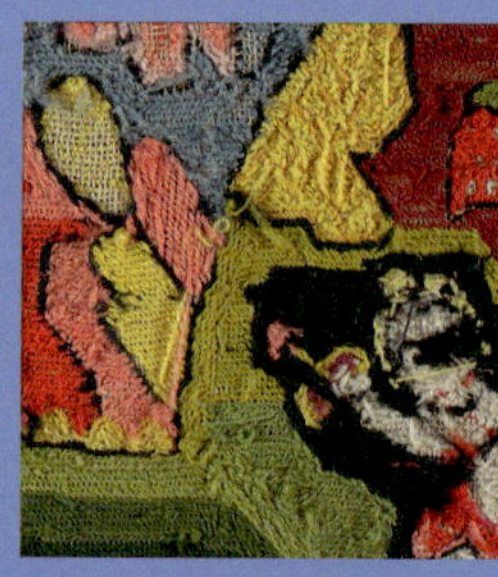
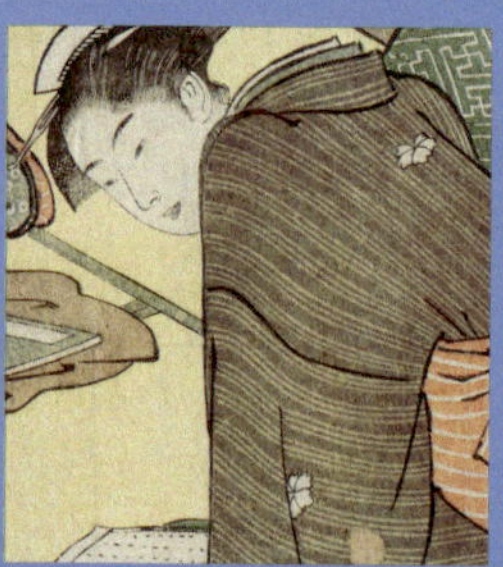
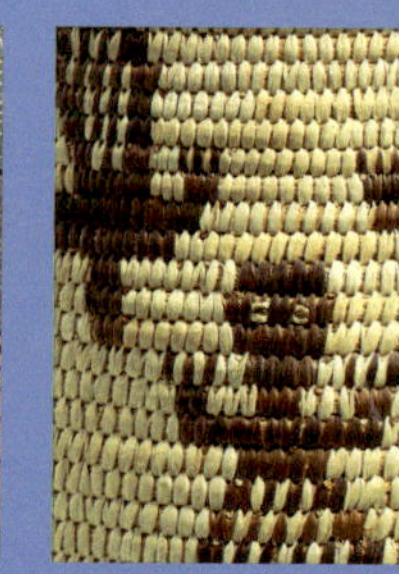

Preserving Art for the Future

Preservation is the ultimate goal of conservation. Museum conservators strive to maintain the integrity of each work of art throughout its life, whenever it is handled, stored, displayed, or shipped to other locations for exhibitions. In the past, preserving a work of art hinged on treating the object itself—making sure that weak parts were firmly attached, applying coatings that slowed the effects of wear and exposure to the atmosphere, using pesticides against different kinds of worms and bugs that feed on art materials, and many other interventions. Conservators and other museum professionals now increasingly concentrate on how the conditions of storage and display affect an object's preservation. They aim to minimize direct interventions and to greatly reduce the possibility of damage or degradation.

Traditional means of art storage and display can be quite damaging. Wooden cases, for example, can speed the deterioration of some objects because many types of wood release acidic gases into the air after the tree has been cut. Since cases are kept closed for long periods of time, the acidic gases stay trapped inside with the art. Even low levels of some common gases in the air can significantly contribute to the breakdown of certain materials such as silver, which tarnishes when exposed to gases containing sulfur.

Conservators must consider many other factors of object preservation. Seasonal swings in relative humidity result in the distortion of wood, cracks in paint, and other changes that often cannot be reversed. Small vibrations or shocks from moving art around a museum can widen or deepen even the finest fractures. Too much light, or the wrong kind of light, can irrevocably change the colors or the mechanical strength of many textiles. Frames can stain and otherwise damage the delicate works on paper they were intended to protect. Even some of the substances used for conservation efforts in the past are now known to cause damage.

Today, museum conservators strive to store and display objects in cabinets made from inert metal coated with stable paints that release no compounds into the air. For practical reasons museums may still use some cases made from wood or wood products (such as plywood), but in such cases conservators line the interiors with metal foil to block out any damaging gases given off by the wood. Both storage and display cabinets can also be designed to glide open and closed with minimal vibrations. Rapid swings in relative humidity are avoided by climate-control equipment in the gallery or storage room, and sometimes by less expensive means of humidity control such as silica gel hidden in the casework. Most museums require such controls in their own building and in that of any institution to which they loan a sensitive work of art. Museums also use special types of lights and light filters to minimize exposure to damaging ultraviolet and infrared radiation. Overall light levels are carefully managed as well, since even visible light can cause damage to some materials. New light sources such as light-emitting diodes (LEDs) may be used more frequently in the future because they are energy efficient and give off virtually no ultraviolet or infrared radiation. By taking into account the possible day-to-day stresses caused by an object's environment, museum conservators do their best to preserve art for generations to come.

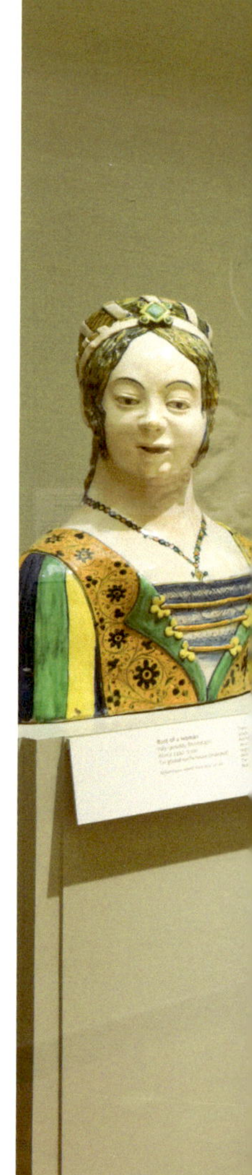

fig. 9. **A display case containing objects from the Italian Renaissance. The platform and pedestals inside the case are made from wood wrapped with metal foil and then covered with fabric. Silica gel hidden from view helps stabilize the relative humidity within the case.**

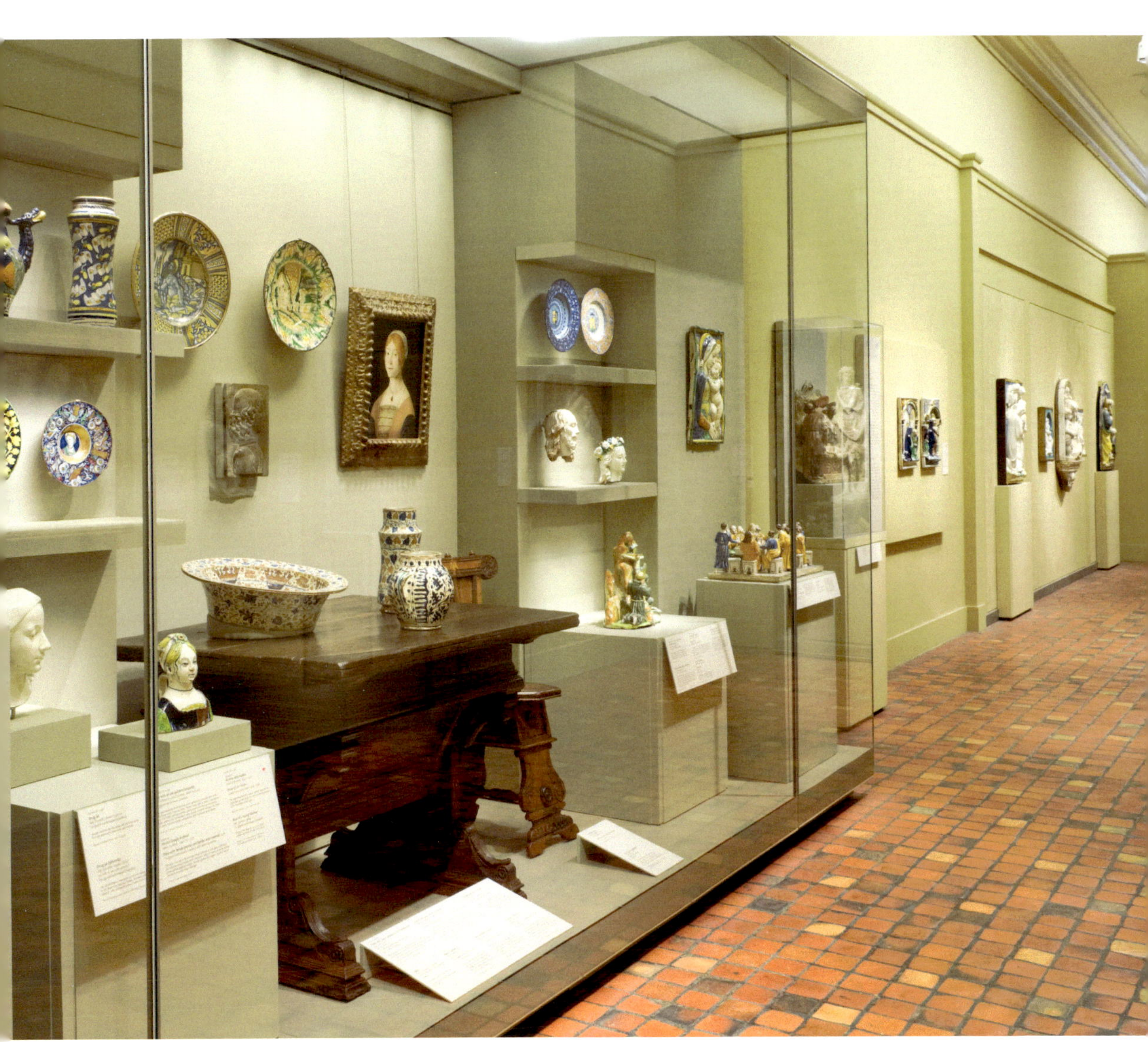

Storage container

Tohono O'odham (Papago)

Southern Arizona, about 1890–1920

Coiled yucca and dyed bear grass

H. 35.6 cm, diam. 25.4 cm (H. 14 in., diam. 10 in.)

Gift of Arthur Beale and Teri Hensick 2009.4626

Carrying basket (or coiled pack basket)

Lataxat (Klikitat)

Columbia River area, Washington, about 1890

Coiled cedar and spruce, with bear grass, wild cherry bark, and horsetail or dyed cedar bark

H. 30.5 cm, diam. 26 cm (H. 12 in., diam. 10¼ in.)

Gift of Arthur Beale and Teri Hensick 2008.1503

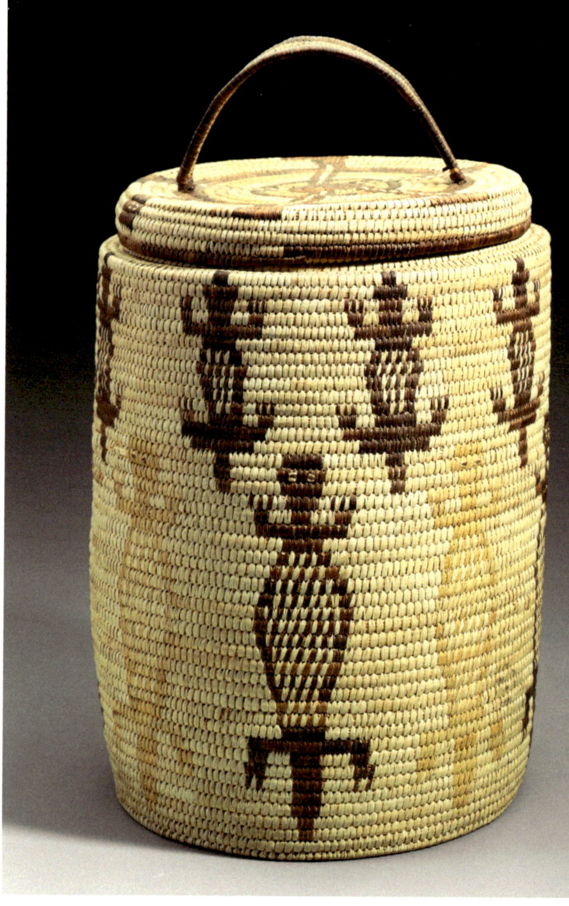

During the late nineteenth and early twentieth centuries, it was common museum practice to treat art made of organic materials with pesticides. Some of the earliest pesticides were safe natural substances, such as lavender or creosote leaves. Others, such as arsenic and mercury salts, were highly toxic and remained in use until the 1970s. Art objects treated with poisons are hazardous to all handlers; even dust falling from the objects can pose health risks. Although research continues, so far no one has developed an entirely satisfactory method for removing such dangerous chemicals without damaging the art.

These Native American baskets were made with natural plant materials that are susceptible to insect damage. When the objects entered the MFA's collection, it was impossible to know without scientific testing whether they had ever been treated with pesticides or what specific compound they had been treated with if they had. To ensure the safety of the staff, Museum scientists removed samples of dust and other surface residues from the baskets and analyzed them with X-ray spectrometry in a scanning electron microscope and with Fourier transform infrared spectrometry.

Fortunately, the tests produced negative results, and the objects can be safely moved for exhibition, study, and storage as usual. If dangerous elements had been detected, however, the objects would have been stored in tightly closed containers with warning labels. Museum staff members would have followed specific protocols when removing them from their storage containers, taking care to ensure that there would be no contact between the objects and a person's skin. Any dust falling from the objects would have been collected on disposable paper and tested if necessary. Special care would also have been taken in displaying such objects so as not to contaminate others.

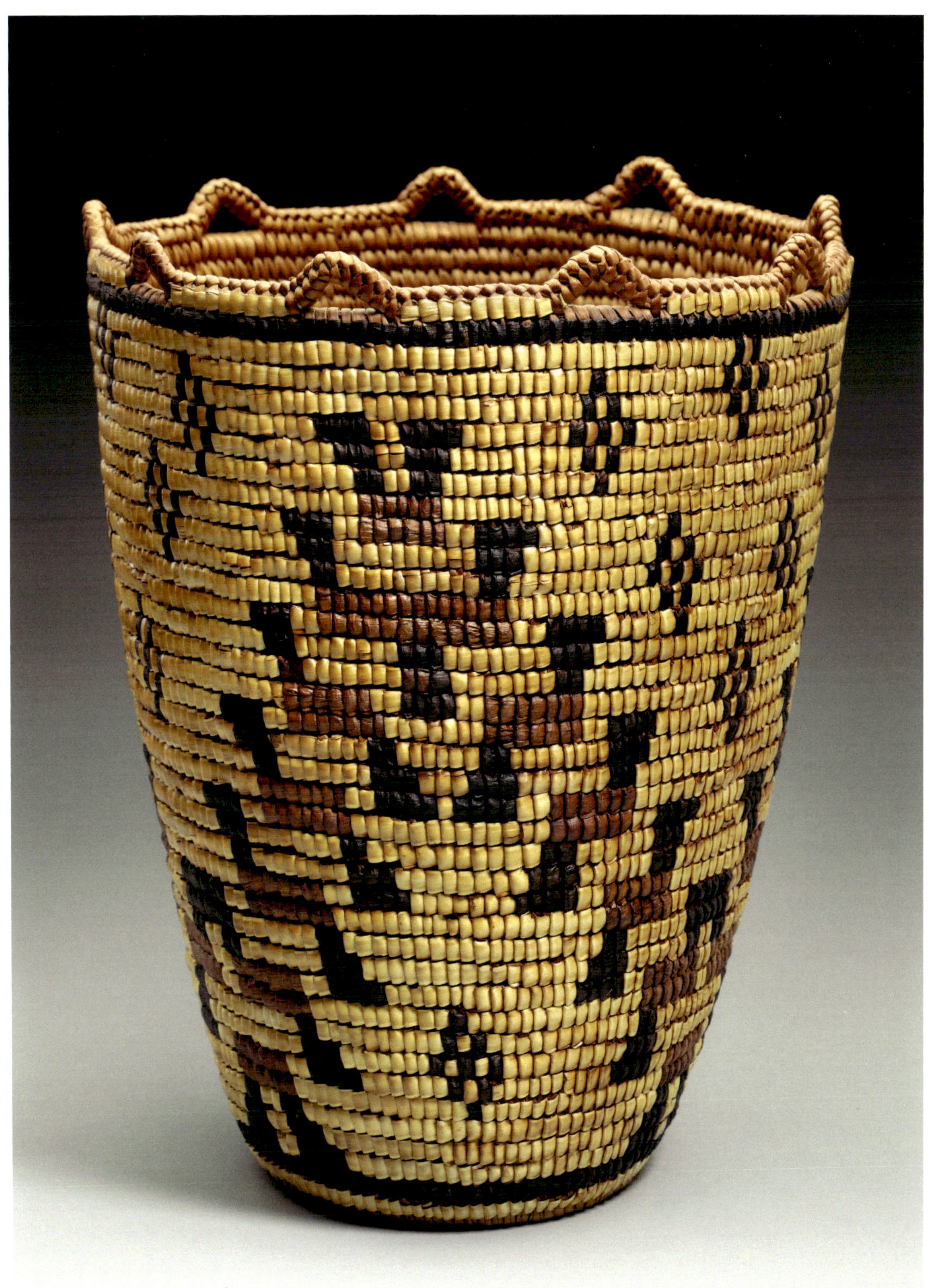

Bed

Attributed to Thomas Hope (English, 1769–1831)

About 1800–1805

Thomas Hope was an influential English furniture designer. This bed is an excellent example of the Regency style he pioneered, and except for an infestation of woodworms, it was in good condition when the Museum acquired it in 2003. To protect the bed from damage and prevent the pests from spreading to other works of art, it was critical to treat the new acquisition before it entered the building.

Conservators completely sealed the bed in a giant impermeable bag and placed an oxygen scavenger inside. In this case, the scavenger was made of fine iron particles. Iron reacts rapidly with oxygen, binding the gas to itself and thereby removing it from the air. With the appropriate amount of scavenger in the sealed environment, the conservators brought the oxygen down from normal air levels of 20 percent to less than 0.1 percent. After about four weeks in containment, all of the bed's woodworms in all life stages suffocated. Then the object could be safely brought into the Museum. No toxic chemicals were involved in the treatment, and the conservators disposed of the spent scavenger safely.

Pests can enter a museum through pipes or vents, or occasionally as hitchhikers on unsuspecting visitors. Once pests get inside, they find many food sources, including the organic materials that make up works of art (such as glues, fabrics, and woods). No museum can achieve a zero-pest environment throughout its building, but it is possible to reduce the pests to extremely low levels. Conservators must be vigilant in this aspect of their preventive care, so that pests found in different areas of a building at different times of the year can be identified, understood, and dealt with as quickly as possible.

Oak and pine veneered with mahogany and painted black, patinated bronze mounts
137.2 x 123.2 x 243.8 cm (54 x 48½ x 96 in.)
Museum purchase with funds donated anonymously and by exchange from a gift given in memory of Dr. William Hewson Baltzell, by his wife Alice Cheney Baltzell, Gift of the Estate of Gertrude T. Taft, Gift of Eben Howard Gay, Helen and Alice Colburn Fund, Gift of Dr. and Mrs. Ronald M. Ferry, Bequest of Mrs. Harriet J. Bradbury, Bequest of Susan Greene Dexter in memory of Charles and Martha Babcock Amory, The Elizabeth Day McCormick Collection, Gift of Miss Anna C. Hoyt, Gift of Mr. and Mrs. Maxim Karolik, Gift of Eugene L. Garbáty, Bequest of Mrs. Thomas O. Richardson, Bequest of George Nixon Black, Gift of Fred Parker and Mary C. Emery, The John Pickering Lyman Collection, Gift of Miss Theodora Lyman, Gift of Mrs. Sidney T. Allen, Gift of Mrs. John Adlen Carpenter, Gift of Dudley Leavitt Pickman, Harriet Otis Cruft Fund, Gift of Mrs. Ruth Kellogg Ferry, Gift of Mrs. Horatio Appleton Lamb in memory of Mrs. Winthrop Sargent, Gift of Miss Evelyn Sears, and Gift of Mrs. Albert J. Beveridge in memory of Delia Spencer Field 2003.258

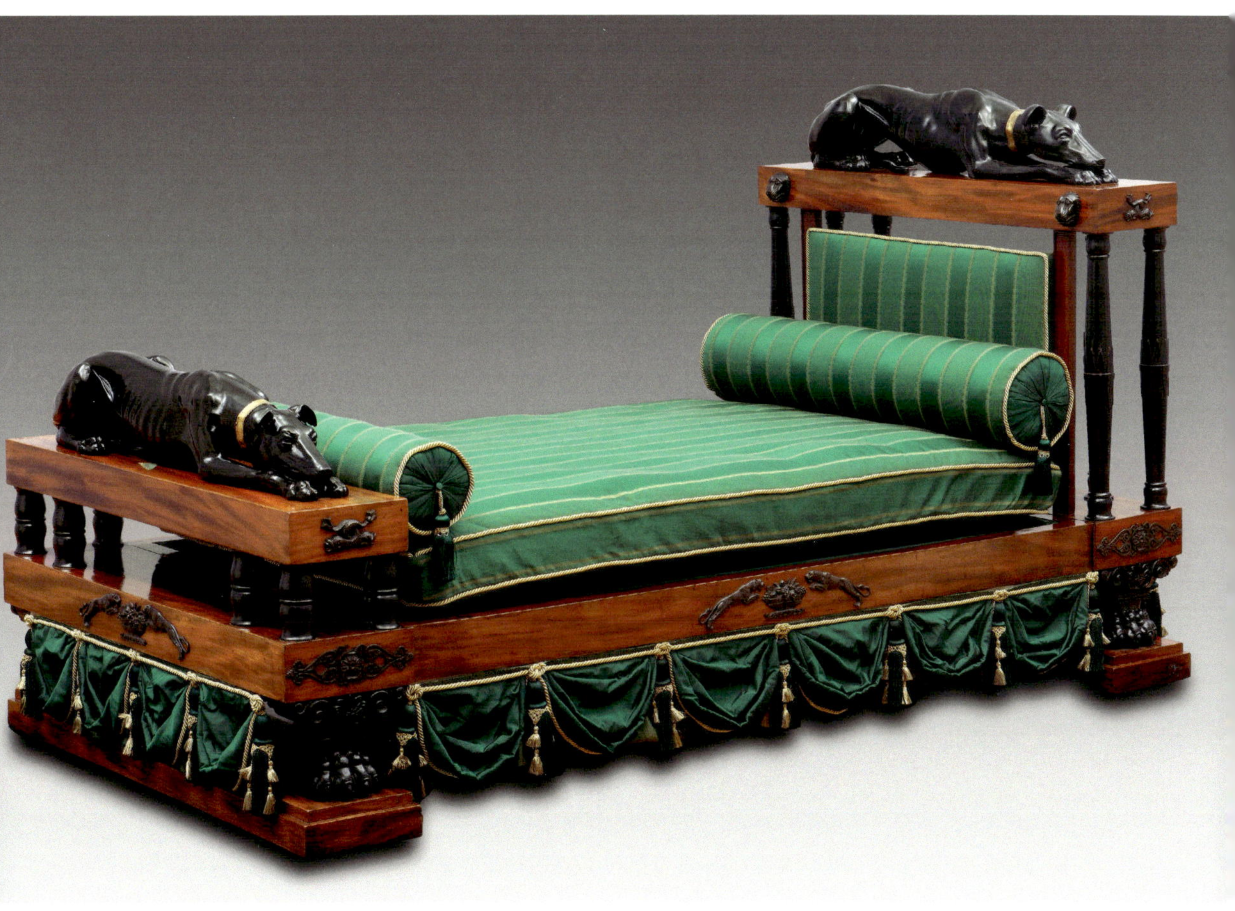

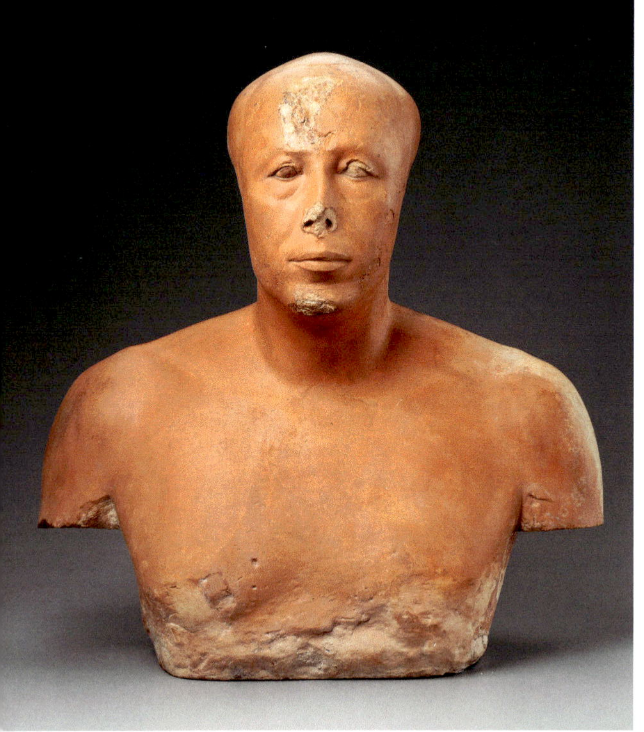

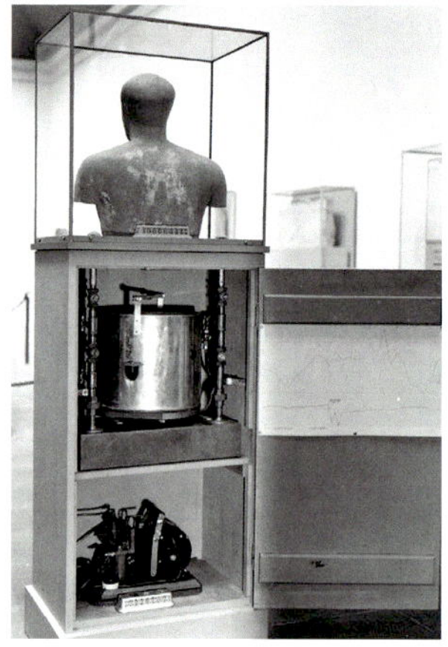

The display case for the sculpture in 1939. The opened back reveals the pump at the bottom and the tank that contained the calcium chloride solution at top.

Bust of Prince Ankhhaf

Egypt, Old Kingdom, 2520–2494 B.C.

The surface of this lifelike bust began to deteriorate shortly after it was excavated from a tomb in Giza, Egypt, in 1925. Carved from limestone and covered with plaster and paint, the sculpture suffered from rapid changes in temperature and relative humidity as it was exposed to air after its long burial. One member of the joint American and Egyptian excavation team noted that the prince looked as if he had broken out in a terrible rash.

The flaking paint and plaster were treated with a consolidating agent, most likely as part of field procedures performed at the archaeological dig site in Egypt. Unfortunately, the applied solution caused even more damage by further weakening the surface's bond with the stone substrate. When the sculpture came to the MFA in 1927, conservators made the surface layers adhere better to the stone and retouched losses to make the bust look more the way it had when it was first excavated.

Because the Museum's galleries did not have air conditioning or humidity controls, conservators installed the bust in a special display case in 1939. They controlled the case's interior climate by enclosing it against the exterior air and by installing a tank of calcium chloride with a pump to circulate the interior air. This allowed the conservators to lower the relative humidity inside the case to 30 percent and keep it constant. The idea of controlling a case's interior environment was new at the time, but now it is common conservation practice. Modern display cases are nearly airtight, making it possible to create independent and almost constant microclimates for the objects inside even if environmental conditions shift outside in the gallery.

Painted limestone
H. 50.48 cm (19 7/8 in.)
Harvard University–Boston Museum of Fine Arts Expedition 27.442

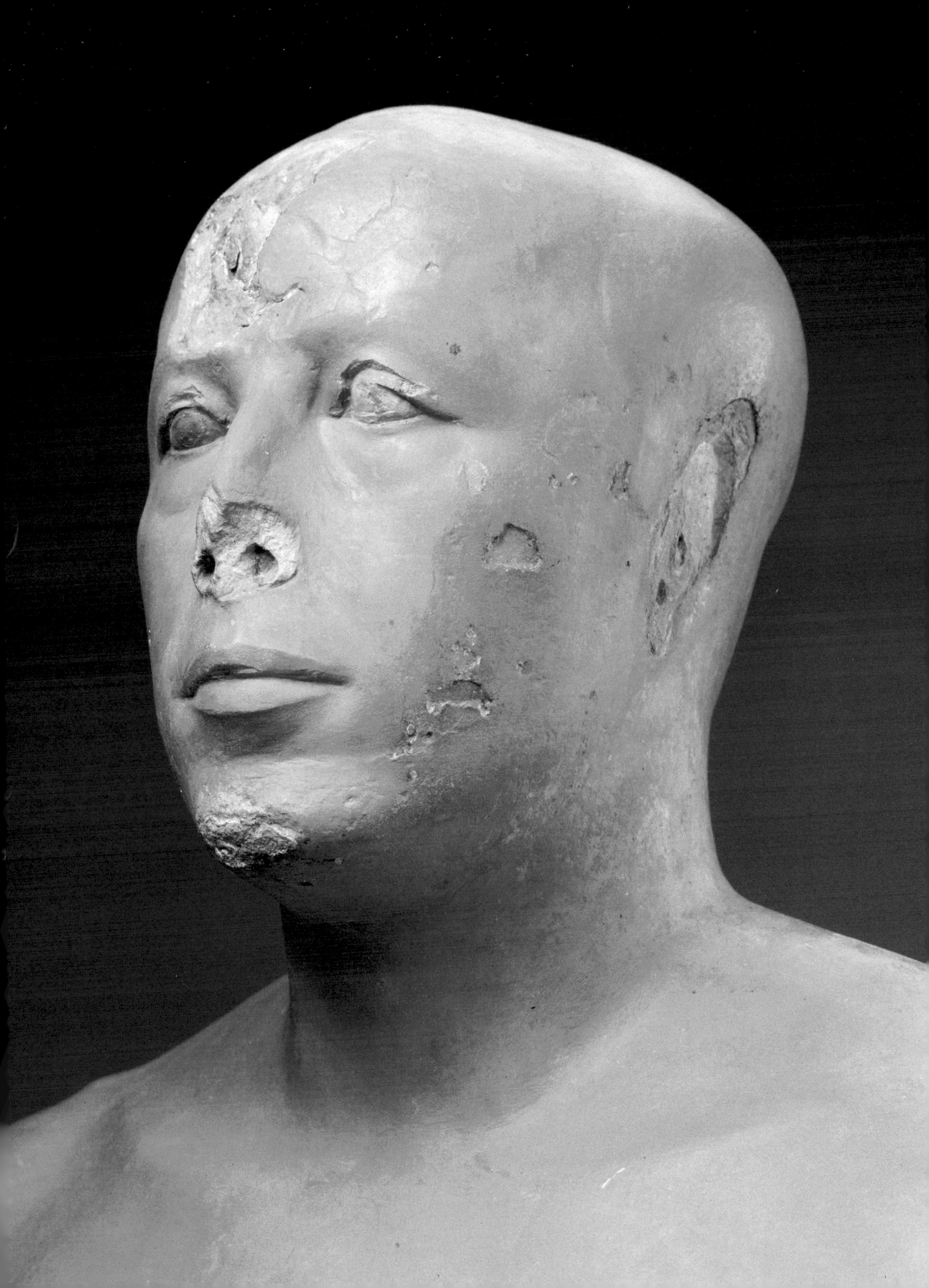

Chessboard and chess pieces

Baltic region or Poland (Danzig), late 17th or early 18th century

Amber, gold foils, wood

Board: 37 x 37 cm (14 9/16 x 14 9/16 in.)

Bequest of William Arnold Buffum

02.205a–gg

Gaming box with counters

Germany, 19th century

Amber

Diam. 3.8 cm (1½ in.)

Bequest of William Arnold Buffum 02.209a–e

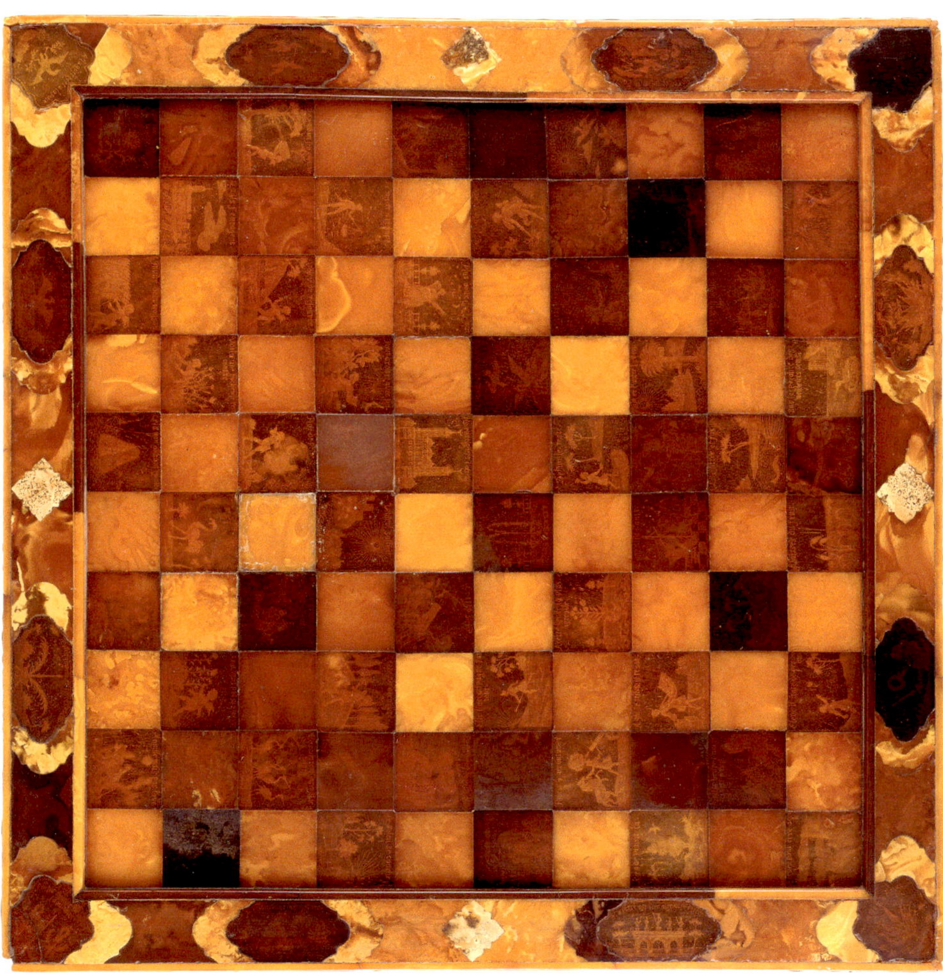

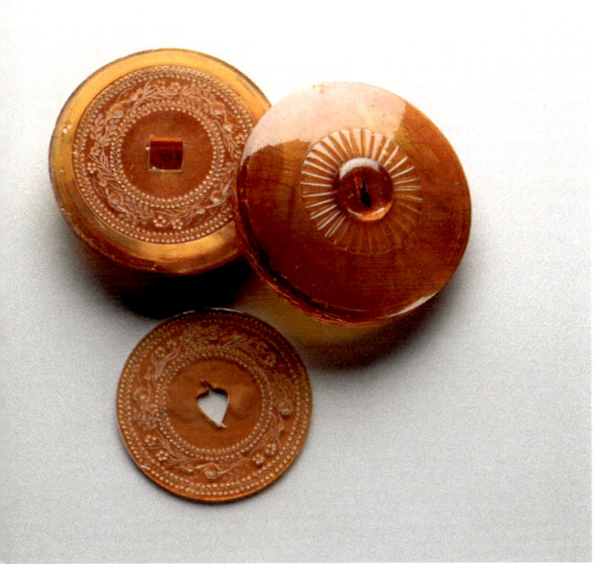

Alternating squares of opaque white and translucent red amber make up this chessboard. Reflective gold leaf painted with aphorisms in French and vignettes of figures, animals, and landscapes back the red areas. The amber was most likely collected along the coast of the Baltic Sea. Other amber specimens, probably from the same area, were carved to make the gaming box, the counters, and the chess pieces.

Amber is the generic name for fossilized resins, some of which can be millions of years old. Treasured by many cultures around the world for its hardness and complete insolubility, as well as its beauty, the material can be carved into small objects of all kinds. There are many sources of amber; the earliest type used in Europe came from the Baltic area, but other sources were known and had long been in use by the time this chessboard and gaming set were created. Artists sometimes also used imitation amber made from certain tree resins, but such materials are neither as durable nor as water-resistant as true amber.

Amber's great weakness is that it can be easily damaged by overexposure to light. The damage usually begins at the surface of an object as a fine network of cracks. When the cracks are shallow, the surface layer can easily flake off; once the cracks have penetrated more deeply, the amber can shatter or break apart. In either case the damage is irreversible. As with flaking paint, great swings in relative humidity further weaken damaged amber because the cracked surfaces can absorb and release moisture, causing them to expand and contract.

Conservators can reattach uplifting amber flakes by running a thin adhesive solution beneath them and gently holding them down as the solution sets. However, they try to avoid such procedures because it may not be possible to remove the adhesive in the future without losing some of those flakes. The best treatment for objects made of amber is preventive: they require an environment with stable levels of humidity and limited exposure to light.

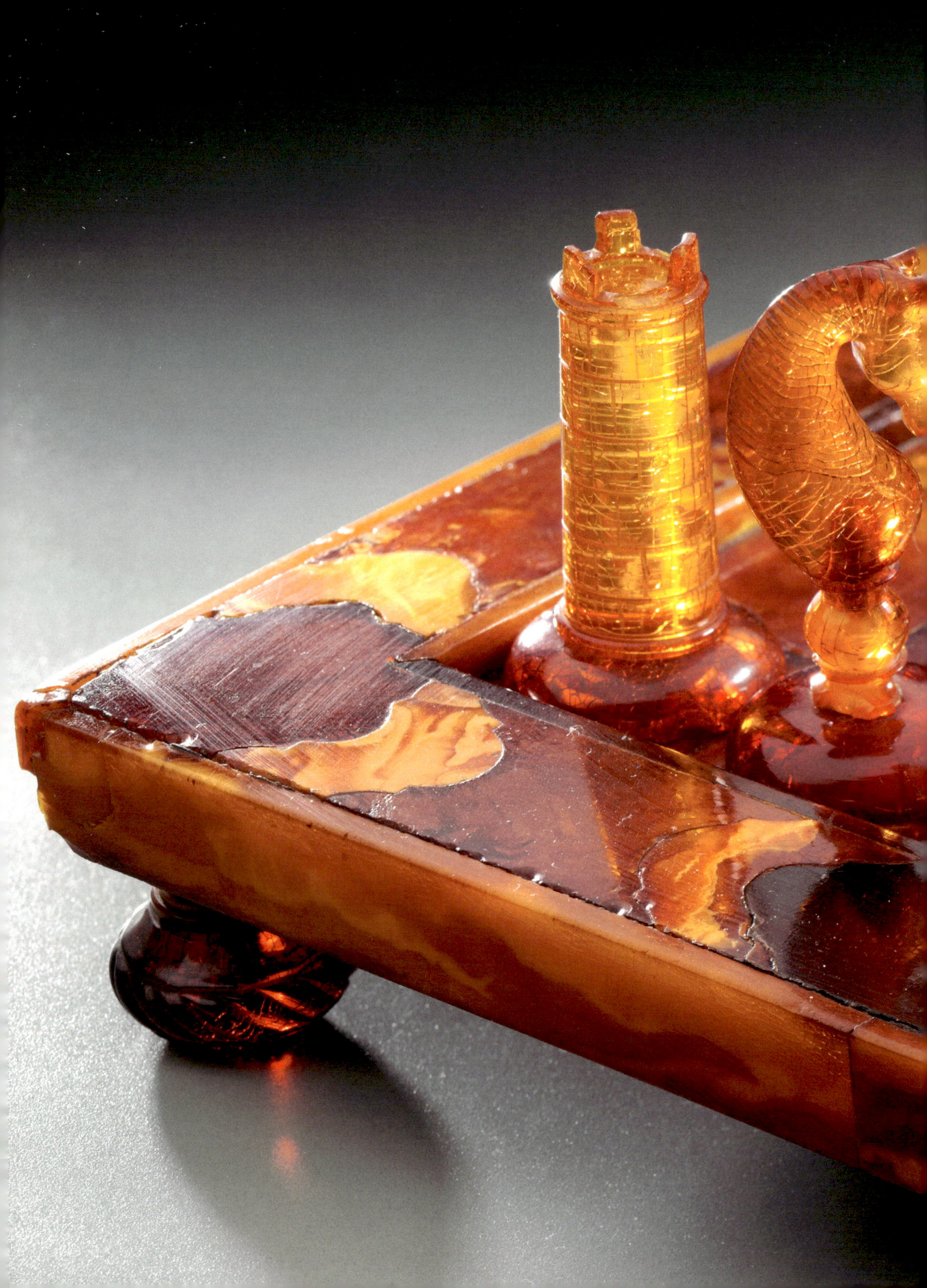

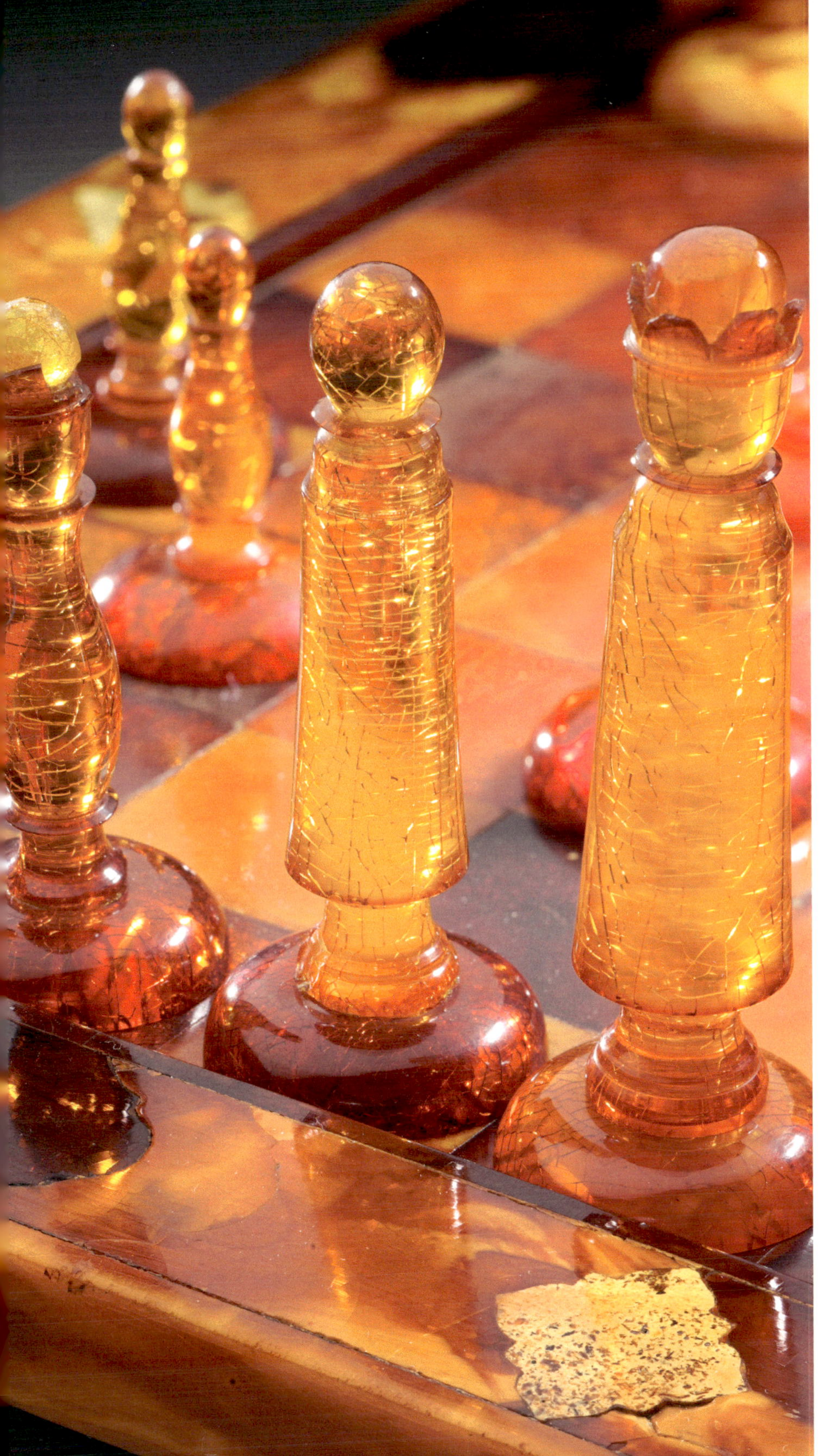

The Calenberg Altarpiece

Master of the Goslar Sibyls (German, working about 1600–1625)

First quarter of the 16th century

Early-sixteenth-century German altarpieces that have remained intact are exceedingly rare. Exceptionally, we know for whom this one was made because of the coat of arms on the central panel in the upper left and right corners. Duke Erich I von Braunschweig-Calenberg and his wife, Katharina von Saxonia, commissioned this triptych for a chapel in Calenberg Castle, located in Pattensen, Germany. The duke is portrayed as a small figure to the right of the Virgin Mary in the central panel; Katharina is on the left. A 1584 report describes Katharina as having been "very painstakingly painted, with her lovely countenance and beautiful red cheeks."

Time has left its marks on this painting. Some of the most devastating ones are due to changes in relative humidity. As is common in large altarpieces, the central panel consists of five or six panels glued together. Sixteenth-century panel makers were well aware that wood expands and contracts, changing in size and shape as humidity in the atmosphere rises and falls, and that such changes eventually lead to permanent cracks and warping. To minimize such problems, they usually used high-quality hard wood least prone to warping, cut along the radius of the tree trunk's cross section. However, the panels in this altarpiece were made from pine, a lower-quality wood, and cut tangentially, causing them to warp much more readily. In addition, because paint does not have the flexibility of wood, as the wood beneath it moved, the paint on the surface cracked, causing small pieces to fall off.

For many years, restorers of wood-panel paintings applied a crisscrossing set of slats (called a cradle) to the backs of paintings to prevent the wood from warping as humidity changed, but this treatment has sometimes backfired, leading to more severe cracking and paint loss than might otherwise have taken place. The central panel of this altarpiece, which had a cradle applied to it, has many vertical cracks. Some occurred along glued joins in the different planks that make up the panel, others along the grain of the wood. Inevitably, some paint was lost as the wood moved and cracked.

The first stages of treatment for this painting involved removing the cradle. Then conservators painstakingly filled and mended cracks in the original panel to stabilize the wood and minimize the distortion of the panel. They filled paint losses on the front to blend with surrounding original paint. To better preserve the painting for the future, they also lightly attached the panel to a secondary structure called a strainer, which supports the original wood panel but gives it freedom to move as relative humidity changes. Future distortion of the wood panels will be minimized by keeping the painting in an environment with a constant level of relative humidity.

Oil on panel

Central panel: 99 x 144.5 cm (39 x 56⅞ in.)

Museum purchase with funds donated anonymously and Charles H. Bayley Picture and Painting Fund 2005.195.1

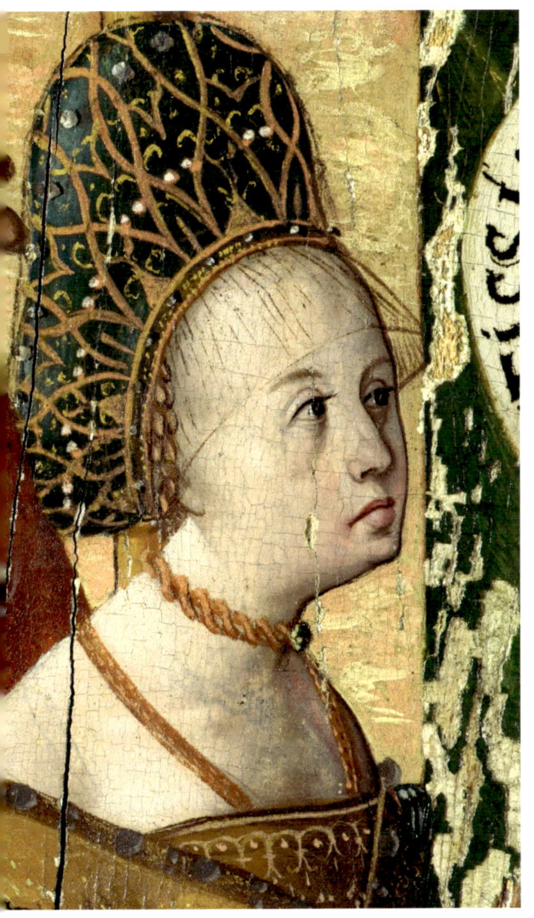

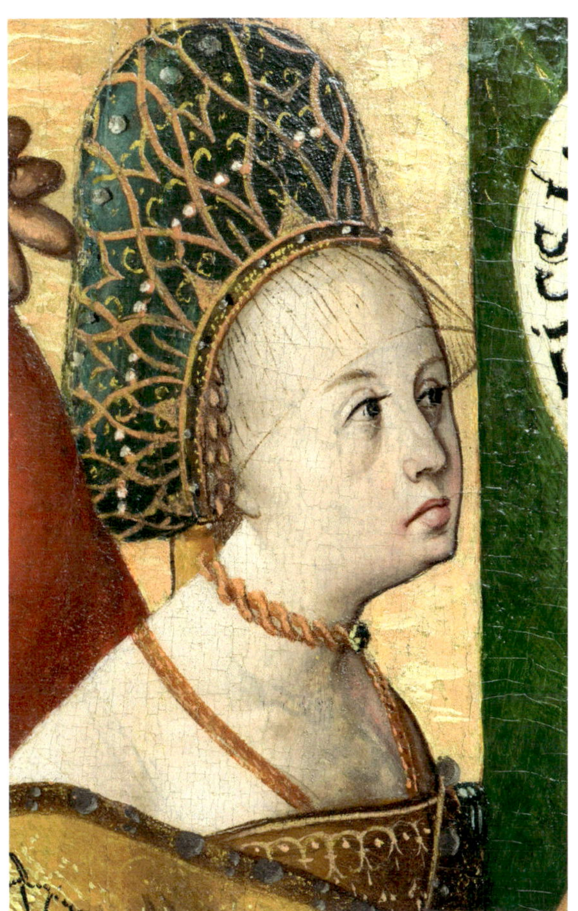

Detail of Katharina von Saxonia kneeling to the left of the Virgin Mary, during and after treatment. Original paint was lost in the many cracks that run vertically along the grain of the wood.

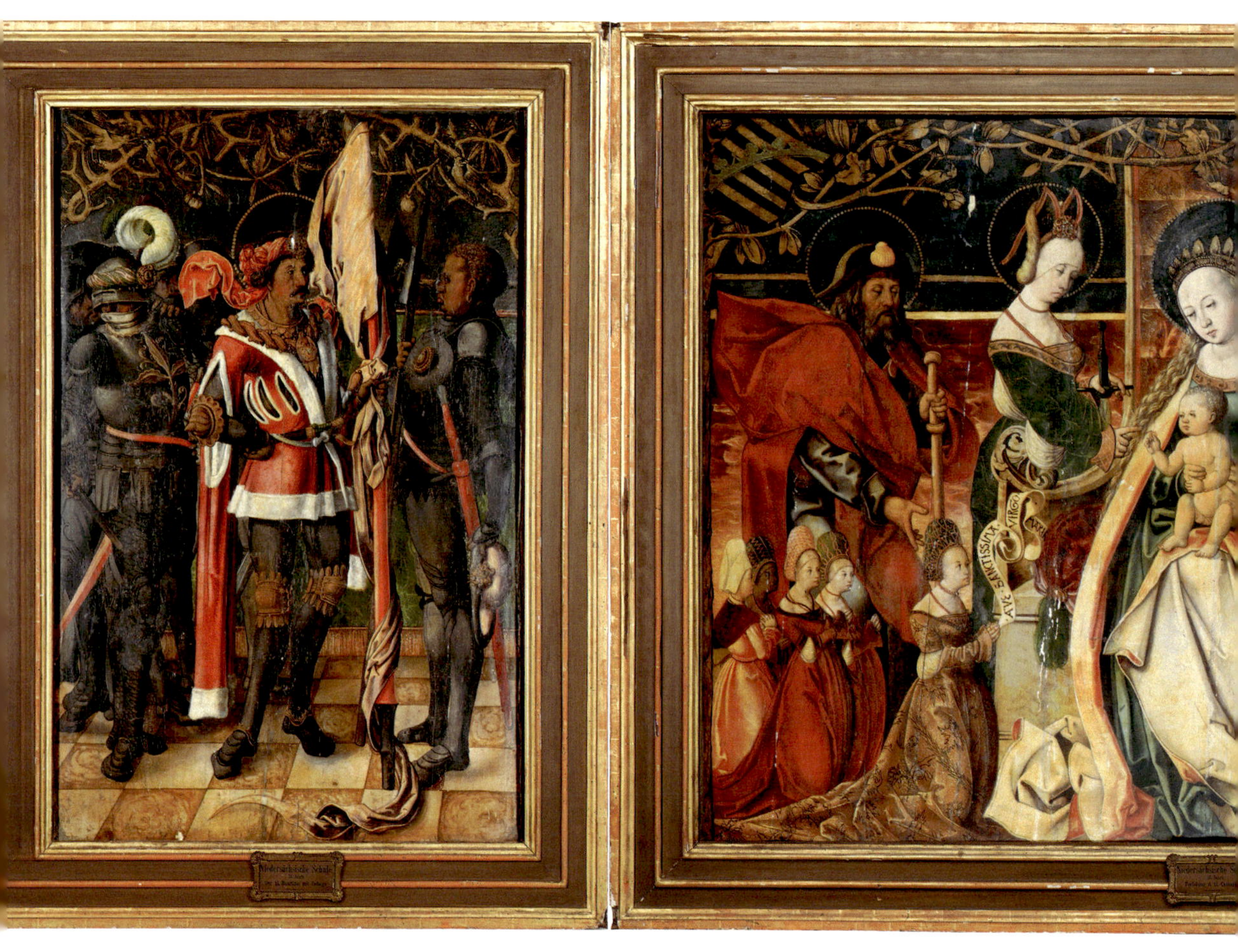

The altarpiece before treatment. The discolored, yellow varnish makes the original colors of the painting difficult to discern. The modern frame shown here will be replaced with a closer approximation of the painting's original frame.

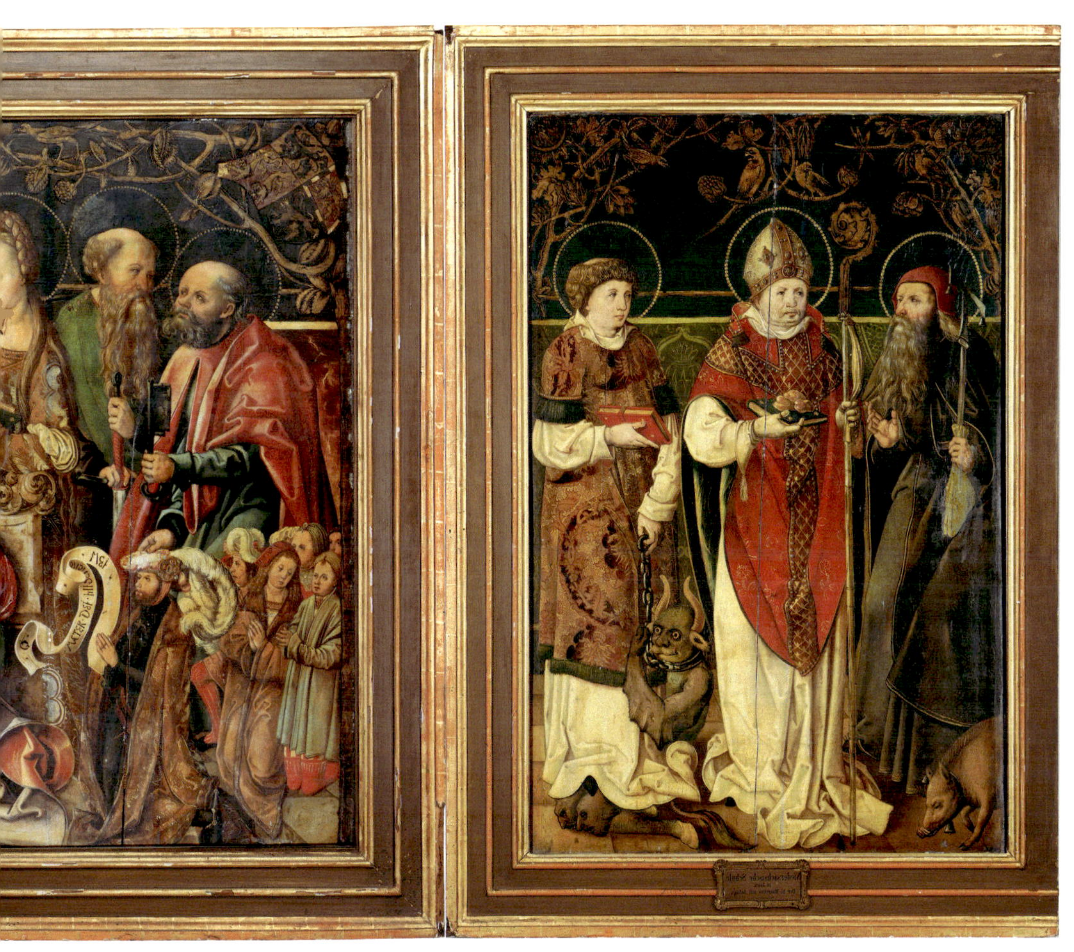

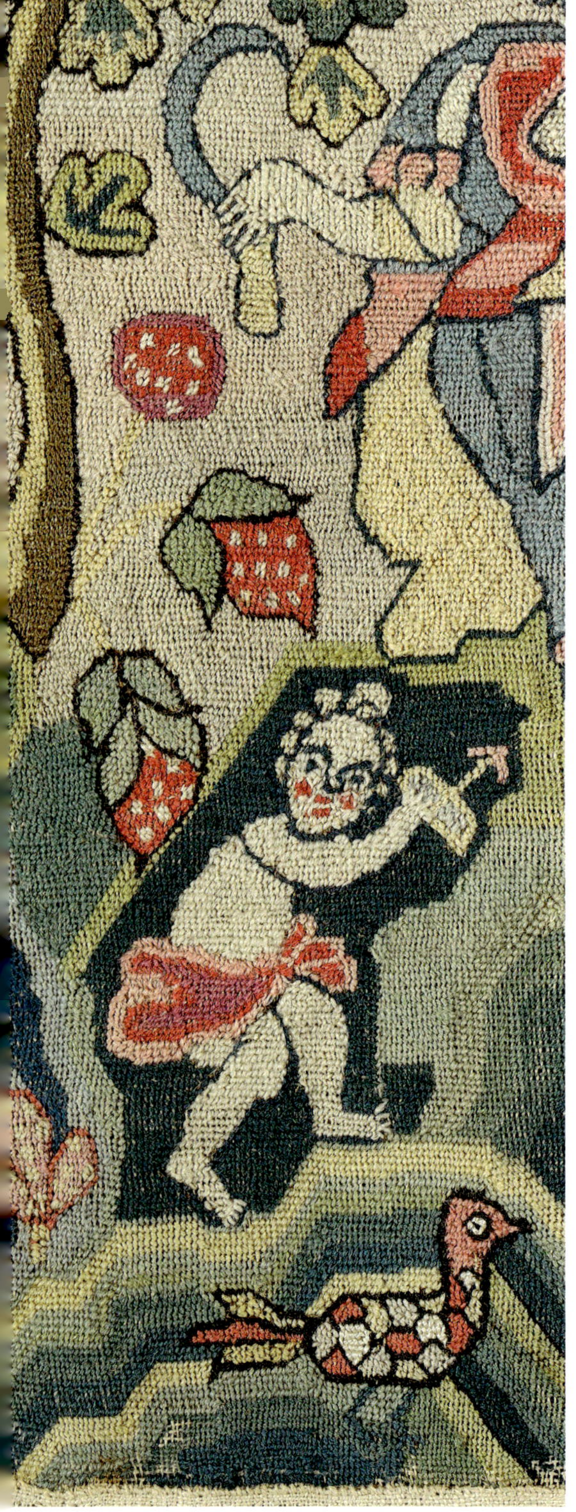

detail, front

Embroidered picture

Ann Peartree (American, working about 1722–44)

1739

The front of this embroidered picture by a colonial-era schoolgirl from Boston was exposed to light each time it was displayed, both by its previous owners and by the MFA for exhibitions. The exposure faded all of the natural dyes of the embroidery threads, although different colors faded at different rates and to different degrees. The blue dye, indigo, faded the least, but the bright yellows (weld and young fustic) are mostly gone. The greens, made from a combination of indigo and yellow dye, are now distinctly blue. Of the two types of red dye, the orchil dye derived from a lichen used in the background has nearly disappeared, whereas the cochineal used in the costume, berries, and leaves is still visible. By comparison, the original colors are better preserved on the back side, which remained hidden against the wall when the object was displayed. The damage to the front is irreversible.

Although fading is the most visible change produced by light, other irreversible changes take place in some materials. For example, silk grows brittle when overexposed, and cellulose-containing textiles and paper become discolored. All such damage occurs because light, in combination with oxygen in the air, triggers chemical reactions in substances exposed to it. Some materials, such as stone and metals, are relatively insensitive to light, but others, such as certain dyes and watercolors, are extremely susceptible.

In addition, both natural and artificial light sources emit infrared and ultraviolet radiation, neither of which is needed for viewing works of art. Infrared radiation creates heat, which accelerates chemical reactions. Museums today therefore place light sources as far away as possible from art on display so that their heating effects can be kept to a minimum. Ultraviolet radiation is particularly dangerous because it is energetic enough to break chemical bonds. Although it is difficult to eliminate ultraviolet radiation completely, it can be minimized with filters placed over a light, in the glass of a display case, or in the glazing of a framed work of art. Frequently changing objects on display and implementing visitor-activated lighting can also help to protect works of art. Some museums have begun to replace standard bulbs with light-emitting diodes (LEDs), which send out neither infrared nor ultraviolet radiation.

Linen plain weave embroidered with wool and silk
27.7 x 23 cm (10 7/8 x 9 1/16 in.)
Bequest of Elsie T. Friedman 59.22

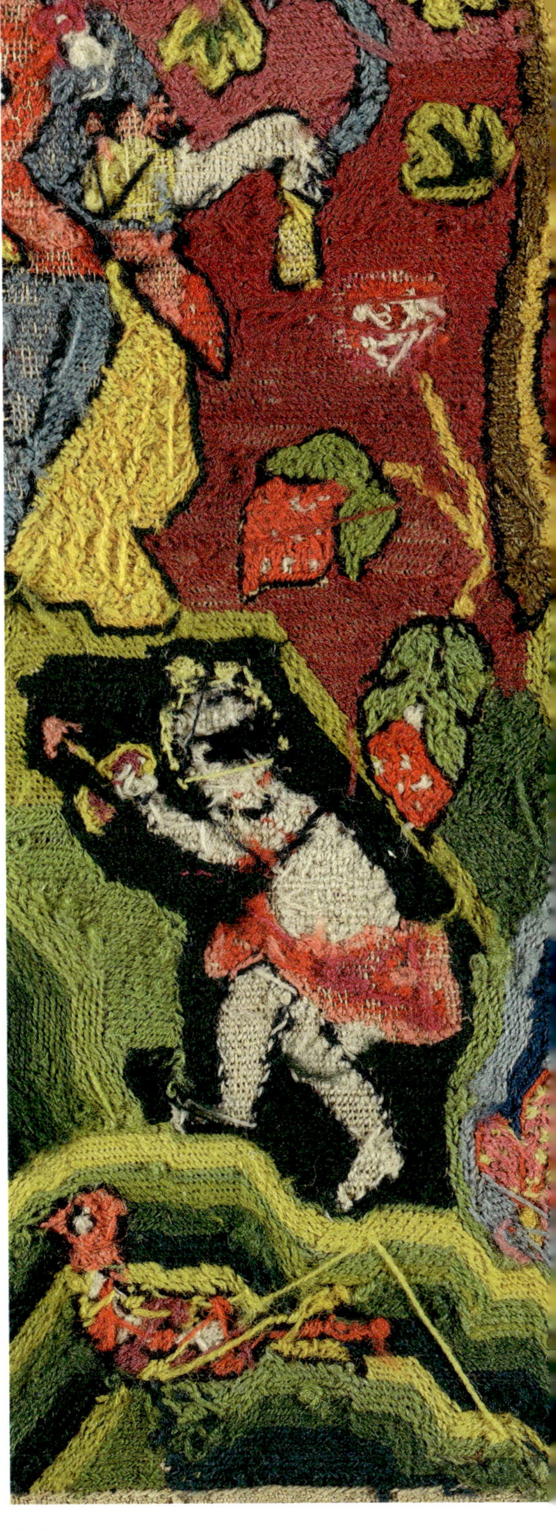

detail, back

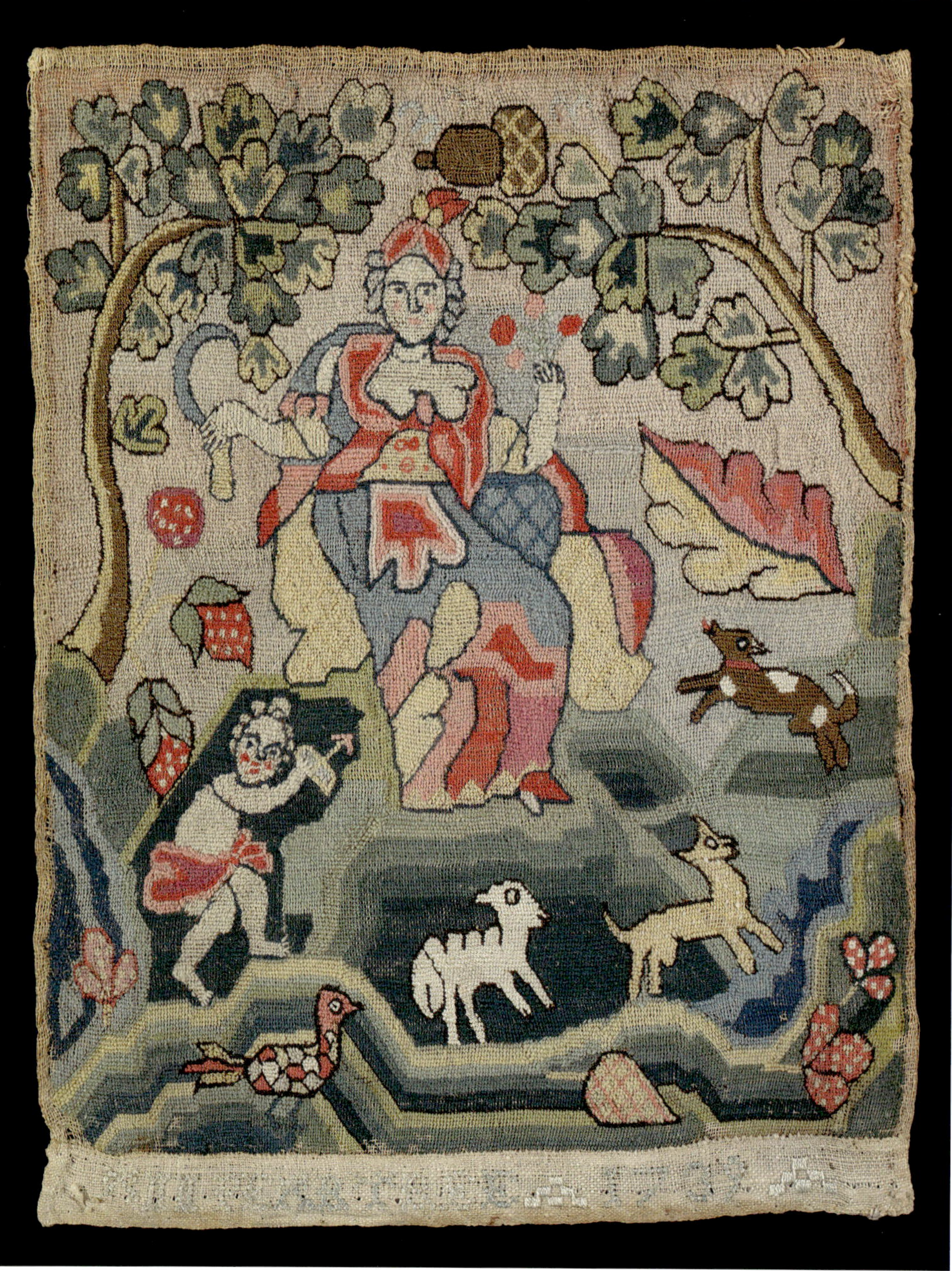

front

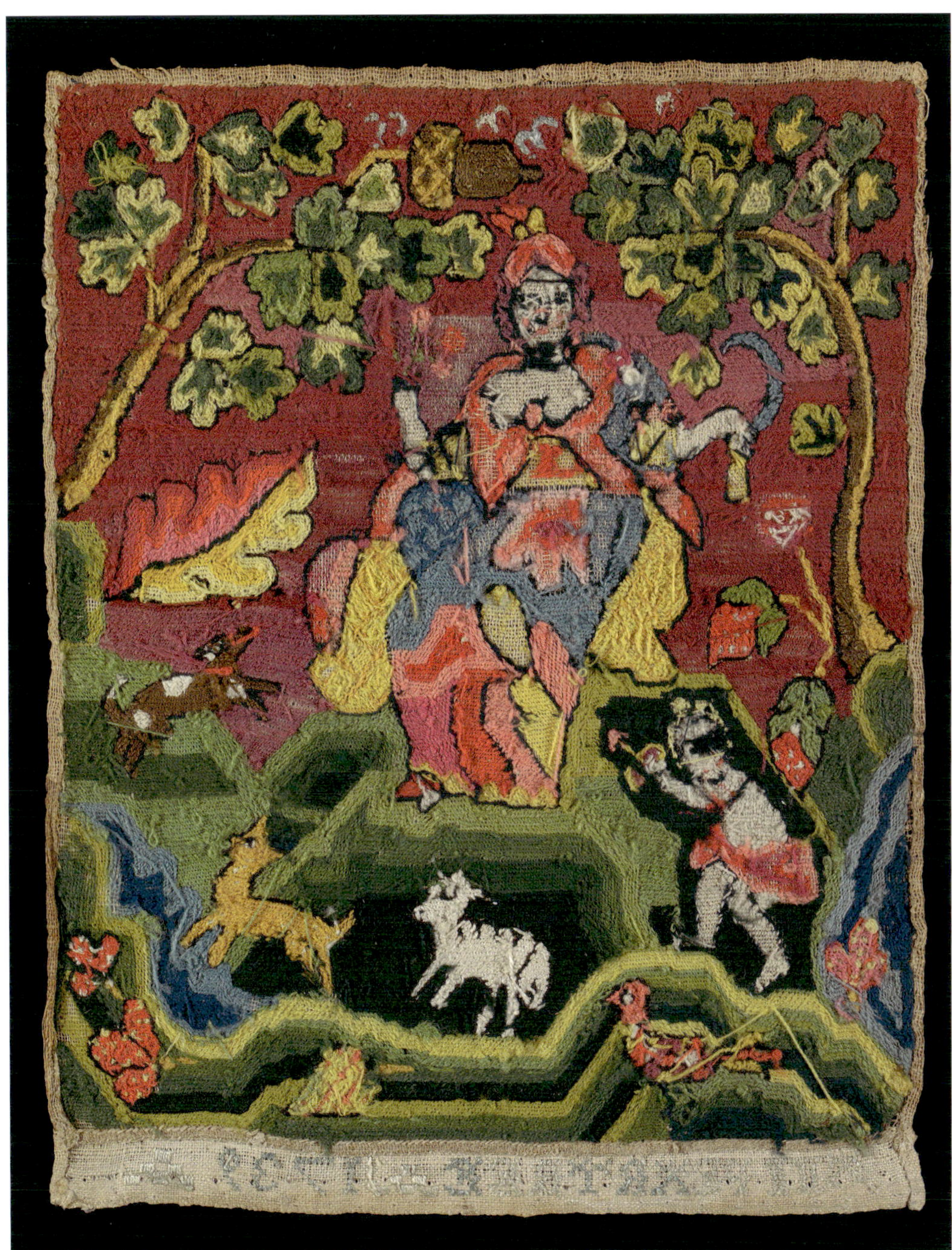

back

Child Prodigy Gyokkashi Shima Eimo Giving a Reading Lesson

Torii Kiyonaga (Japanese, 1752–1815)

About 1785

Full-color Japanese woodblock prints from the eighteenth century began with an artist's design carved into several woodblocks. One block carved with outlines and printed with black ink was followed by multiple other blocks printed in different colors for various design elements. A single design could involve as many as thirteen separate blocks with as many different colors.

One of the common colorants in Japanese woodblock prints of this period was a blue made from juice extracted from dayflower petals. By mixing this extract with different quantities of water and binder, printers obtained a variety of blue shades ranging from a warm purple to an ethereal gray-yellow. Like other plant-based colorants, dayflower blue is sensitive to light. It is also uniquely susceptible to damage from prolonged exposure to humidity, which causes the color to shift to a pale greenish yellow. Dayflower blue was often the last color to be printed because of its high water solubility.

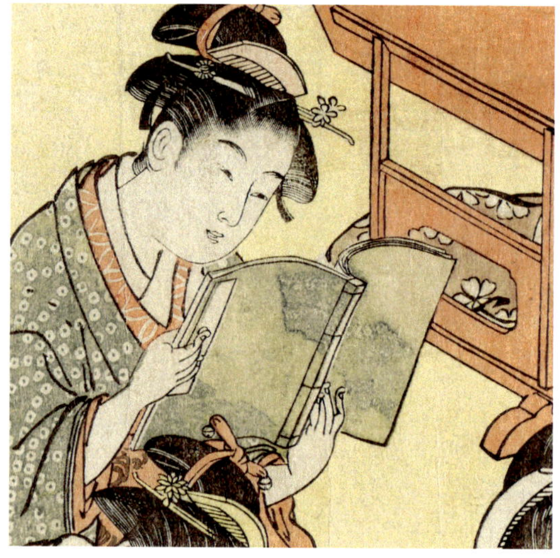

detail, showing water damage

Drops of water accidentally fell on this Japanese print, dissolving areas of dayflower blue and forming tide lines of concentrated color as the water evaporated. This irreversible damage can be seen in the book cover held up by one of the figures on the left and at the sleeve and hem of the figure in the foreground on the right. More subtle shifts of color from exposure to humidity may also be seen in this print at the extreme lower-right corner and at the opening of the vase located near the right edge. Ironically, conservators often use these aspects of dayflower blue as a visual means by which to identify the color's use on a print. When handling, exhibiting, and storing prints with dayflower blue, they must take special care to monitor relative humidity and avoid moisture in the form of water or other liquids.

Woodblock print; ink and color on paper

38 x 25.1 cm (14 15/16 x 9 7/8 in.)

Weld Fund 54.565

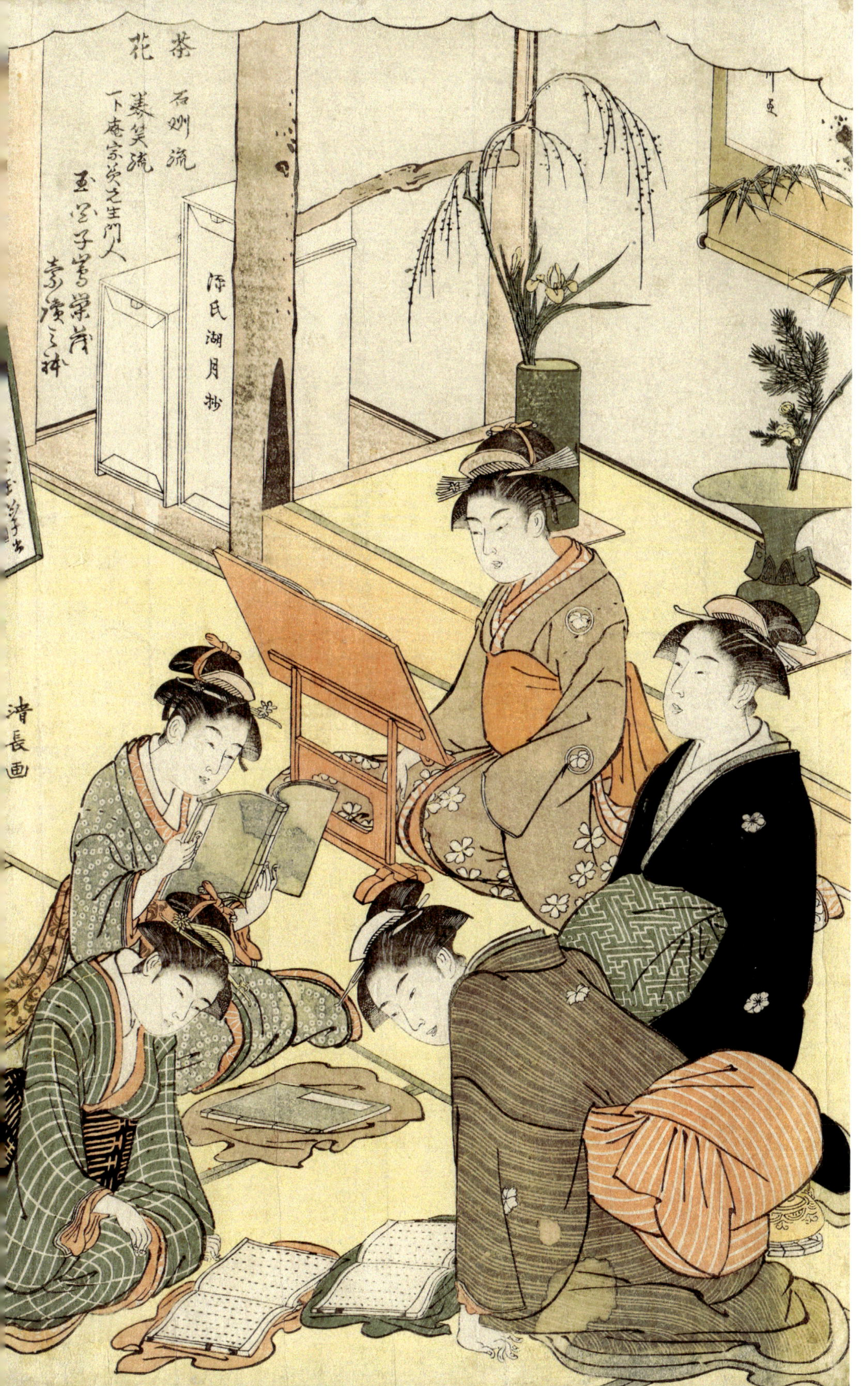
茶 石州流
花
源氏湖月抄
清長画

Jug

Nubian, Meroitic Period, 270 B.C.–A.D. 320

Inappropriate repair materials can damage an object as much as or more than accidents of time and nature. After an early-twentieth-century conservator removed thick layers of uneven corrosion from this jug caused by the object's long burial, he or she reattached the handle with cellulose nitrate, a synthetic material commonly used as an adhesive in the past. A white cement was also used around the joins to the body. New corrosion products, specifically salts of formic acid, developed around the handle when the copper in the jug's bronze material reacted to compounds probably given off by that cement. Formate salts can also emerge on objects in display or storage cases made of certain woods, fabrics, or glues.

Bronze
H. 17 cm, diam. 7.3 cm (H. 6 11/16 in., diam. 2 7/8 in.)
Harvard University–Boston Museum of Fine Arts Expedition 24.964

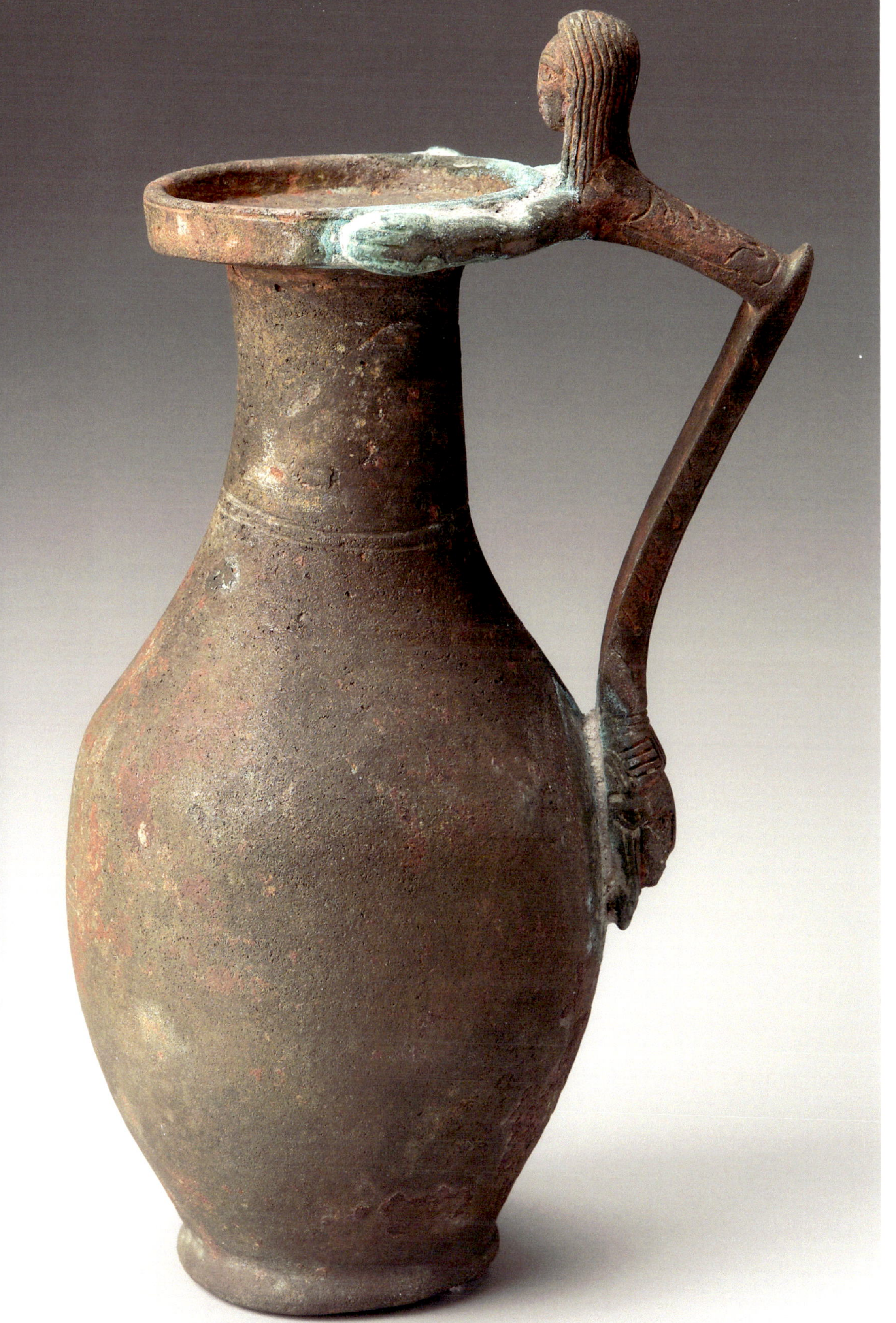

Water jar

Greek, Late Archaic Period, about 500–490 B.C.

Although the black glaze on the surface of this ancient Greek water jar is nonporous, the ceramic body within is still able to absorb moisture. Like most other ancient objects, this vessel was broken and discarded at some point. Under the ground, salts from the soil impregnated the broken pieces; these salts remained even after the sherds were dug up. As the relative humidity in the air changes, these water-soluble salts can become liquid again, move through small pores in the ceramic, and recrystallize. Repetitions of this process can weaken the vessel and cause pieces of it to break off.

In the late nineteenth century, a restorer made the jar whole again by gluing its pieces together with a natural adhesive, probably animal glue. He filled losses with plaster, and then painted the filled areas to blend in with the jar's original surface. After a hundred years, the old adhesive began to pull away bits of the original ceramic. The nineteenth-century paint also discolored, spoiling the jar's decoration.

Conservators at the MFA decided to take the jar apart completely. Once it was in pieces, they soaked some of the sherds in highly purified water. Tests of the water containing the sherds showed evidence of ions (electrically charged atoms), confirming the presence of salts, which might have caused the jar's deterioration. After determining that the pieces were strong enough to withstand a longer period of immersion, the conservators soaked all of them for many days, changing the water regularly. When the quantity of salt drawn into the water had fallen to an extremely low level, they dried the sherds and reassembled them with a synthetic adhesive known to remain stable for a long time. Unlike animal glues, this adhesive poses no danger to the ceramic. Although it is impossible to remove all of the soluble salts in the sherds, this treatment will reduce the likelihood of future problems. Storage and display environments with constant levels of relative humidity will also help preserve this jar.

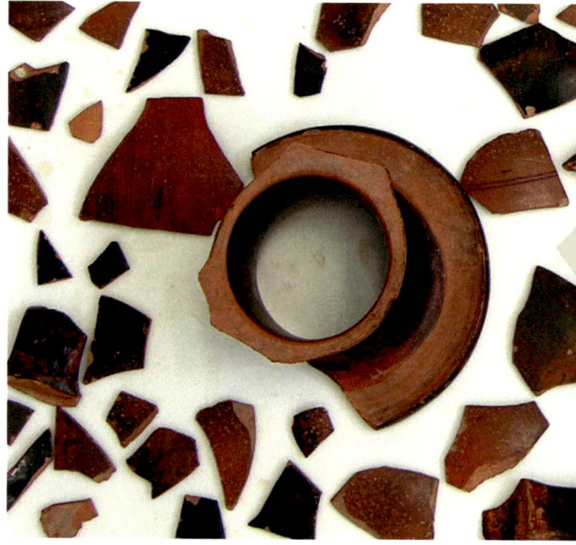

Disassembled fragments of the water jar

Ceramic, red-figure technique

H. 53 cm, diam. 32.5 cm (H. 20⅞ in., diam. 12 13/16 in.)

Henry Lillie Pierce Fund 98.878

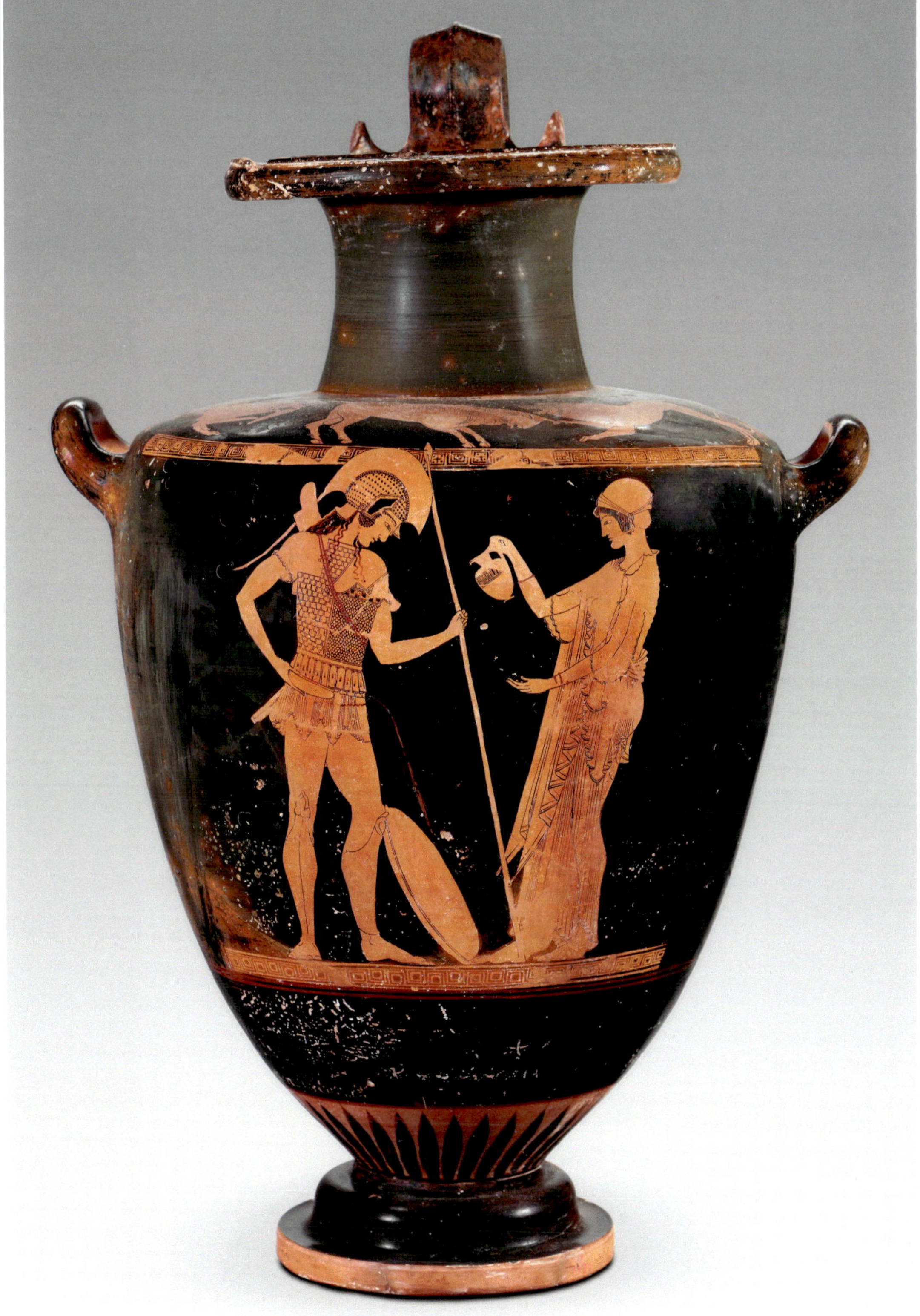

The water jar after reassembly, filling, and inpainting

Orpheus and Cerberus

Thomas Crawford (American, about 1813–1857)

1843

The American sculptor Thomas Crawford created this grand-scale sculpture as a commission for the Boston Athenaeum while living in Rome. He carefully packed and shipped it to Boston via New York in 1843. Unfortunately, the sculpture was damaged along the way. Chips broke off from the lyre, Orpheus's legs fissured above the knees and at the ankles, and the dog snapped into two pieces. The Athenaeum hired a local sculptor to repair Crawford's work and first showed it in its restored state at the beginning of 1844. The sculpture was a part of the Athenaeum's collection until 1872, when it was deposited on permanent loan to the Museum of Fine Arts, which acquired it in 1975.

Over the years, MFA conservators have had to repair small new losses and breaks alongside areas damaged by the transatlantic voyage of 1843. The sculpture's tremendous weight—over a ton at 1,061 kilograms, or 2,335 pounds—makes it difficult to move. Therefore, some of the later damage may have been caused by handling or perhaps the flexing of old joins as Museum staff transferred the piece between galleries and storage spaces.

In 1986, concerned about the stability of the areas joined together by the mid-nineteenth-century restorer, conservators partly disassembled the sculpture. They were surprised to find a bronze rod an inch in diameter extending from the top of one dog's head, through the dog's body, and into the base. Running a rod through a sculpture is unusual by today's conservation standards because the metal can corrode, expanding as it does so and causing cracks in the surrounding stone. However, in this case, because the metal did not pose a danger to the sculpture and in fact provided a strong connection between the largest of the broken pieces, and

The sculpture on its steel mount

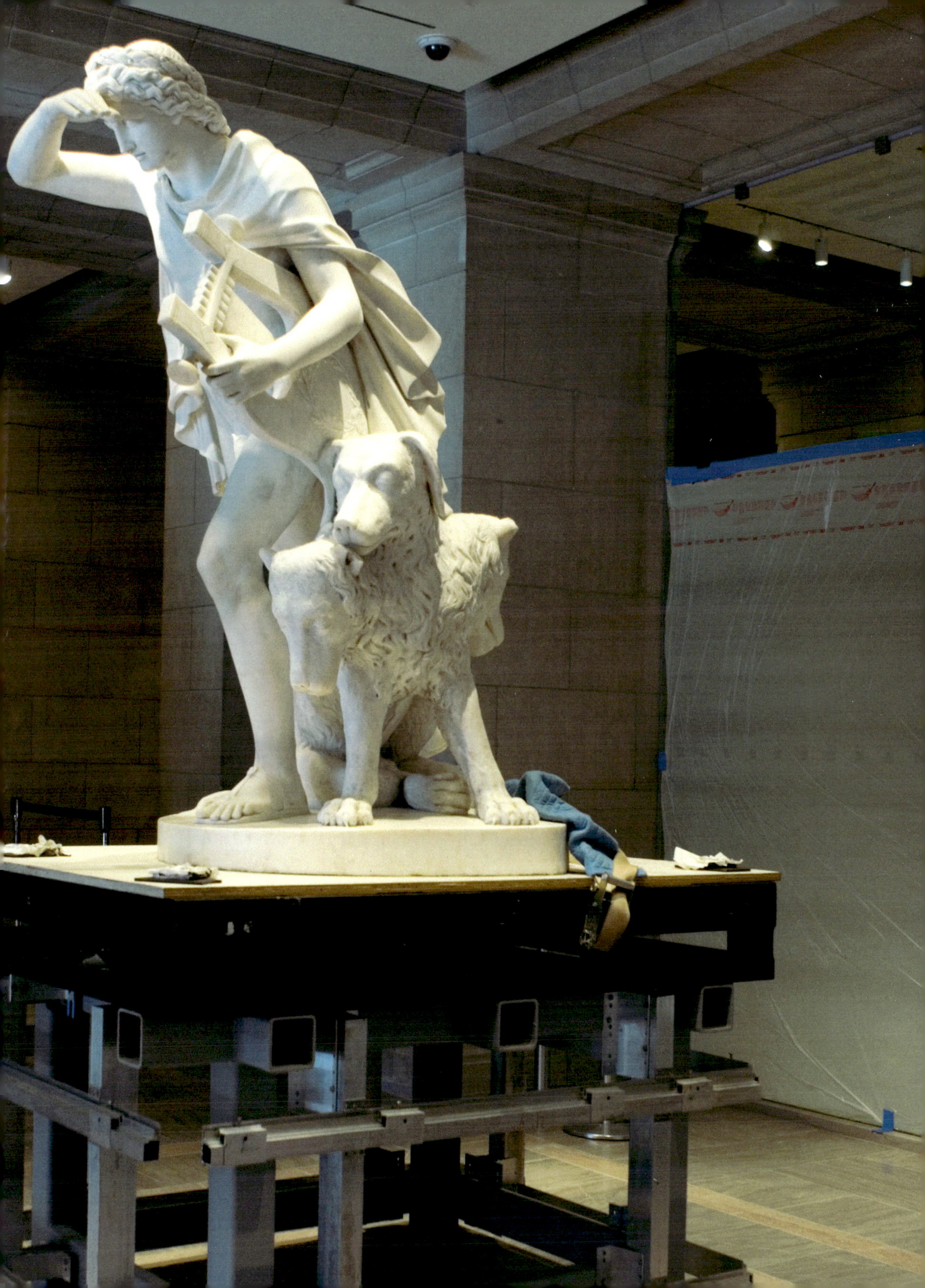

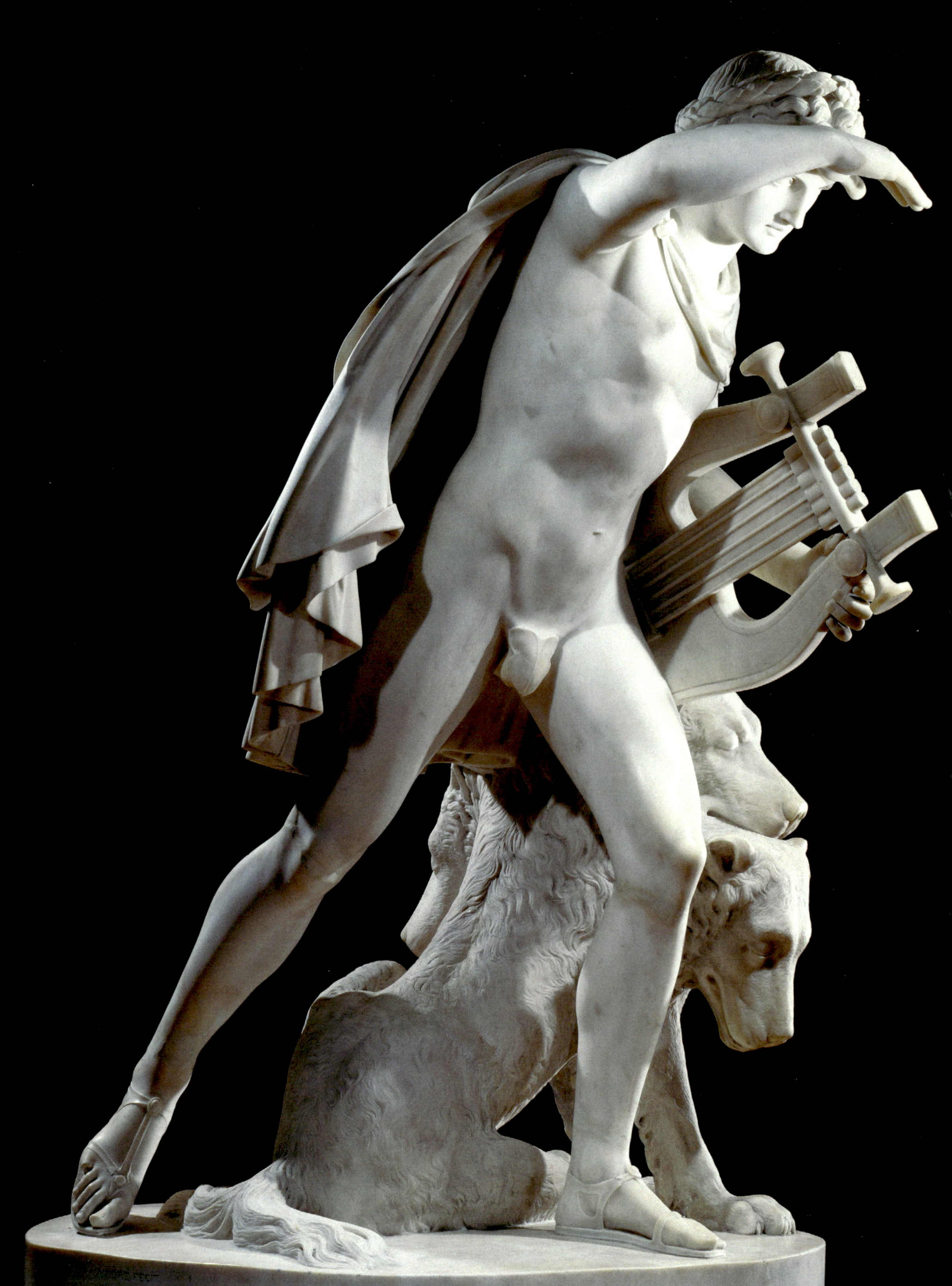

because any attempts to remove the rod might cause additional damage, the conservation team left it in place.

To strengthen some of the other breaks, including those in Orpheus's right foot and both knees, the conservators inserted new brass pins into the marble. They carefully drilled holes into the pairs of pieces to be joined, fixed the pins into the holes with an adhesive, and then fitted the pinned pieces together with the same adhesive applied to the broken surfaces. They chose brass pins at that time, but conservators today favor stainless steel because it is more resistant to corrosion. The adhesive is of a kind that can be softened with solvents should the joins need to be taken apart in the future. Adhesives used in the past can sometimes be removed only by mechanical means such as chisels and scalpels, which can damage the original stone even when used with extreme care.

The conservators joined other breaks with adhesive alone because these did not support enough weight to require the extra strength of metal pins. Finally, they filled small losses with mixtures of marble dust and adhesive, and in some areas they painted over the fills to closely match the original marble surface. They carefully documented every step of the restoration process and carried it out only with materials that are weaker than the marble and that can be removed.

More recently, conservators collaborated with engineers to construct a new steel pedestal designed to accommodate the prongs of a forklift. The sculpture is now securely attached to this framework so that Museum staff can move it without touching the marble at all. The pedestal prevents furthcr handling of the sculpture to the greatest extent possible, protecting its surface from further stress along the joins of the early breaks.

Marble

171.5 x 91.4 x 137.2 cm (67½ x 36 x 54 in.)

Gift of Mr. and Mrs. Cornelius C. Vermeule III 1975.800

Portrait of Charles Bartlett Roberts

Joseph H. Davis (American, 1811–1865)

1835

Buffeted by function and fashion, the aesthetics of framing have varied over time. Curators and conservators consider original frames or mounts to be significant to the history of the art they surround and therefore preserve them whenever possible. However, when original framing contributes to the deterioration of an object, they take steps to isolate, modify, or replace its harmful components.

The edges of this watercolor by Joseph H. Davis are brown and brittle and have suffered numerous losses due to direct contact with an old wooden frame. The paper is also stained, likely from prolonged contact with a wooden backing board. A backing board may be made of any stiff, flat material and is placed behind the work of art to hold it firmly in the frame. Shingles were commonly used as backing materials in the nineteenth century and may be what was used in the original framing of this watercolor. Because wood is acidic and resinous, direct contact with paper results in staining and deterioration. This type of staining often takes on the pattern of the wood's grain, knots, and splits of the backing board. Although such stains may respond to conservation treatment, the deterioration of the paper's fibers, called embrittlement, is not reversible. To avoid further harm to this watercolor, the Museum uses only high-quality, nonacidic mat board, hinges, and adhesives to store and display it.

Watercolor over graphite

Sheet: 20.5 x 16.7 cm (8 x 6 7/16 in.)

Gift of Maxim Karolik for the M. and M. Karolik Collection of American Watercolors and Drawings, 1800–1875 60.868

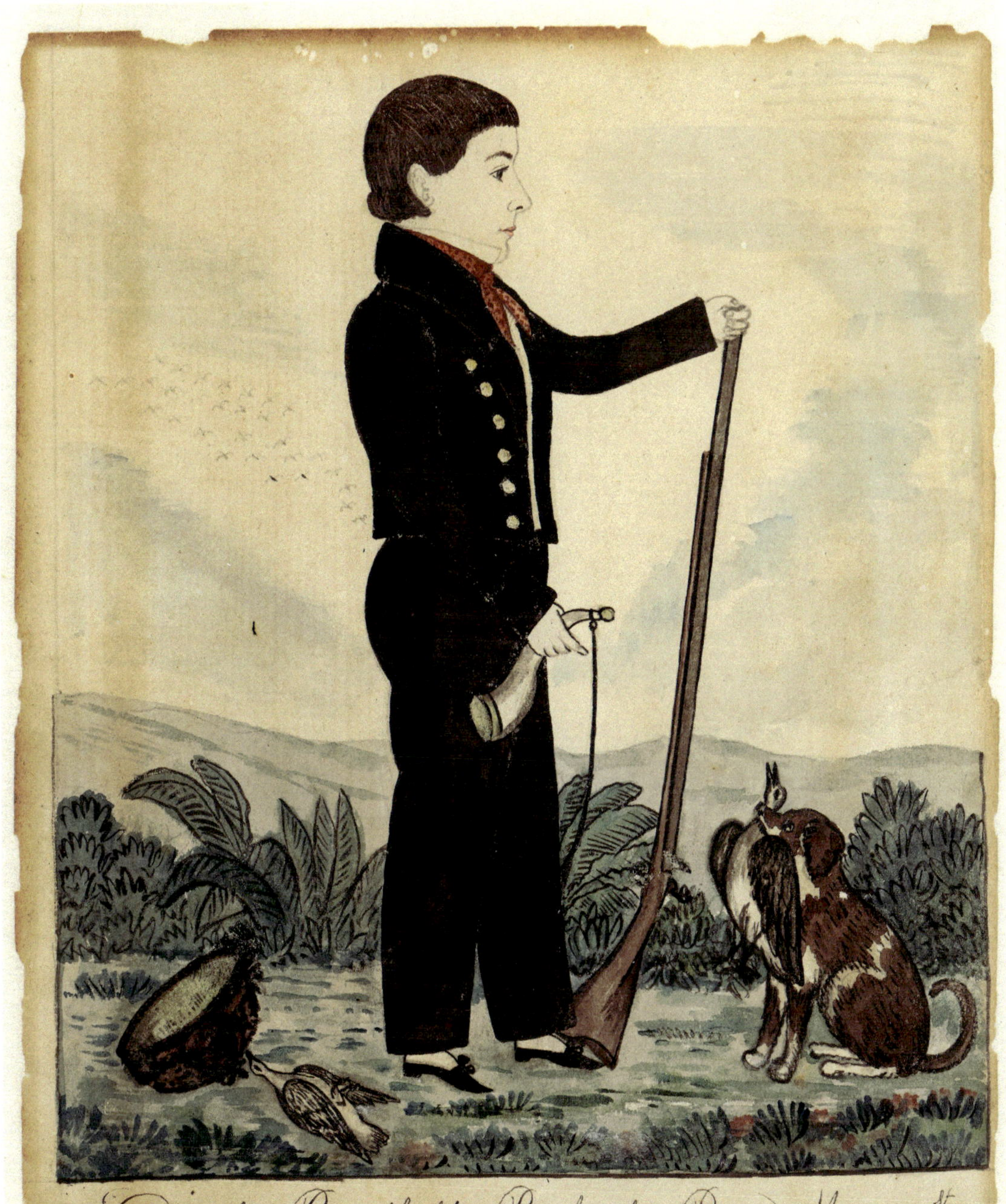
Charles Bartlett. Roberts. Born May 21st 1822.
Painted at the Age of 13 years.

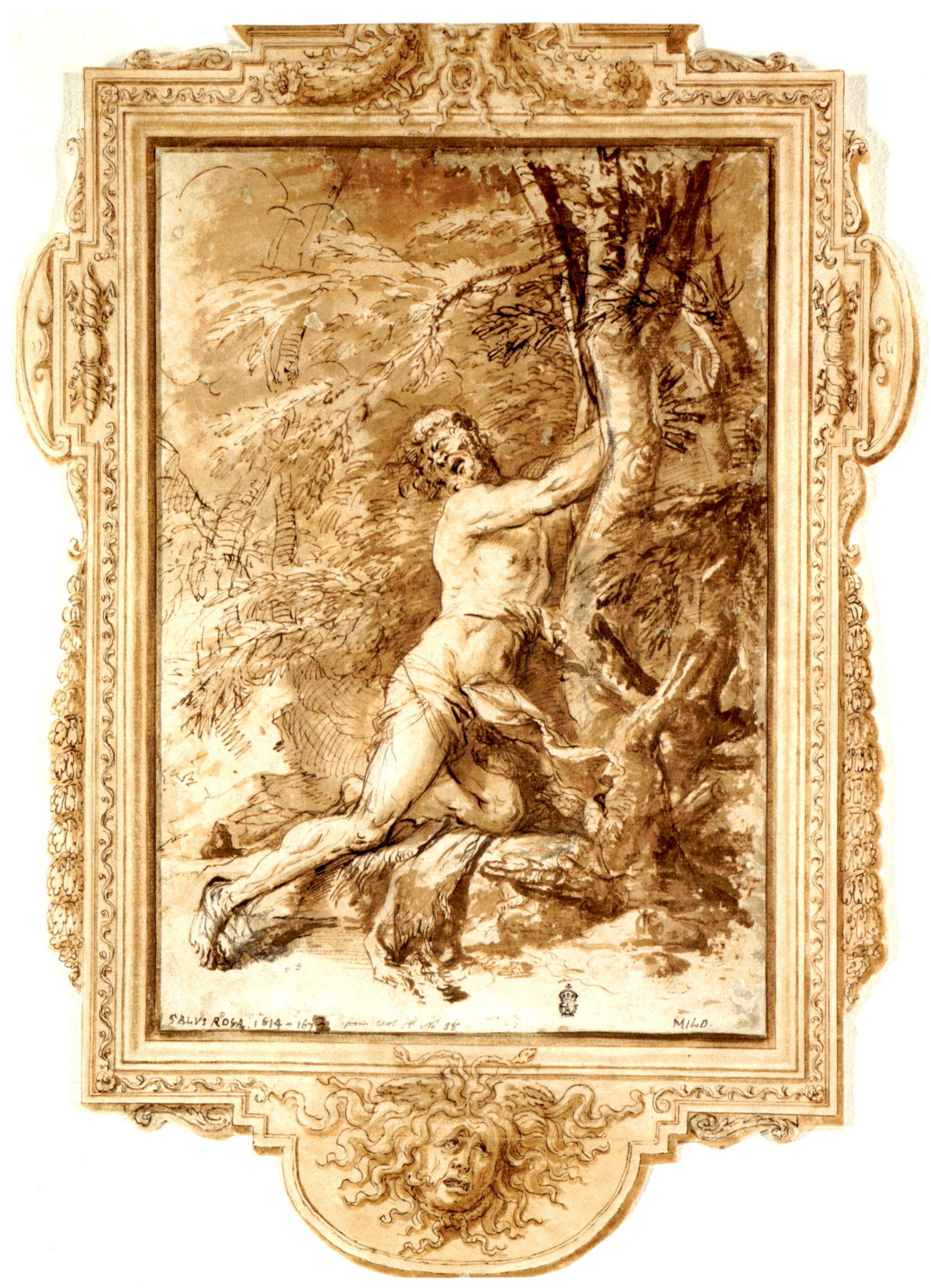
SALV: ROSA. 1614 - 1673
MILO.

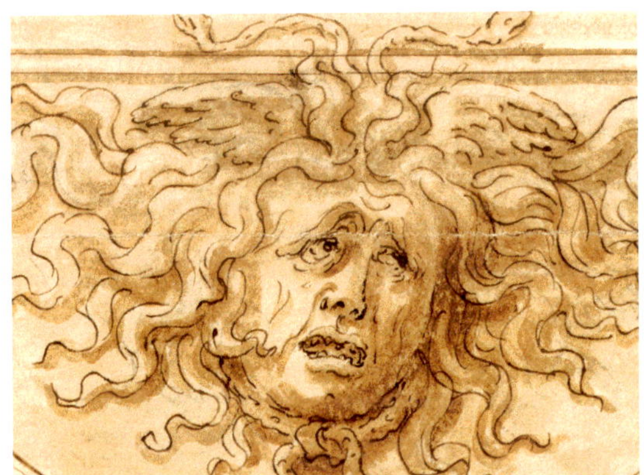

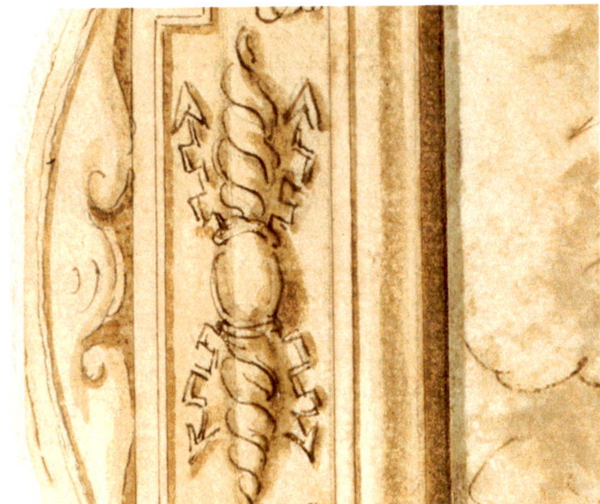

Milo of Croton

Salvator Rosa (Italian, 1615–1673)

About 1666

Borders serve as both adornment and physical protection for prints and drawings. The practice of artists and collectors adding borders to images has a long history. Current scholarship suggests that a collector, not the artist, added the elaborately designed paper margin of Gorgon heads and scrolls to Salvator Rosa's *Milo of Croton*. Collectors sometimes commissioned embellishments of this kind to highlight prized works of art in their collections. While likely not original to Rosa, the decorative paper frame on this drawing speaks to the history of collecting and offers a spectacular example of a historical mount in a manner that does not compromise the safety or preservation of the art.

Pen and brush in brown ink, with additions in white and graphite
Sheet: 31.1 x 22.2 cm (12 1/4 x 8 3/4 in.)
Mount: 44.2 x 32.8 cm (17 3/8 x 12 15/16 in.)
Charles H. Bayley Picture and Painting Fund 1986.579

Helen Freeman

Alfred Stieglitz (American, 1864–1946)

1921–22

In the early twentieth century, Alfred Stieglitz challenged art museums to accept photographs on an equal footing with paintings, sculpture, and prints. Museums had been slow to accept, let alone purchase, photographs for their collections, regarding the images as products of science instead of creative expression. However, curators at the MFA saw value in Stieglitz's work and persuaded him to make a gift of some of his photographs to the Museum. Stieglitz's enthusiasm for the project eventually led him to select and mount twenty-seven of his finest photographs for the MFA.

Stieglitz made clear the critical importance of size and presentation when he wrote on December 31, 1923, "I find it impossible to mount [my photographs] on the Museum standard sizes of mounts. I find I have through years of experience worked out such a right way of making my prints and mounts, one that changing anything in the relative sizes changes the spirit and robs my work of its life and significance. . . . Photography is still on trial—I can't possibly go ahead feeling the Museum's standard sizes come before photography in this particular case."

In accepting Stieglitz's gift, the MFA honored his aesthetic. Original mounts and relative sizes remain unchanged to this day. Due to age and fragility, the original Stieglitz frames are no longer in use. Current frames are faithful replicas, with original frames preserved in museum storage. However, to better protect the photographs, glazing and mat board have been upgraded to archival, museum-quality materials that were not available to Stieglitz at the time of the gift.

Photograph, palladium print
Image: 18.7 x 23.2 cm (7 3/8 x 9 1/8 in.)
Gift of Alfred Stieglitz 24.1729

The photograph matted and framed according to Stieglitz's specifications

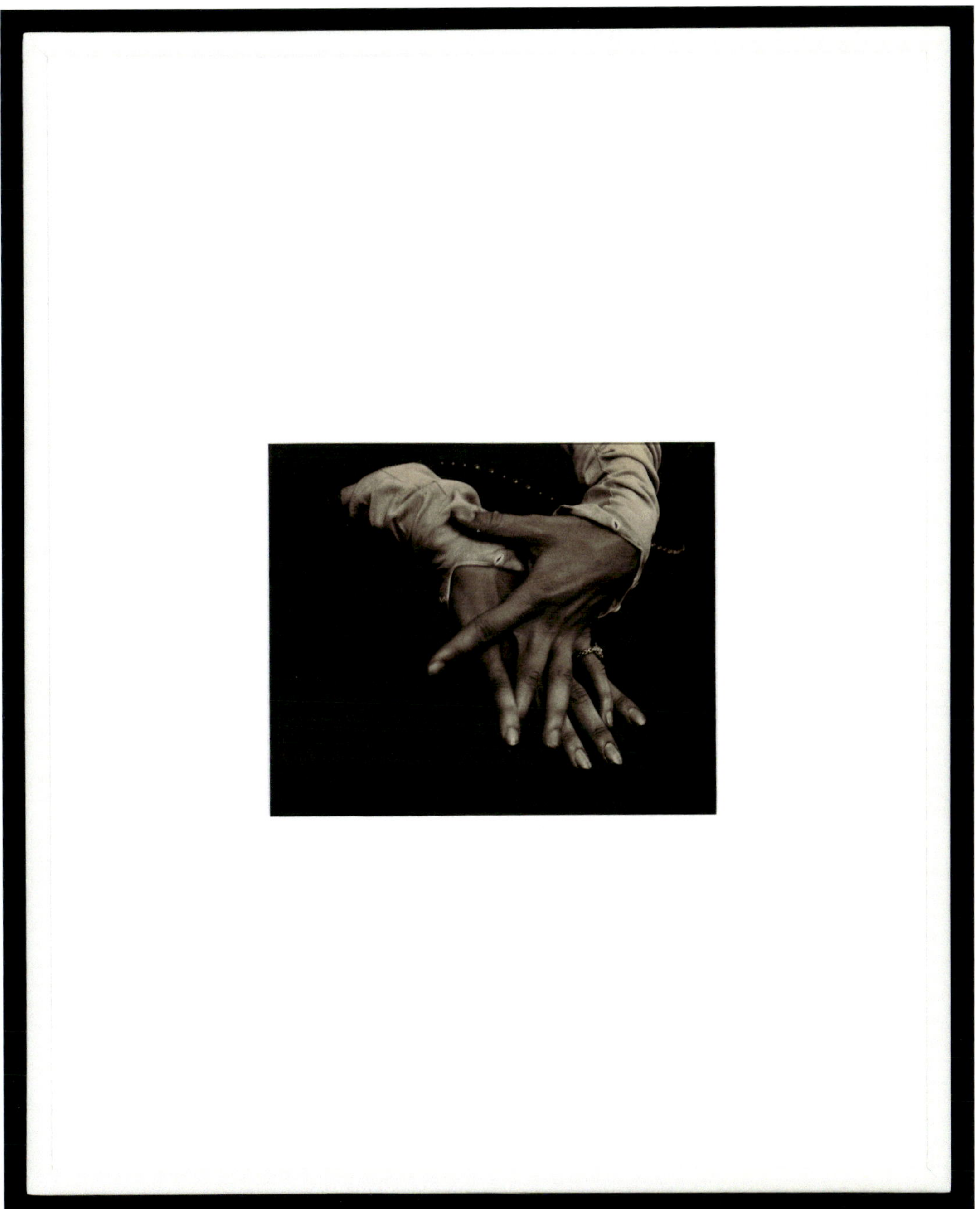

Como tea and coffee service

Lino Sabattini (Italian, born in 1925), designer

Orfèvrerie Christofle (France), manufacturer

Paris, designed 1956

Silver objects tarnish easily because they react with even small amounts of sulfur in the air. Sulfur slowly dissolves the metal, leaving behind a layer of corrosion. The most common corrosion product is silver sulfide, a very thin layer of which produces an iridescent surface, whereas thicker layers are black.

Various methods have been developed to clean tarnished silver, but many remove some of the metal surface along with the disfiguring corrosion. The best method for preserving silver objects is to eliminate the chemicals that cause corrosion from their surroundings. The Museum stores this tea and coffee service and other polished silver objects in sealed environments from which sulfur gases and other pollutants have been removed with scavengers. One effective scavenger consists of fine particles of copper, which rapidly react with any sulfur-containing gases before they can corrode the silver. The scavenger can be embedded in special fabric and installed in display cases, hidden from view. Because the relative humidity in the air can also affect the rate of corrosion, conservators often place silica gel in cases to absorb moisture and keep the environment inside at a low relative humidity level (35 percent). Even with these measures, highly polished silver objects may slowly tarnish over time. When this service needs to be cleaned for exhibition, conservators use a very mild method—a soft abrasive in a slurry of liquids applied with cotton swabs. Because all corrosion, including tarnish, consumes original metal, it is important to try to halt the process.

Silver with wooden handles

Coffeepot: H. 21 cm (8¼ in.) Sugar bowl: H. 7 cm (2¾ in.)

Teapot: 13.7 cm (5⅜ in.) Tray: 4.2 x 49.8 cm (1⅝ x 19⅝ in.)

The John Axelrod Collection 1999.256.1–5

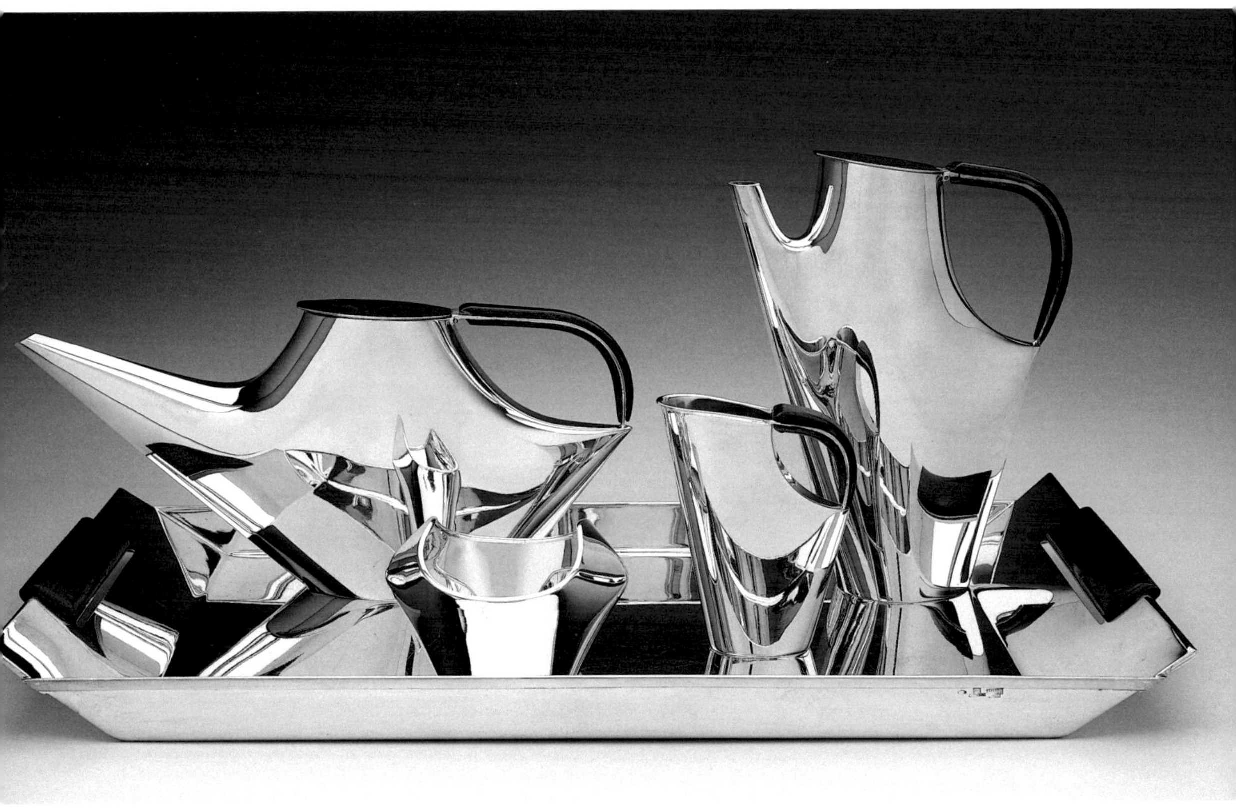

Jar

Egypt, Predynastic Period,
Naqada II–III, 3650–2960 B.C.

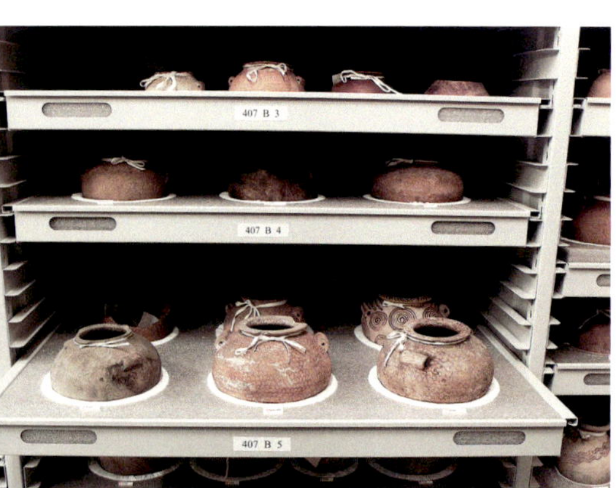

The jar in its protective storage cabinet

The Museum of Fine Arts, Boston, has a rich collection of ancient Egyptian artifacts from expeditions it sponsored in the early years of the twentieth century. The sheer number and varied quality of the objects make it impractical to display them all, and visitors usually prefer to see only the best examples in the galleries. The rest, like this jar, spend most of their time in storage, waiting for specialists to come and study them.

This jar lives in a cabinet with others like it from the Naqada culture of Upper (southern) Egypt. Despite their age, neither the ceramic bodies nor the painted decorations of this group are particularly fragile. The MFA stores them in a manner that preserves the objects' sound condition and allows them to be studied with minimum handling. For example, the cabinet is made of metal coated with a type of paint that will not deteriorate as it ages. Compared with natural or manufactured wood products (such as plywood) traditionally used to make storage cabinets, these materials release no volatile chemicals that can damage the art. Such chemicals can be particularly dangerous if they become trapped and therefore concentrated in the small space of a closed cupboard. The open design of this jar's storage also allows any off-gassing compounds to quickly dissipate into the air in the room.

Nonreactive plastic foam in the cabinet drawers serves to prevent physical damage. The jar sits in its own snug space carved to fit its unique shape. The drawers move smoothly as they are opened and closed so that vibrations are kept to a minimum. Visiting archaeologists can view all of the ceramics in a drawer at once, and then choose individual jars for closer examination without disturbing the other objects nearby.

Pottery
16 x 22 cm (6 5/16 x 8 11/16 in.)
Harvard University–Boston Museum of Fine Arts Expedition Eg.Inv.4820

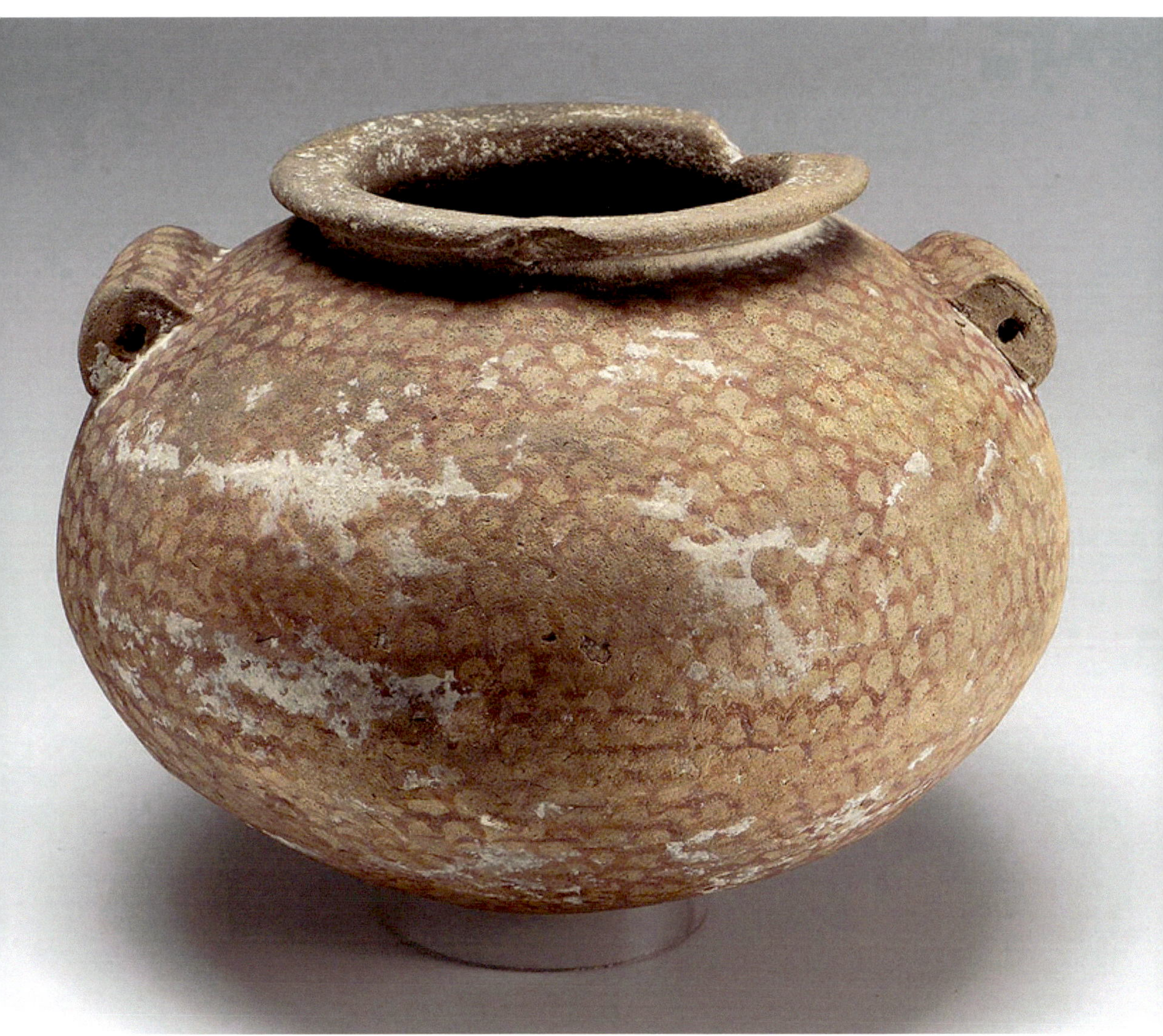

Capri-Batterie

Joseph Beuys (German, 1921–1986)

From an edition of 200, 1985

Lightbulb, socket, and lemon
18.4 x 18.4 x 17 cm (7¼ x 7¼ x 6 11/16 in.)
Gift of Lucio Amelio 1986.531

Sculptor, painter, installation artist, and performance artist Joseph Beuys's *Capri-Batterie* consists of a yellow lightbulb, a socket, and a fresh lemon. The lemon is one of the main agricultural products of the Italian island of Capri, where Beuys created *Capri-Batterie* in an edition of two hundred while recovering from a lung infection in the last year of his life. With the plugs of the socket pushed into it, the lemon acts as a battery and makes the lightbulb glow.

Beuys left tongue-in-cheek instructions to replace his "battery" every one thousand hours, but when the MFA exhibited the work in 1994, staff members replaced the lemon after only 168 hours due to the stench of rotting fruit in the gallery. The artist intentionally provided no guidance about how to deal with the natural consequences of the lemon's acidic juice, which will eventually corrode all the metal elements with which it comes in contact.

Beuys is one of many twentieth-century artists who deliberately used materials that cannot be preserved in their original state. About works like *Capri-Batterie*, he explained: "The nature of my sculpture is not fixed and finished. Processes continue in most of them: chemical reactions, fermentations, colour changes, decay, drying up. Everything is in a state of change."[1] Because Beuys's ideas are inextricably linked to the materials he used to express them, and because processes of decay are critical to those ideas, conservators' basic assumptions about preservation fail for works such as *Capri-Batterie*.

---

1. Beuys, quoted in *In Memoriam Joseph Beuys: Obituaries, Essays, Speeches*, trans. Timothy Nevill (Bonn: Inter Nationes, 1986), 22.

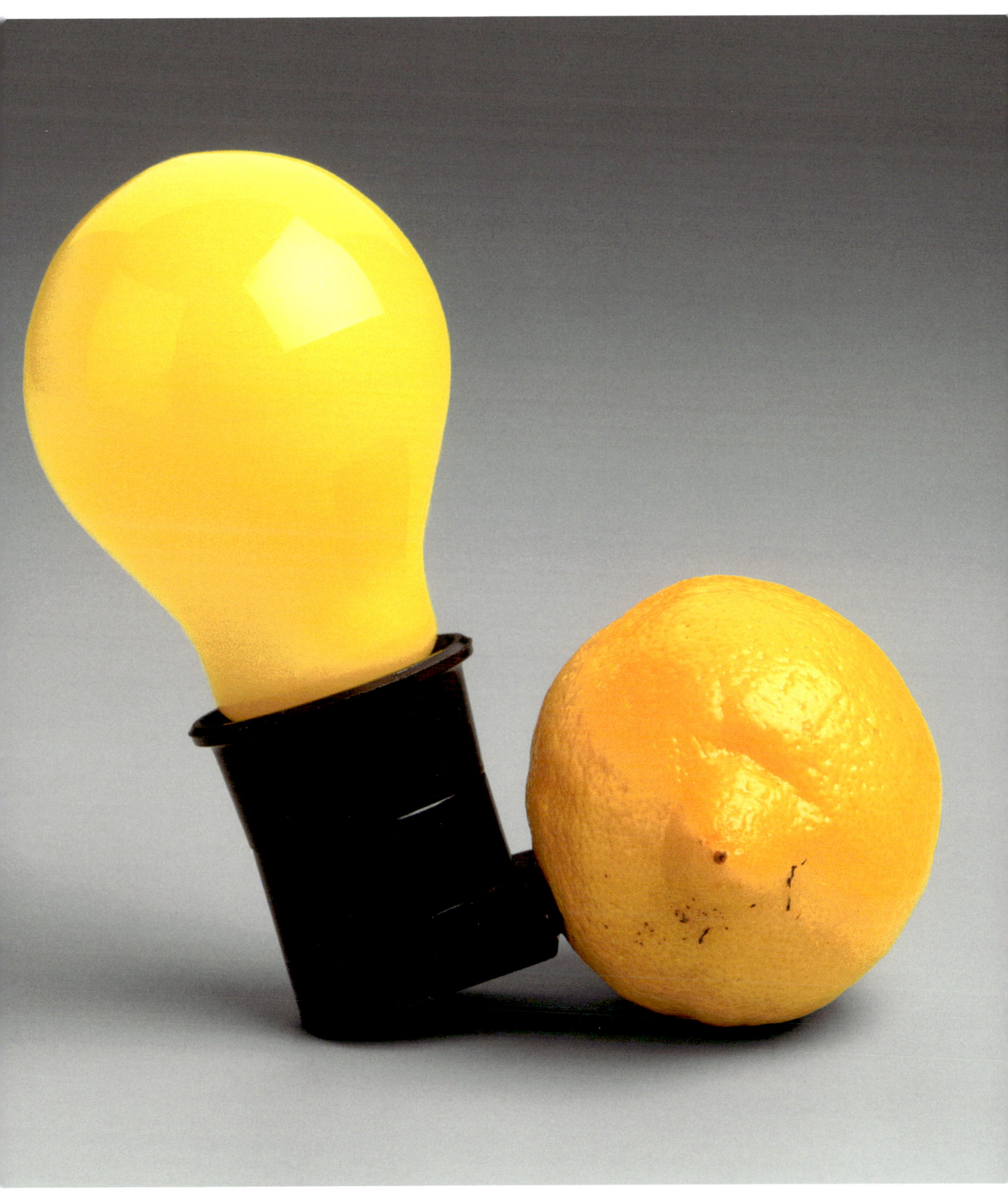

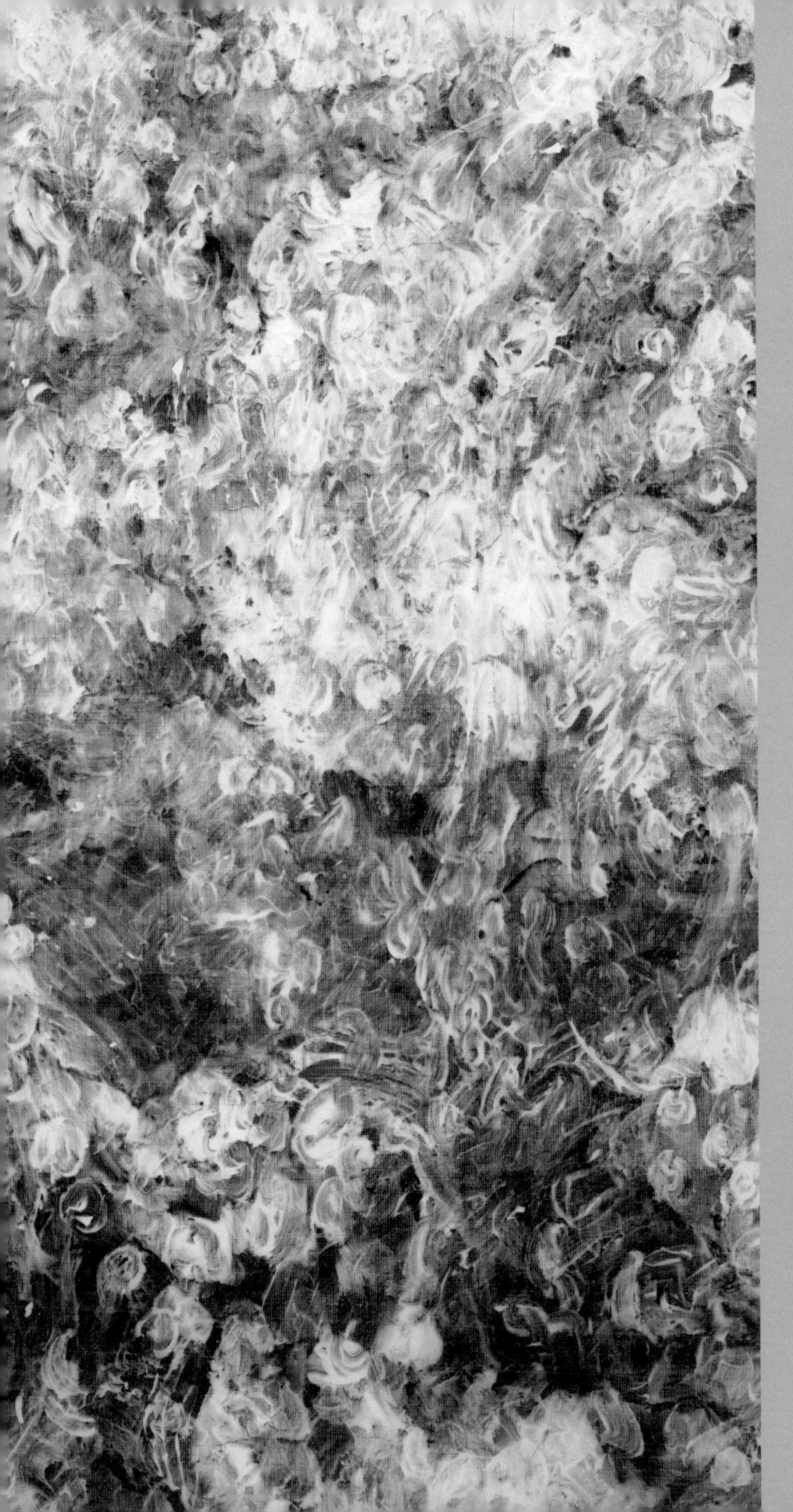

glossary, further reading, figure illustrations, index

Glossary

cleaning
A process for removing material from the surface of a work of art. Cleaning can be performed with the aid of chemicals (to dissolve varnishes, for example) or by physical means (such as using scalpels to remove corrosion products on metal objects). The materials removed can vary, from dirt or grime to weathering products from exposure to the elements to varnishes and coatings applied during conservation treatments.

consolidation
A process used for both two-dimensional and three-dimensional works of art when the surface becomes weakened by small cracks or fissures. It involves applying an adhesive solution, which strengthens weakened material or more firmly adheres it to a stronger surface below. Consolidants are chemically stable materials, different in nature from any original organic binder, that do not change or only minimally change the glossiness of the surface.

cross section
A small, solid sample from a work of art that has been placed in a liquid resin, such as epoxy, and allowed to set. Part of the sample is exposed by sanding and polishing the hardened resin. The sample can be a millimeter or less in size. If it comes from a section of the work of art in which multiple layers are present, as is common in most paintings, it can be sanded in such a way that the individual layers are revealed. The cross section can then be studied by numerous analytical techniques.

electromagnetic spectrum
A range of radiation types that differ in wavelength and energy. Visible light (the only section of the spectrum that our eyes can detect) has wavelengths between 400 and 700 nanometers (a nanometer is a billionth of a meter). Infrared radiation has longer wavelengths than visible light, ultraviolet radiation has shorter wavelengths, and X-radiation has even shorter wavelengths. Artificial light sources often emit ultraviolet and infrared radiation in addition to visible light.

embrittlement
The process of deterioration of paper or textile fibers whereby the material becomes more brittle, or weak and fragile.

fading
The process of change in a material's color, usually caused by exposure to light in the presence of oxygen. Fading is often the visible result of chemical change and cannot be reversed.

fills
The materials added to a loss in a work of art to make the object appear more complete. Fills can be applied so as to be nearly undetectable, as is often the case on easel paintings, or engineered so that they are obvious even on casual observation, as on some three-dimensional objects.

Fourier transform infrared spectroscopy
An analytical technique that measures by wavelength the amount of infrared radiation transmitted or reflected. The resulting infrared spectrum can be used to identify different compounds or mixtures of compounds, particularly organic materials.

gas chromatography/mass spectrometry
A specialized analytical technique used to separate mixtures of compounds and identify the individual compounds in each mixture. It can provide very detailed information on both natural and synthetic materials such as paint binders, adhesives, and varnishes.

infrared radiation
See *electromagnetic spectrum*

infrared reflectography
An examination technique most often used with paintings to detect underdrawings or underpaintings. In this method, a painting is exposed to infrared radiation, which is reflected off of it and picked up by a special detector. Some materials are more transparent when viewed under infrared radiation, which allows one to see layers underneath the surface that may or may not be visible in normal light.

inpainting
The process of painting a filled area, often on top of a thin film, so it blends in with the rest of the original artwork. Stable pigments that will not fade or discolor are used in media that can be easily removed without affecting the surrounding original material.

laser cleaning
A method of cleaning objects using fine laser beams to burn or blast away surface materials, such as dirt, dark encrustations, and other accretions. Conservators have a great deal of control with laser cleaning, so even very fragile materials may be safely treated with this process.

microclimate
A controlled climate within a small space, such as a display case or storage cabinet. In museums, a microclimate is often created within a display case to establish a relative humidity level that is more stable and sometimes lower than that of the gallery.

patina
A layer on the surface of a work of art that can be the result of natural aging or weathering or that can be artificially applied. Patinas may be disfiguring to a surface but can also protect what lies beneath. Removal of a patina during a conservation treatment is carried out only after careful consideration of its composition and origin(s).

radiocarbon dating
An archaeological dating technique that can be applied to any plant- or animal-based material (such as wood, ivory, and bone), measuring its age up to fifty thousand years. A tiny fraction of all carbon in living things consists of a radioactive isotope of the element C^{14}. Radiocarbon dating determines the amount of C^{14} still present in a sample and uses the known rate of the isotope's decay to calculate the time that has passed since the sample was living.

raking light
The visible light reflected off an object when the light source is directed at its surface at a very low angle. Such lighting accentuates surface texture by causing raised features to cast shadows.

relative humidity
The amount of water vapor in the air relative to the maximum possible content at a given temperature. As the temperature of the air increases, the maximum amount of water vapor in the air also increases. Some materials, such as wood and fabric, always contain a certain amount of water, which changes as the relative humidity of the environment changes.

scanning electron microscope
An analytical instrument that uses a focused high-electron beam, scanned over the surface of a sample, to create an image at magnifications much higher than are possible with visible light microscopes. When attached to a scanning electron microscope, X-ray fluorescence spectrometers can be used for chemical analysis of the scanned area.

scavengers
Materials capable of absorbing or reacting with gaseous compounds in the air. Oxygen scavengers, for example, can be used to lower the oxygen content of air in a closed container in treatments to kill pests. Other scavengers absorb pollutants and can be used to better preserve certain reactive materials, such as those that absorb sulfur, which tarnishes silver.

silica gel
A material manufactured in various forms that is capable of controlling the relative humidity of a small space in which it is placed. Museums often use silica gel conditioned to a certain relative humidity in display cases to maintain a microclimate that is different or more stable than that of the gallery.

stereobinocular microscope
A type of optical instrument with two eyepieces used to look at objects at magnifications of up to one hundred times.

tesserae
Small pieces of stone, tile, or glass used in a mosaic.

thermoluminescence dating
An archaeological dating technique that can indicate the amount of time that has passed since a ceramic material was last fired, or manufactured. Although not highly precise, the technique can be used to distinguish an original ceramic from a copy or forgery made many hundreds (or more) years later.

ultraviolet radiation
See *electromagnetic spectrum*

X-radiography
A technique using X-rays to reveal features of an object that are not visible on its surface under normal light. A tube emits a spectrum of X-rays with a certain energy distribution; film or a digital imaging system then records the amount of radiation transmitted through an object. Thin objects, such as paintings, require much lower energy X-rays than thicker, more dense objects, such as metal or stone sculptures.

X-ray fluorescence
An analysis technique that uses a high-energy beam of X-rays in a stand-alone spectrometer (or electrons in a scanning electron microscope) to create characteristic, fluorescent X-rays of the material on which the beam is focused. These secondary X-rays have specific energies that can be used to identify chemical elements in the area being analyzed.

Further Reading

General

Appelbaum, Barbara. *Conservation Treatment Methodology*. Oxford: Butterworth-Heinemann, 2007.

Bachmann, Konstanze. *Conservation Concerns: A Guide for Collectors and Curators*. Washington, DC: Smithsonian Books, 1992.

Bewer, Francesca G. *A Laboratory for Art: Harvard's Fogg Museum and the Emergence of Conservation in America, 1900–1950*. Cambridge, MA: Harvard Art Museum, 2010.

Brill, Thomas. *Light: Its Interaction with Art and Antiquities*. New York: Springer, 1980.

Hatchfield, Pamela. *Pollutants in the Museum Environment*. London: Archetype Books, 2007.

Muñoz-Viñas, Salvador. *Contemporary Theory of Conservation*. Oxford: Butterworth-Heinemann, 2004.

National Committee to Save America's Cultural Collections. *Caring for Your Collections*. Washington, DC, 1992.

Richmond, Alison, and Alison Bracker, eds. *Conservation: Principles, Dilemmas and Uncomfortable Truths*. Oxford: Butterworth-Heinemann, 2009.

Thomson, Garry. *The Museum Environment*. Oxford: Butterworth-Heinemann, 1986.

European Paintings

Bomford, David, ed. *Underdrawings in Renaissance Paintings*, exh. cat. London: National Gallery, 2002.

Bomford, David, Jill Dunkerton, Dillian Gordon, Ashok Roy, and Jo Kirby. *Italian Painting before 1400*, exh. cat. London: National Gallery, 1989.

Bomford, David, Sarah Herring, Jo Kirby, Christopher Riopelle, and Ashok Roy. *Art in the Making: Degas*, exh cat. London: National Gallery, 2005.

Bomford, David, Jo Kirby, Ashok Roy, Axel Ruger, and Raymond White. *Rembrandt*, rev. ed. London: National Gallery, 2006.

Bomford, David, John Leighton, Jo Kirby, and Ashok Roy. *Impressionism*, exh. cat. London: National Gallery, 1990.

Bomford, David, and Mark Leonard, eds. *Issues in the Conservation of Paintings*. Los Angeles: Getty Conservation Institute, 2005.

Callen, Anthea. *The Art of Impressionism: Painting Technique and the Making of Modernity*. New Haven: Yale University Press, 2000.

Crook, Jo, and Tom Learner. *The Impact of Modern Paints*. New York: Watson-Guptill, 2000.

Dunkerton, Jill, Susan Foister, Dillian Gordon, and Nicholas Penny. *Giotto to Dürer: Early Renaissance Painting in the National Gallery*. New Haven: Yale University Press, 1994.

Dunkerton, Jill, Susan Foister, and Nicholas Penny. *Dürer to Veronese: Sixteenth-Century Painting in the National Gallery*. New Haven: Yale University Press, 2002.

Garland, Patricia Sherwin, ed. *Early Italian Paintings: Approaches to Conservation*. New Haven: Yale University Press, 2003.

Hermans, Erma, ed. *Looking through Paintings*. London: Archetype Publications, 1998.

Kirsch, Andrea, and Rustin S. Levenson. *Seeing through Paintings: Physical Examination in Art Historical Studies*. New Haven: Yale University Press, 2002.

Learner, Tom, Jay W. Krueger, and Michael R. Schilling, eds. *Modern Paints Uncovered: Proceedings from the Modern Paints Uncovered Symposium, May 16–19, 2006, Tate Modern*. Los Angeles: Getty Publications, 2008.

Nicolaus, Knut. *The Restoration of Paintings*. Cologne: Konemann, 1999.

Price, Nicholas Stanley, M. Kirby Talley, Jr., and Alessandra Melucco Vaccaro, eds. *Historical and Philosophical Issues in the Conservation of Cultural Heritage*. Los Angeles: Getty Publications, 1996.

Wetering, Ernst van de. *Rembrandt: The Painter at Work*. Berkeley: University of California Press, 2009.

Furniture and Frames

Barclay, Robert L., ed. *The Care of Historic Musical Instruments*. Ottawa: Canadian Conservation Institute, 1997.

Bigelow, Deborah, ed. *Gilded Wood: Conservation and History*. Madison, CT: Sound View Press, 1980.

Dorge, Valeri, and F. Carey Howlett, eds. *Painted Wood: History and Conservation*. Los Angeles: Getty Conservation Institute, 1998.

Gill, Kathryn, and Dinah Eastop. *Upholstery Conservation: Principles and Practice*. Oxford: Butterworth-Heinemann, 2000.

Hoadley, R. Bruce. *Identifying Wood*. Newtown, CT: Taunton Press, 1990.

———. *Understanding Wood*. Newtown, CT: Taunton Press, 2000.

Karraker, D. Gene. *Looking at European Frames: A Guide to Terms, Styles, and Techniques*. Los Angeles: Getty Publications, 2010.

Powell, Christine, and Zoe Allen. *Italian Renaissance Frames at the V & A: A Technical Study*. Oxford: Butterworth-Heinemann, 2009.

Rivers, Shayne, and Nick Umney. *Conservation of Furniture*. Oxford: Butterworth-Heinemann, 2003.

Sawicki, Malgorzata. *Non-traditional Gilding Techniques in Gilded Objects Conservation*. Saarbrücken: VDM–Verlag Dr. Müller, 2010.

Schniewind, Arno P., ed. *Concise Encyclopedia of Wood and Wood-Based Materials*. Oxford: Pergamon Press, 1989.

Unger, Achim, Arno P. Schniewind, and Wibke Unger. *Conservation of Wood Artifacts: A Handbook*. New York: Springer, 2001.

Webb, Marianne. *Lacquer: Technology and Conservation*. Oxford: Butterworth-Heinemann, 2000.

Asian Paintings and Works on Paper

Connors, Sandra A., Paul M. Whitmore, Roger S. Keyes, and Elizabeth I. Coombs. "The Identification and Light Sensitivity of Japanese Woodblock Print Colorants: The Impact on Art History and Preservation." In *Scientific Research on the Pictorial Arts of Asia: Proceedings of the Second Forbes Symposium at the Freer Gallery of Art*, ed. Paul Jett, John Winter, and Blythe McCarthy, 35–47. London: Archetype Publications, 2005.

Gulik, Robert H. van. *Chinese Pictorial Art as Viewed by the Connoisseur*. Rome: Istituto Italiano per il Medio ed Estremo Oriente, 1958.

Hirayama, Ikuo, Kyotaro Nishikawa, Akiyoshi Watanabe, Hiromitsu Washizuka, and Naohachi Usami, eds. *Restoration of Japanese Art in European and American Collections*. Tokyo: Chuokoron-sha, 1995.

Keyes, Roger S., and Elizabeth I. Coombs. "Color as Language in Traditional Japanese Prints." In *The Broad Spectrum: Studies in the Materials, Techniques and Conservation of Color on Paper*, ed. Harriet K. Stratis and Britt Salvesen, 184–89. London: Archetype Publications, 2006.

Koyano, Masako. *Japanese Scroll Paintings: A Handbook of Mounting Techniques*. Washington, DC: Foundation of the American Institute for Conservation, 1979.

Meredith, Philip, and Tanya Uyeda. "Mountings and Painting Techniques of Ukiyo-e Hanging Scrolls." In *Drama and Desire: Japanese Paintings from the Floating World 1690–1850*, ed. Anne Nishimura Morse, 222–27. Boston: MFA Publications, 2007.

Newland, Amy Reigle, ed. *The Hotei Encyclopedia of Japanese Woodblock Prints*. Amsterdam: Hotei Publishing, 2005.

Sasaki, Shiho, and Elizabeth I. Coombs. "Dayflower Blue: Its Appearance and Lightfastness in Traditional Japanese Prints." In *Scientific Research on the Pictorial Arts of Asia: Proceedings of the Second Forbes Symposium at the Freer Gallery of Art*, ed. Paul Jett, John Winter, and Blythe McCarthy, 48–57. London: Archetype Publications, 2005.

Uyeda, Tanya. "Urazaishiki in Ukiyo-e Paintings: Examples from the Bigelow Collection of the Museum of Fine Arts, Boston." *Kokka* 1377 (2010): 34–44.

Walsh, Judith. "The Identification of Deliberately Discolored Red Leads in Sino- and Russo-Japanese War Prints." In *In Battle's Light: Woodblock Prints of Japan's Early Modern Wars*, exh. cat., ed. Elizabeth de Sabato Swinton, 133–35. Worcester, MA: Worcester Art Museum, 1991.

Wang, Zi-qiang, and Heng Shi. *Illustrations of Chinese Traditional Mounting Techniques for Paintings and Calligraphy*. Hangzhou: Zhejiang Photographic Press, 2010.

Paper, Photographs, and Digital Materials

Baldwin, Gordon, and Martin Jürgens. *Looking at Photographs: A Guide to Technical Terms*. Los Angeles: Getty Publications, 2009.

Batterham, Ian. *The Office Copying Revolution: History, Identification and Preservation*. Canberra: National Archives of Australia, 2008.

Brunner, Felix. *The Handbook of Graphic Reproduction Processes*. Teufen, Switzerland: Arthur Niggli, 1962.

Ellis, Margaret Holben. *The Care of Prints and Drawings*. Walnut Creek, CA: AltaMira Press, 1995.

Gascoigne, Bamber. *How to Identify Prints: A Complete Guide to Manual and Mechanical Processes from Woodcut to Ink-Jet*. New York: Thames and Hudson, 1986.

James, Carlo, Caroline Corrigan, Marie Christine Enshaian, and Marie Rose Greca. *Old Master Prints and Drawings: A Guide to Preservation and Conservation*. Trans. and ed. Marjorie B. Cohn. Amsterdam: Amsterdam University Press, 1997.

Jürgens, Martin C. *The Digital Print: Identification and Preservation*. Los Angeles: Getty Conservation Institute, 2009.

Kissel, Eléonore, and Erin Vigneau. *Architectural Photoreproductions: A Manual for Identification and Care*. New Castle, DE: Oak Knoll Press; New York: New York Botanical Garden, 1999.

Lavédrine, Bertrand. *A Guide to the Preventive Conservation of Photograph Collections*. Los Angeles: Getty Conservation Institute, 2003.

———. *Photographs of the Past: Process and Preservation*. Los Angeles: Getty Conservation Institute, 2009.

Reilly, James M. *Care and Identification of 19th-Century Photographic Prints*. Rochester: Eastman Kodak Company, 1986.

Shweidler, Max. *The Restoration of Engravings, Drawings, Books and Other Works on Paper*. Translated, edited, and with an appendix by Roy Perkinson. Los Angeles: Getty Conservation Institute, 2006.

Stratis, Harriet K., and Britt Salvesen, eds. *The Broad Spectrum: Studies in the Materials, Techniques, and Conservation of Color on Paper*. London: Archetype Publications, 2002.

Wilhelm, Henry. *The Permanence and Care of Color Photographs: Traditional and Digital Color Prints, Color Negatives, Slides, and Motion Pictures*. Grinnell, IA: Preservation Publishing Company, 1993.

Zigrosser, Carol, and Christa M. Gaehde. *A Guide to the Collecting and Care of Original Prints*. New York: Crown Publishers, 1965.

Objects and Sculptures

Buys, Susan, and Victoria Oakley. *The Conservation and Restoration of Ceramics*. Oxford: Butterworth-Heinemann, 1996.

Considine, Brian, Julie Wolfe, Katrina Posner, and Michael Mark Bouchard. *Conserving Outdoor Sculpture*. Los Angeles: Getty Conservation Institute, 2010.

Drayman-Weisser, Terry, ed. *Gilded Metals: History, Technology and Conservation*. London: Archetype Books, 2000.

Florian, Mary-Lou, Dale Paul Kronkright, and Ruth E. Norton. *The Conservation of Artifacts Made from Plant Materials*. Los Angeles: Getty Conservation Institute, 1991.

Grattan, David W., ed. *Saving the Twentieth Century: The Conservation of Modern Materials*. Ottawa: Canadian Conservation Institute, 1993.

Koob, Stephen B. *Conservation and Care of Glass Objects*. London: Archetype Publications, 2006.

Oakley, Victoria, and Kamal K. Jain. *Essentials in the Care and Conservation of Historical Ceramic Objects*. London: Archetype Books, 2002.

Peachey, Claire, and Emily Williams, eds. *Conservation of Archaeological Materials: Current Trends and Future Directions*. Oxford: British Archaeological Reports, 2011.

Scott, David A., Jerry Podany, and Brain A. Considine, eds. *Ancient and Historic Metals: Conservation and Scientific Research*. Los Angeles: Getty Publications, 1995.

Teutonico, Jeanne Marie, and John Fidler, eds. *Monuments and the Millennium*. London: Maney Publishing, 2001.

Textiles

Boersma, Foekje. *Unraveling Textiles: A Handbook for the Preservation of Textile Collections*. London: Archetype Publications, 2009.

Cardon, Dominique. *Natural Dyes: Sources, Tradition, Technology and Science*. London: Archetype Publications, 2007.

Flecker, Lara. *A Practical Guide to Costume Mounting*. Oxford: Butterworth-Heinemann, 2006.

Joseph, Marjory L. *Joseph's Introductory Textile Science*. Revised by Peyton B. Hudson, Anne C. Clapp, and Darlene Kness. Fort Worth: Harcourt Brace Jovanovich College Publishers, 1992.

Kajitani, Nobuko. "Care of Fabrics in the Museum." In *Preservation of Paper and Textiles of Historic and Artistic Value*, ed. John C. Williams, 161–80. Washington, DC: American Chemical Society, 1978.

Lennard, Frances, and Patricia Ewer, eds. *Textile Conservation: Advances in Practice*. Oxford: Butterworth-Heinemann, 2010.

Mailand, Harold F., and Dorothy Stites Alig. *Preserving Textiles: A Guide for the Nonspecialist*. Indianapolis: Indianapolis Museum of Art, 1999.

Figure Illustrations

figs. 1a and 1b
Marine mosaic
Roman, Eastern Mediterranean, Imperial Period, A.D. 200–230
Mosaic (stone and glass tesserae)
Overall: 291.5 x 287 cm (114¾ x 113 in.)
Museum purchase and conservation with funds donated by George D. and Margo Behrakis, The Getty Foundation, Jane's Trust, John F. Cogan, Jr. and Mary L. Cornille, Daphne and George Hatsopoulos, the Estate of Dr. Harold Amos, Peter and Widgie Aldrich, Mrs. I. W. Colburn, Mary B. Comstock, The Hellenic Women's Club, Inc., an anonymous donor, Katherine R. Kirk, Peter Vlachos, Mrs. James Evans Ladd, Irene and Grier Merwin, Suzanne R. Dworsky, Mr. and Mrs. Robert K. Faulkner, Francis J. Jackson and Nancy M. McMahon, Meg Holmes Robbins, Otis Norcross Fund, Helen and Alice Colburn Fund, Arthur Tracy Cabot Fund, Charles Amos Cummings Fund, and by exchange from the John Wheelock Elliot and John Morse Elliot Fund, Henry Lillie Pierce Fund, Benjamin Pierce Cheney Donation, Bequest of Benjamin Rowland, Jr., Gift of a "class of young ladies," Museum purchase by contribution, Gift of Barbara Deering Danielson, General Funds, William Sturgis Bigelow Collection, Gift of Mr. and Mrs. G. W. Wales, Gift of Paul E. Manheim, Bequest of Mrs. May Sheppard Jordan, Gift of Mr. and Mrs. William de Forest Thomson, Francis Bartlett Donation, Gift of James Howe Proctor, Gift of Benjamin W. Crowninshield, Gift of the Estate of Dana Estes, Gift of Thomas Gold Appleton, Gift of Edward Perry Warren, Gift of an anonymous donor, Gift of Francis Amory, Gift of J. J. Dixwell, Gift of Edward Austin, Gift of Edward Robinson, Gift of Horace L. Mayer, Everett Fund, Gift of the Misses Norton, Gift of the Misses Amy and Clara Curtis, Gift of Charles C. Perkins, Gift of Mrs. Walter Scott Fitz, Gift of Harold Murdock in memory of his brother, Rear-Admiral J. B. Murdock, Gift of the Estate of Alfred Greenough, and Gift of Edward Southworth Hawes 2002.128.1

figs. 2, 3a and 3b
Thomas Sully
(American, born in England, 1783–1872)
The Passage of the Delaware
1819
Oil on canvas
372.1 x 525.8 cm (146½ x 207 in.)
Gift of the Owners of the old Boston Museum 03.1079

fig. 4a
Model shouldered jar
Egyptian, end of Dynasty 5,
reign of Djedkare, about 2414–2375 B.C.
H. 6.5 cm, diam. 5.3 cm
(H. 2 7/16 in., diam. 2 1/16 in.)
Copper
Harvard University–Boston Museum of Fine Arts Expedition 12-11-20b

fig. 4b
Neckless jar
Egyptian
Old Kingdom, Dynasty 6, reign of Neferkare Pepy, 2246–2152 B.C.
H. 5 cm, diam. 4.2 cm
(H. 1 15/16 in., diam. 1⅝ in.)
Copper
Harvard University—Boston Museum of Fine Arts Expedition 13.2957

figs. 5a and 5b
Interior finish from the Oak Hill dining room
Carving attributed to Samuel McIntire
(American, 1757–1811)
Danvers, Massachusetts, United States, early 19th century
Wood, paint
Variable dimensions
Charles Amos Cummings Fund and anonymous gift 22.806

figs. 6a and 6b
Chest with drawers
Probably New York State, United States, about 1840–60
Painted pine, brass
Overall: 72.4 x 110.5 x 47cm
(28½ x 43½ x 18½ in.)
Museum purchase with funds donated by a Friend of the Department of American Decorative Arts and Sculpture and Frank B. Bemis Fund 1982.400

fig. 7
Rhona MacBeth, Head of Paintings Conservation and Eijk and Rose-Marie van Otterloo Conservator of Paintings, inpainting a work by John Singer Sargent:
John Singer Sargent (American, 1856–1925)
The Daughters of Edward Darley Boit
1882
221.9 x 222.6 cm (87⅜ x 87⅝ in.)
Oil on canvas
Gift of Mary Louisa Boit, Julia Overing Boit, Jane Hubbard Boit, and Florence D. Boit in memory of their father, Edward Darley Boit 19.124

fig. 8
X-ray fluorescence spectrometer analyzing pigments on a Japanese scroll:
Minister Kibi's Adventures in China, Scroll 3
Japan
Heian period, 12th century
Handscroll; ink, color, and gold on paper
32.0 x 721.8 cm (12⅝ x 284 3/16 in.)
William Sturgis Bigelow Collection, by exchange 32.131.3

fig. 9
Photograph of cases containing objects from the Italian Renaissance
2010
Museum of Fine Arts, Boston

Index

Page numbers in italics indicate illustrations.